THE WAR ON KIDS

THE WAR ON KIDS

HOW AMERICAN JUVENILE JUSTICE LOST ITS WAY

CARA H. DRINAN

OXFORD
UNIVERSITY PRESS

OXFORD
UNIVERSITY PRESS

Oxford University Press is a department of the University of Oxford. It furthers
the University's objective of excellence in research, scholarship, and education
by publishing worldwide. Oxford is a registered trade mark of Oxford University
Press in the UK and certain other countries.

Published in the United States of America by Oxford University Press
198 Madison Avenue, New York, NY 10016, United States of America.

CIP data is on file at the Library of Congress
ISBN 978–0–19–060555–1

1 3 5 7 9 8 6 4 2
Printed by Edwards Brothers Malloy, United States of America

For Cooper and William

CONTENTS

———⊰◆⊱———

ACKNOWLEDGMENTS

I first read the *Graham v. Florida* opinion on an airplane six years ago, and I remember thinking at the time, I'm a criminal law professor. How did I not know that the United States was the only developed nation that sentenced children to die in prison? I realized that if I was largely unaware of the extremity of our juvenile sentencing practices, so too was most of America. Since that day, the questions of how children end up in the criminal justice system and how we treat them inside that system have haunted me. My aim in this book is to shine a light on the reality of juvenile sentencing practices in America, to humanize the experiences of those juveniles within the system, and to contribute to the momentum for juvenile justice reform.

I am grateful to many individuals who helped translate the concept for this book into a reality. First, I am indebted to Terrence Graham. Meeting Terrence and hearing his story during a personal interview in 2012 was the immediate impetus for this book. Over the last few years, Terrence has been a contributor through written correspondence, and he has been an ongoing source of motivation. When a book project seemed overwhelming, I would simply re-read his words of encouragement, telling me that he and others inside were counting on me and reminding me to "let God use me." I am equally thankful to Terrence's mother, Mary Graham, for her willingness to reflect on and share very personal details of her story and those of her children. Bryan Gowdy, Terrence's excellent lawyer who won his case before the United States Supreme Court and who represented Terrence when he was resentenced in the Florida courts, also provided key assistance at the beginning of this project.

I thank all those who have written to me and shared their experiences of youth incarceration. Your correspondence grounds my research and reminds me that my scholarship is useful only if it contributes to the common good and gives voice to those who don't otherwise have one.

I am also indebted to many fellow academics who helped me with the manuscript at various stages of development. Over the last few years, I have shared portions of the manuscript with faculty and workshop participants at Florida State University, William & Mary, Duke, the University of New Orleans, and the Southeastern Association of Law Schools. I received especially helpful comments and motivation from Doug Berman, Jancy Hoffel, Megan La Belle, Heidi Schooner, George Smith, Kathryn Kelly, Catherine Hancock, John Stinneford, Allison Larsen, Daniel Attridge, Marin Scordato, and A.G. Harmon. Eric Braun brought his surgical skills to bear, providing editorial structure—and cheerleading—when I needed it most. I am also thankful to Mark Holden and the Charles Koch Foundation for its generous financial support of this endeavor.

Finally, I am grateful to my family. My circle of female friends kept me sane and helped me with logistics. My parents, David and Helen Drinan, taught me that hard work pays off and that when you have opportunity and grace you have to share both. Cooper and William overlooked my absence at many events and patiently waited while I finished just one paragraph more. They even asked me, "how'd your writing go today?" My boys are the greatest gifts I have ever received and my motivation for ending the war on kids.

NOTE ON SOURCES

The bulk of the research for this book was conducted in the typical fashion of a legal academic. Case law, statutes, and secondary sources on which I rely are noted throughout the text as endnotes.

It is worth noting that, unlike many academic works, this book relies heavily upon the personal experiences and words of individuals who were sent to prison as juveniles. In some cases, I reached out to these individuals because of the pivotal nature of their case to the development of law in this area. In those instances, I obtained continuous consent from the individuals who shared their histories and their words. In countless other cases, though, people wrote directly to me to share their experience as a juvenile coming of age in prison. In those cases, if I relied upon their words or experiences, I have employed pseudonyms in order to protect their identity.

Introduction

I MET TERRENCE ON a muggy August morning at the Taylor Correctional Institution (TCI) in Perry, Florida. Perry is about a two-and-a-half hour drive west from Jacksonville on the edge of Florida's panhandle. Despite its nearly deserted Main Street and depressed feel, Perry is less than 10 miles from the Gulf of Mexico and only one hour from the state's capital. The town has approximately 7,000 residents; the prison can hold nearly 3,000 inmates. TCI employs more than 550 staff members, and a quarter of the town's residents live below the poverty line. Perry is a prison town, and a Confederate flag greets its visitors.

Months of research had brought me to Perry. As a law professor whose scholarship focuses on criminal justice reform, I'd become especially interested in juvenile justice in 2010. That year, the United States Supreme Court had considered the case of Terrence Jamar Graham, who, at 17, had been sentenced to life without parole for his involvement in an attempted robbery of a barbeque restaurant. The Supreme Court, in *Graham v. Florida*, held that life without parole sentences for juveniles who commit non-homicide offenses are cruel and unusual—that they violate the Eighth Amendment. As a result, Terrence was entitled to a new sentencing hearing and ultimately received a 25-year sentence.

After months of researching and writing about the *Graham* case, I had decided that I needed to meet the young man at the center of the Court's decision. I asked Terrence's lawyer, Bryan Gowdy, who had successfully argued Terrence's case before the Supreme Court, if I could do

I

so. Like a good lawyer, mindful of his client's autonomy, Bryan told me to "ask Terrence." Terrence and I exchanged letters; he agreed to meet me; the Florida Department of Corrections allowed me to schedule a visit; and several months later, my visit day had arrived.

The night before my scheduled visit, I had landed in Jacksonville and driven to Perry, wanting to be on time for my 9 a.m. slot the next day. Thirty minutes outside Jacksonville the landscape grew sparse. I shifted back and forth between radio static and a half-audible talk radio host ranting about President Barack Obama. With the 2012 presidential campaign at fever pitch, the host declared that Clinton had been our first black president and that Obama was our first gay president because he supported the "gay Gestapo."

I reached Perry at dusk. As I wound along a narrow residential road heading into the center of town, I was struck by the beauty of its huge oak trees and dangling Spanish moss. At the same time, two images from that short stretch have stayed with me. First: a man coming out of a trailer home, picking up a small dog by the neck in a terribly cruel manner. I looked away, fearing what was to come. Second: a closed-down store that advertised "gun alternatives." This was a town that had seen more prosperous days.

After a fitful night's sleep at the Perry Holiday Inn Express, I woke early and drove the short distance to the prison. TCI comprises three separate facilities, and I visited them all before reaching the right one. Walking toward the gates of each facility, I was conscious of the men who were already out and about working in the prison yard under the merciless sun and the supervision of guards. The inmates were black; the guards were white. It had rained the night before, so everything was damp, and with the growing heat, a mist rose from the concrete. The air smelled like the coat of a wet dog.

Before beginning the security process, I left all valuables in my car—cash, laptop, phone. I was allowed to bring in my audio recorder, a pad of paper, and a pen. The metal detector beeped loudly at me. After several passes, I suggested to the skeptical-looking guard that my underwire bra might be causing the problem. I took off my light suit jacket at his instruction and stood there awkwardly in my bra and tank top. He waved the wand over me again. "Yup. It's the bra," he said. As I hurriedly got my jacket back on, he looked at me sternly and said: "keep the jacket on."

The guard led me to the interview room and handed me a small, cigarette-pack-shaped alarm. There was a single button on it. He said to me casually: "call if you need me; press the alarm to call for more people if there's an incident." He didn't describe what would constitute an incident. The "interview room" was closer to a storage closet than a room. Approximately three feet by five feet with a door on each side, strangely, the room had a sink on one wall. Someone had set up a scratched, shaky card table with two folding chairs. I was led into the space through one door (that was left open), and the door opposite me was open, as well. I was told that Terrence would be brought in through the opposite door. Where was he coming from? What would he look like? Would the guard escorting him be polite? Was I being recorded? My mind raced as I set up my recorder and waited for Terrence to arrive. The room was dirty.

My pre-interview jitters disappeared when Terrence was led into the room. He was my height, trim, and well groomed. Terrence had kind, deep brown eyes, and he was incredibly polite. I began by asking him to describe his typical daily routine, and after that question, I never relied upon another one that I'd drafted in advance. We just talked—about his life in prison, his family, and how he passes the time. When several hours had passed, I knew I should be heading back to Jacksonville—I was scheduled to present a paper at an academic conference hours away. I felt sad and guilty leaving. I promised Terrence we'd stay in touch, and that I would be back. I had to say it, and I felt like he needed to hear it. As I packed up my things, I asked Terrence if he knows what he'll do when he's released. He didn't miss a beat: "first I gotta make it outta here."

HOW DID THIS HAPPEN? How is it that Terrence and thousands of other juveniles were sentenced to die in prison before they were legally old enough to get a tattoo, vote, or enlist in the army? It wasn't always this way. The United States was once, not too long ago, a pioneer on juvenile justice matters.[1] Legislators in Illinois invented the concept of a juvenile court at the end of the 19th century. Quickly thereafter, every state in the union instituted its own juvenile court system, and developed nations around the world emulated the American juvenile court model. The "ethic of parens patriae" governed these early juvenile courts, and the judge was focused on the juvenile's rehabilitation. Juvenile court proceedings were largely informal; the judge enjoyed great discretion and was able to tailor the intervention to the particular child in each case. Most important, the juvenile court itself was premised on the notion that childhood is a period of dependency and risk; the state's obligation was to assist a child in jeopardy, typically by providing social services.

Dramatically and rapidly, though, the United States became an international outlier in the severity of its juvenile sentencing practices. Each year in America, police arrest more than one million juveniles,[2] and about 250,000 of those kids are charged with a crime and processed in adult court.[3] In some states, children as young as six can be transferred out of juvenile court into adult court without any judicial oversight.[4] Once there, they face sentences—often mandatory ones—that were drafted with adults in mind.[5] If convicted, these children are sentenced to a term of years in a correctional facility fraught with problems, not the least of which is that it was designed for adults. Until 2005, the United States was the only developed country that subjected children to the death penalty, and today we are the only nation that employs juvenile life without parole. Because of their physical and mental vulnerability, youth inmates experience the highest rates of sexual and physical assault, as well as suicide.[6] The pope, U.N. officials, and international human rights organizations have condemned American juvenile sentencing practices.[7]

So how did we abandon the groundbreaking model of juvenile justice that we constructed only a little more than a century ago? Part of the answer to that question lies in the arc of criminal justice in America across the board. As recently as the 1970s, the corrections system impacted only a small percentage of Americans—approximately 300,000 people were imprisoned, while the nation's population hovered around 200 million.[8] Between 1960 and the mid-1990s, though, violent crime rose consistently, reaching an all-time peak in 1994.[9] The War on Drugs was ushered in, and lawmakers on both sides of the aisle adopted tough-on-crime rhetoric and policies to match. Today, more than two million adults and children are behind bars[10]—1 in 99 adults in America. An even larger number of people—1 in 31 adults— are under some form of correctional control, whether incarceration, parole or probation.[11] With only 5 percent of the world's population and 25 percent of the world's prison inmates, the land of the free has become the world's largest jailer.[12]

While there are many explanations for mass incarceration in America, at bottom, two shifts in policy are responsible: we send more people to prison and we sentence them for longer periods of time than ever before. These two changes have not simply generated a bloated prison population; they have also altered the fabric of American society. In some states, correctional costs have outstripped education expenditures. Prison overcrowding is rampant, and the conditions often horrific as a result. The Supreme Court's 2011 decision in *Brown v. Plata* revealed the dire state of California's prisons: they were at more than double their capacity.[13] Mentally ill inmates were being held in telephone-booth-sized cages because there were no hospital beds for them;[14] inmates were dying because of systemic delays in medical treatment.[15]

Moreover, as Michelle Alexander explained so well in *The New Jim Crow*, this explosion in correctional supervision has not impacted all Americans equally.[16] While African Americans and Hispanics make up less than one-third of the U.S. population,[17] they comprise more than half of all prisoners.[18] As of 2001, one in six black men had been incarcerated at some point.[19] If current trends continue, one in three black males born today can expect to spend time in prison during his lifetime.[20] American penal practices have spun out of control, and poor people of color are paying the greatest price.

As tough-on-crime policies took over America, children, again usually from poor minority communities, were swept up into the justice system in ways intentional and unintentional. For example, as discussed in *Chapter 1*, states both made it easier to move a child into the adult court system and shifted toward mandatory sentences for those in adult court. With these two forces at work, kids were caught in the crosshairs, perhaps unintentionally. At the same time, though, some legislative efforts were specifically targeted at kids in the criminal justice system. In the 1980s almost every state passed legislation imposing harsher penalties for juvenile offenders.[21] A decade later, criminologists predicted a wave of juvenile "super-predators" that would terrorize the American streets.[22] The super-predator theory was eventually debunked,[23] but that came decades later. Amid rising homicide rates, the terrifying prediction resonated with voters, and Congress enacted the expansive 1994 Crime Bill, which, among others things, created incentives for states to impose harsher sentences and narrow parole provisions, including those applicable to juveniles.[24] Quite simply, in the 1980s and 1990s we lost sight of the ways in which children are vulnerable and susceptible to rehabilitation, and we erroneously accepted a vision of kids as one of the greatest threats to our safety.

Mercifully, in the last two decades there has been a growing social awareness of the scope of the criminal justice system and its chokehold on certain communities. Some of that awareness can be attributed to the United States Supreme Court. In *Brown v. Plata*, the nation's high court ordered California to remedy the overcrowding issue or to release inmates.[25] Taxpayers, balking at the prospect of spending more money on corrections, rejected any plans for further prison expansion and swiftly expressed their outrage at the polls. In 2012, Californians voted to drastically scale back the state's three-strikes law—a law that had mandated 25 years to life for any defendant convicted of three felonies, even nonviolent ones.[26] The law had been the most severe of its kind in the nation and arguably the source of the state's prison overcrowding. At the same time, California voters only narrowly favored maintaining the state's death row.[27] Other states, motivated by the threat of similar lawsuits and taxpayer resistance to ever-increasing correctional costs, have explored ways to reduce incarceration rates and foster re-entry.

The Great Recession also can take credit for some of the emerging awareness that criminal justice in this country has gone awry. After 2008, facing shrinking budgets, politicians from both parties began to look for ways to reduce corrections expenditures. Organizations like Right on Crime emerged. Founded in 2010 with the leadership of individuals like Grover Norquist and Newt Gingrich, Right on Crime seeks to reduce mass incarceration by promoting the principles of personal responsibility and limited government.[28] In early 2015, Koch Industries, the conglomerate led by the conservative brothers Charles and David Koch, partnered with the Center for American Progress to undertake criminal justice reform.[29] The unexpected alliance is attributable, in part, to the Koch's recognition that the American corrections model today stifles economic freedom and prosperity.

If America is rethinking its criminal justice practices generally, a revolution in juvenile justice is afoot, and to a large extent that revolution can be traced to Terrence Graham. By the early 21st century, as Columbia Law School Professor Elizabeth Scott explains, there had been a marked dissipation of the "moral panic" of the 1990s: "Many lawmakers and politicians—from the Supreme Court to big city mayors—appear[ed] ready to rethink the punitive approach of the 1990s."[30] At just that time, Terrence entered the criminal justice system. In 2003, when he was 16, Terrence and three other teens attempted to rob a barbeque restaurant in Jacksonville.[31] They entered the restaurant through an unlocked back door at closing time, fled when the manager started yelling at them, and left with no money.[32] A Florida judge sentenced Terrence to life without parole for his involvement in that crime.[33]

In 2010, the Supreme Court of the United States overturned his sentence, holding that life without parole was cruel and unusual in light of his crime and age.[34] Writing for the Court, Justice Kennedy relied upon what neuroscientists had been saying for some time: given their stage of development, [children are both less culpable for their crimes and more amenable to reform than adults.] As a result, the Court held, a juvenile who commits a non-homicide crime may not be sentenced to die in prison: "A State is not required to guarantee eventual freedom to a juvenile offender convicted of a nonhomicide crime. What the State must do, however, is give defendants like Graham some meaningful opportunity to obtain release based on demonstrated maturity and rehabilitation."[35] When his case was sent back to the Florida courts for a resentencing hearing, Terrence received a 25-year sentence, and if he survives prison, he will be released at the age of 38.

Only two years later, the Supreme Court revisited the issue of extreme juvenile sentences in America and held once again in favor of the juvenile petitioner. Evan Miller had been sentenced to mandatory life without parole for a homicide he committed at the age of 14. In *Miller v. Alabama*, the Court held that his sentence, like Terrence's, was cruel and unusual.[36] As the *Miller* Court explained, "[life without parole] is an 'especially harsh punishment for a juvenile,' because he will almost inevitably serve 'more years and a greater percentage of his life in prison than an adult offender. . . . The penalty when imposed on a teenager, as compared with an older person, is therefore 'the same . . . in name only.' "[37] Under the *Miller* decision, states may still impose a life without parole sentence upon a juvenile homicide defendant, but only after taking into account youth and all of its mitigating attributes.[38] Together, the *Graham* and *Miller* decisions stand for the proposition that children are different in the eyes of the law, and state and federal sentencing practices must reflect that fact.

The Supreme Court's decisions in *Graham* and *Miller* were about much more than life without parole sentences for kids. The *Miller* Court, in particular, made clear that its opinion was an indictment of broader juvenile justice practices, such as transfer laws that permit children to be tried in adult court and sentencing guidelines that render youth irrelevant. Perhaps most important, the Court sent the message loud and clear that *kids are different*—their brains have not fully developed, and thus they are less culpable and more amenable to rehabilitation. Because of this biological difference, it violates basic notions of fairness for the state to proceed with criminal charges against juveniles "as though they [are] not children."[39]

The Court's moral leadership in these opinions has prompted states to begin addressing these deeply misguided juvenile justice practices. Since the *Graham* decision in 2010, 12 states have abolished juvenile life without parole and another 6 ban the sentence in most juvenile cases.[40] A majority of state courts that considered whether *Miller* applies retroactively concluded that it must, and the Supreme Court later affirmed that position.[41] One state supreme court has held that, under *Miller*, mandatory minimums will be inapplicable to juveniles across the board, and another has held that juveniles have a right to be resentenced in light of *Graham* and *Miller* and that they have a right to counsel during that resentencing hearing.[42] Five years before Terrence's case was heard, these changes would have been unthinkable.

Yet, as promising as these developments are, there remains much to be done for children swept up in the criminal justice system. The Supreme Court's recent decisions can only take juvenile justice reform so far. As a function of institutional design, the Court can address only those cases brought before it, and to date, the Court has addressed only the two harshest sentences available under law—capital punishment and life without parole—as they apply to children. Juveniles may still be sentenced to life without parole in some cases, and on a more regular basis, they may face 30-, 40-, even 60-year sentences. Moreover, while the Court has addressed extreme sentencing, it has not yet addressed the legitimacy of practices that put children in adult court in the first place. Nor has it set limits on the conditions of confinement for children. These issues have been left to the states, with dire consequences, as evidenced by the high rates of physical and sexual assault and suicide among young inmates.

Most Americans would be shocked by how harshly children accused, let alone convicted, of a crime are treated in the criminal justice system. Newspapers report on parents being charged with criminal neglect for permitting their children to walk to a playground unsupervised.[43] College administrators complain that freshmen are incapable of doing anything independently because they have been smothered and stunted by well-meaning "helicopter parents." In a recent *New Yorker* article entitled "Spoiled Rotten," Elizabeth Kolbert wrote, "contemporary American kids may represent the most indulged young people in the history of the world."[44]

But this is not true for all children in America. Indeed, there is a subclass of children whom we have deemed expendable. These children enter guilty pleas without the advice of a lawyer, and they serve time in prisons, sometimes shackled and hog-tied. These children are physically abused, raped, and emotionally traumatized. Some of them committed heinous crimes, but most of them did not.[45] Even for those who did commit a serious crime, we ought not be comfortable with a system that treats them as adults, because they are not adults, regardless of the legal fiction that treats them as such. Neuroscience tells us that we cannot hold them responsible in the same way that we can adults. Yet, we have written these children off and sentenced them to a life of limited opportunities if not an excessive term of years in a penitentiary. Who are these kids? How did this happen? And how do we fix it? These are the questions that this book seeks to answer.

The War on Kids explains how American juvenile justice lost its way. The book juxtaposes theoretical failings of the juvenile justice system

with actual experiences at the hands of that system. *Chapter 1* reveals
the severity of juvenile sentencing practices and explains how age-
appropriate sentencing disappeared from our system almost inadvert-
ently and in such a short period of time. Having explained the current
state of affairs and how we got here, the book then turns to exposing
the machinery of juvenile justice: how certain kids are more likely than
others to end up in the system and what that bleak experience looks like
for a juvenile inside the system. *Chapter 2* draws upon Terrence's life
experience and broader social science to explain that, for some children
in America, crime is practically their destiny. Race, poverty, parental
incarceration, and exposure to violence dramatically increase a child's
likelihood of contact with the criminal justice system. *Chapter 3* identifies legal and policy mechanisms that make that destiny a reality, specifically the school-to-prison pipeline, transfer laws, ineffective assistance
of counsel, and mandatory minimums. *Chapter 4* then lays bare the
reality of children coming of age in prison, drawing upon corrections
studies and upon the experiences of the inmates with whom I correspond. This chapter also documents the ways in which young inmates
seek to survive while incarcerated both in a physical, day-to-day sense
and in a psychic sense.

Having looked in depth at how certain children are swept into
a criminal justice system that treats them as adults, the book then
turns to examine the prospects for reform on the horizon. *Chapter 5*
presents evidence that today's climate is ripe for juvenile justice
reform by unpacking recent Supreme Court juvenile sentencing decisions and related state legislative responses. *Chapter 6* examines early
implementation efforts in the wake of these recent Supreme Court
decisions, looking specifically at three cases of individuals who have
been impacted by those decisions. The three cases demonstrate the
ways in which implementation of new laws can be painfully unpredictable and uneven. Finally, *Chapter 7* maintains that, while these
recent Supreme Court decisions and legislative trends are promising,
there remains much work to be done for kids in the criminal justice
system. Specifically, *Chapter 7* argues that we must launch a war *for*
kids, and the chapter outlines policy measures that such a war must
entail, including the nationwide elimination of juvenile life without

parole sentences, the abolition of mandatory minimums for kids, and a shift away from juvenile incarceration altogether. This book intends to shine a light on the brutal reality of children in our criminal justice system and to inspire its readers to pursue reform efforts that are so desperately needed.

I

Pioneer to Pariah

The Arc of American Juvenile Justice

IN 1999, WHEN HE was 14 years old, Kuntrell Jackson and two friends decided to rob a video store in Arkansas.[1] Kuntrell learned while en route to the store that one of his friends had brought along a sawed-off shotgun; he decided to wait outside the video store.[2] Once inside, Kuntrell's friend pointed the gun at the clerk and demanded money from her.[3] She refused. After a few minutes, Kuntrell walked inside the store to find his friend insisting that the clerk "give up the money."[4] At trial, it was disputed whether Kuntrell said to the clerk, "we ain't playin," or whether he said to his friends, "I thought you all was playin."[5] Either way, the clerk refused to hand over money and threatened to call the police. Kuntrell's friend shot and killed her. All three boys fled the store empty-handed.

Arkansas law allows prosecutors to unilaterally transfer 14-year-olds out of the juvenile court system into adult court if they are charged with certain serious crimes.[6] In Kuntrell's case, the prosecutor exercised this discretion and charged him as an adult with capital felony murder and aggravated robbery—even though Kuntrell was barely old enough to attend high school.[7] Felony murder, the capital charge in Kuntrell's case, has long been disputed as unjust in American criminal law, even as it applies to adults. The theory of a felony murder charge is this: certain felonies are so inherently dangerous that if a person intends to engage in the felony, the law holds them responsible for any death that occurs during the commission of that felony, whether the defendant intended that death or not. Some have argued that this "transferred intent" is inherently unfair; it's one thing to be held responsible for one's intention to rob a store, but it's another thing to impute the intent to kill when death appears an accident incidental to the felony. Even more contentious, though, is that in the felony murder context, code-fendants can be held responsible for the actions of each other. So, in Kuntrell's case, not only is it questionable whether he intended to carry out the robbery, but also he was not the triggerman—he definitely did not intend to shoot and kill the clerk. Yet the theory of felony murder holds him responsible for her death. Once in adult court, a jury convicted Kuntrell of both crimes, and Arkansas law at the time permitted only one sentence: life without parole.]

Terrence Graham was also sentenced to life without parole, but his case was even more shocking because it was not a homicide conviction. Recall the facts of his case from the Introduction. In 2003, when he was 16, Terrence and some friends tried to rob a restaurant in Jacksonville. Confronted by an undoubtedly angry manager, they fled and took no money. Before fleeing, one of Terrence's accomplices struck the manager in the head with a metal bar. The manager required stitches for his head wound. Terrence was arrested and charged with armed burglary and attempted armed robbery.[8]

The prosecutor, who, under Florida law, enjoyed sole discretion regarding whether to charge Terrence as a juvenile or adult, chose to file his case in adult court.[9] Terrence pleaded guilty to both charges and received a term of three years' probation.[10] He was required to spend the first year of his probation in the (adult) county jail, but he received credit for the time he had spent in that jail awaiting trial and was released in 2004.[11]

Less than six months later, Terrence was arrested again, allegedly for his involvement in a home invasion robbery.[12] The state never pursued those new charges because Terrence's probation officer filed with the trial court an affidavit asserting that he had violated several conditions of his probation, including associating with persons engaged in criminal activity and fleeing from law enforcement.[13] A different trial judge from the one who had accepted Terrence's previous guilty plea presided over a sentencing hearing for the probation violations.[14]

Terrence insisted that he had no involvement in the home invasion robbery, but he did admit to violating his probation conditions by fleeing from police. Violating his probation terms exposed him to the original sentence hanging over him from the attempted robbery of the barbeque restaurant.

Under Florida law, Terrence faced anywhere from 5 years to life imprisonment.[15] The state asked for a 45-year sentence—30 years on the armed burglary count and 15 years on the attempted robbery count.[16] Terrence's lawyer requested the 5-year minimum sentence, and the Florida Department of Corrections recommended that Terrence receive even less prison time—4 years maximum.[17] The judge imposed life without parole.[18]

Before announcing the sentence, the judge made the following statement:

> Mr. Graham, as I look back on your case, yours is really candidly a sad situation. You had, as far as I can tell, you have quite a family structure. You had a lot of people who wanted to try and help you get your life turned around including the court system, and you had a judge who took the step to try and give you direction through his probation order to give you a chance to get back onto track. . . . And I don't know why it is that you threw your life away. I don't know why.
>
> But you did, and that is what is so sad about this today is that you have actually been given a chance to get through this, the original charge, which were very serious charges to begin with. . . . The attempted robbery with a weapon was a very serious charge.
>
> And I don't understand why you would be given such a great opportunity to do something with your life and why you would throw it away. The only thing that I can rationalize is that you decided that this is how you were going to lead your life and that there is nothing that we can do for you. And as the state pointed out, that this is an escalating pattern of criminal conduct on your part and that we can't help you any further. We can't do anything to deter you. This is the way you are going to lead your life, and I don't know why you are going to. You've made that decision. I have no idea. But, evidently, that is what you decided to do.

So then it becomes a focus, if I can't do anything to help you, if I can't do anything to get you back on the right path, then I have to start focusing on the community and trying to protect the community from your actions. And, unfortunately, that is where we are today is I don't see where I can do anything to help you any further. You've evidently decided this is the direction you're going to take in life, and it's unfortunate that you made that choice.

I have reviewed the statute. I don't see where any further juvenile sanctions would be appropriate. I don't see where any youthful offender sanctions would be appropriate. Given your escalating pattern of criminal conduct, it is apparent to the Court that you have decided that this is the way you are going to live your life and that the only thing I can do now is to try and protect the community from your actions.[19]

Nothing in the judge's decision reflected Terrence's youth, the mitigating circumstances of his childhood, or the various ways in which the state of Florida had failed him as a minor.[20] The judge failed to account for the fact that Terrence had grown up in abject poverty with two crack-addicted parents or the fact that Terrence had been physically and verbally abused from the time he was a toddler. The judge made no mention of the fact that the Florida Department of Children and Families (DCF) had files on incidents relating to Terrence's mother and her children dating back to when Terrence was only 3 years old, including questions whether Terrence and his brothers should be removed from the home because there was no food. Apparently, none of this history made it into the judge's decision-making process; it certainly was not mentioned at sentencing. Terrence was an adult in the eyes of the law, and the law permitted a life without parole sentence. At the age of 17, he was sentenced to die in prison.

Like Terrence Graham and Kuntrell Jackson, more than 200,000 juveniles are charged in adult criminal court each year.[21] Their experiences in the adult criminal court system would be inconceivable to those Americans who invented the juvenile court at the turn of the 20th century. To begin, it is very easy and common for children today to be removed from juvenile court and charged as adults. Many states set no minimum age at which a child can be removed from juvenile court and, as a result, children as young as six in some states can be transferred out of juvenile court into adult court without any judicial oversight.[22]

Once in adult court, a juvenile defendant enjoys the right to counsel as other defendants, but there is no guarantee that this attorney will be experienced in representing juveniles.[23] Precisely because they are young, juvenile defendants are less equipped to assist in their own representation: they're less capable of considering the long-term consequences associated with a plea bargain or sentence, and they're more susceptible to coercion by the state.[24] If convicted, children can be jailed with adult inmates, even in dormitory-style arrangements.[25] This practice continues despite the fact that Congress has enacted legislation advising of the dire risks of sexual and physical assault, and despite research demonstrating that juveniles housed in adult prisons are exponentially more likely to commit suicide than if confined in a facility for juveniles.[26] On the other end of the spectrum, sometimes for infractions and sometimes "for their own safety," juvenile inmates can be housed in solitary confinement, a practice prohibited by the United Nations more than 20 years ago and opposed by the American Academy of Child & Adolescent Psychiatry.[27]

In a little more than 100 years, the United States went from being a leader on juvenile justice to being an international outlier in its harsh treatment of juvenile criminal defendants. How did this happen? And how did it happen in such a dramatic and rapid fashion? Chapter 1 answers these questions in three subparts. Part A of Chapter 1 provides a brief historical overview of American juvenile justice. In Parts B and C, the chapter demonstrates how two developments in American criminal procedure converged to expose juveniles to mandatory sentences, in some cases extreme ones: the transfer of juvenile delinquents to adult criminal court and the trend toward determinate sentencing schemes.

A. The Arc of American Juvenile Justice

First established in Illinois in 1899, juvenile justice is now a well-established feature of our criminal justice system. Every jurisdiction in the country has a separate juvenile justice system.[28] Prompted by Progressive Era reformers, the early juvenile court was attentive to the differences between adults and children and emphasized age-appropriate punishment and treatment for juvenile offenders.[29] As described by Professor Aaron Kupchik, an expert on juvenile justice, "Founders of the juvenile justice system believed that juveniles who misbehaved were products of pathological environments rather than intrinsically evil. The target of the juvenile justice system was the deprivation, not the depravation, of delinquent youth. The court's mission was to resocialize youth and provide them with the necessary tools for adopting a moral lifestyle."[30] Over time, several features emerged as defining attributes of the juvenile justice system: (1) a degree of informality relative to criminal court proceedings; (2) great discretion afforded to the judge who was able to tailor the intervention to the particular juvenile in each case; and (3) a fundamental shared belief that childhood is a period of dependency and risk where the state had a role to play for a child in jeopardy.[31] Today, developed countries around the world have installed juvenile justice systems modeled after the American system.[32]

Vanderbilt Professor of Law Terry Maroney has described three primary phases in the development of American juvenile justice prior to the immediate era that we are entering.[33] The first phase, already discussed, was prompted by the rehabilitative ideal of the late 19th century, and it expressed optimism about the juvenile's capacity for change and society's obligation to support that change.[34] The Supreme Court explained this first phase in the following way: "The child—essentially good, as [early reformers] saw it—was to be made 'to feel that he is the object of (the state's) care and solicitude,' not that he was under arrest or on trial. The rules of criminal procedure were therefore altogether inapplicable. The apparent rigidities, technicalities, and harshness which they observed in both substantive and procedural criminal law were therefore to be discarded. The idea of crime and punishment was to be abandoned."[35] While the intentions of early juvenile justice advocates may have been noble, in practice juvenile courts did not always live up to their paternalistic aims.

By the middle of the 20th century, juvenile advocates argued that the flexibility of the juvenile court, while born of a caretaking concept, was resulting in arbitrary outcomes for juveniles and the denial of basic procedural rights familiar to American law. In 1966 the Supreme Court confronted these claims in *Kent v. United States*.[36] The case centered on Morris Kent, Jr., who first entered Washington, D.C.'s juvenile justice system at age 14. At that time, Kent was arrested for breaking into homes and for an attempted purse snatching; he was placed on probation and released to his mother's custody.[37] Two years later, during his probation period, D.C. police identified Kent as the primary suspect in a burglary and rape case.[38] Police apprehended Kent, took him into custody, interrogated him, and detained him for a week. Ultimately, with no hearing and over the objection of counsel retained by Kent's mother, the juvenile court judge transferred Kent's case to adult criminal court. He was ultimately found guilty and sentenced to serve between 30 and 90 years.[39]

The Supreme Court focused on the narrow issue of the transfer decision and held that while the judge enjoyed great latitude under the relevant transfer statute, that "latitude [was] not complete."[40] Moreover, the Court held that the statute did "not confer upon the Juvenile Court a license for arbitrary procedure."[41] At the same time, the Court noted that the state had deprived Kent of basic procedural safeguards that he would have enjoyed had he been an adult. For example, Kent was deprived of liberty for more than a week without any kind of a probable cause hearing before a judge; and he was interrogated in the absence of counsel and without any advice regarding his right to remain silent and the right of access to counsel.[42] The Court held that juveniles like Kent were entitled to a hearing before the transfer decision to adult court could be made, that his lawyer had a right of access to material relevant to the transfer decision, and that the juvenile court was required to provide some articulation of reasons for transferring his case.[43]

One year later, the Supreme Court dealt with a similar claim from a juvenile charged with a crime in the case of *In re Gault*.[44] An Arizona juvenile court judge sentenced Gault, 15 years old, to six months' probation for "being in the company of another boy who had stolen a wallet from a lady's purse."[45] During that six-month probationary period, Gault and another teenager were accused of making a lewd phone call to a neighbor.[46] Police picked Gault up at his home while both of his parents were at work, arrested him, and took him to a juvenile detention center, without notifying his parents.[47] In the following days and weeks, the entire process for determining Gault's guilt or innocence was informal and ill-informed. The complaining neighbor never appeared in court; the state never presented Gault's parents with notice of formal charges against their son; and no rationale was offered either for detaining Gault initially or for releasing him pending his final hearing.[48] Ultimately, the juvenile judge determined that Gault had made the lewd phone call, and he sentenced Gault to six years in a state industrial school, with only a conclusory explanation: "after a full hearing and due deliberation the Court finds that said minor is a delinquent child."[49] Had Gault been an adult convicted of the same lewd phone call, he would have faced a penalty of "$5 to $50, or imprisonment for not more than two months."[50]

The Supreme Court acknowledged that, regardless of the history of the juvenile court model and its paternalistic ethos, there was nothing "civil" about the proceedings that resulted in Gault's six-year prison sentence—they were criminal proceedings for all intents and purposes. Accordingly, the Court held that Gault had a right to notice of the charges against him; a right to counsel during the proceedings, at the state's expense if necessary; the right to be free from self-incrimination; and a right to confrontation and cross-examination of witnesses.[51] In both *Kent* and *Gault*, the Supreme Court recognized that the juveniles in question were dealing with the worst of both worlds: they neither enjoyed the procedural safeguards accorded to adult criminal defendants nor the solicitude of a juvenile court focused on rehabilitation. According to Professor Maroney, these cases marked the zenith of the "due process era" of juvenile justice, the second phase in the development of American juvenile law.[52]

Despite these added procedural protections for kids, the American juvenile justice system shifted radically to a posture of fear and containment in the late 20th century—the third phase in juvenile law development. As discussed in the Introduction, the nation experienced rising violent crime rates for most of the latter half of the 20th century, and legislators responded by enacting a host of generally applicable tough-on-crime policies. In the 1990s, Princeton political scientist John J. DiIulio predicted the emergence of a juvenile "super-predator"—"that there would be hordes upon hordes of depraved teenagers resorting to unspeakable brutality, not tethered by conscience."[53] He was wrong, and he later admitted as much; in the 17 years between 1994 and 2011, murders by children actually fell by two-thirds.[54] Before his theory was debunked, though, lasting damage to kids in the system was done, as state laws shifted to expose children to ever-harsher procedures and punishments.[55]

By the beginning of the 21st century, the United States was an international outlier in its harsh sentences for juvenile criminal defendants. Until 2005, the United States was the only developed country that subjected children to the death penalty,[56] and today we are the only nation that employs juvenile life without parole.[57] Two recent developments, in particular, led to the practice of extreme sentences for juvenile offenders: juvenile transfer laws that removed children from juvenile proceedings and placed them under the jurisdiction of adult criminal courts, and the general trend toward determinate sentencing schemes.

B. Juvenile Transfer Law: Kids in Adult Court

From the inception of the juvenile court to the mid-1970s, a child who was accused of committing a crime was initially and usually processed in the juvenile justice system.[58] In that system, the judge enjoyed great power and flexibility relative to today's criminal court judges. The "ethic of parens patriae" permeated the juvenile court and typically prompted judges to provide social services that were lacking for the youth offender.[59] In this context, it was the juvenile judge's decision when and if to transfer a child to adult court.[60] Moreover, the transfer decision involved a hearing at which the state had to persuade the juvenile judge that the juvenile was not amenable to rehabilitation, had committed a crime too serious for adjudication in juvenile court given its punitive limits, or both.[61] Transfer was not common; it was the exception.

Beginning in the 1970s, states amended their laws, making it easier for children to be prosecuted in adult criminal court.[62] These laws operated in a number of ways. Some laws lowered the age at which a child could be transferred into adult court; some *required* transfer when a juvenile was charged with certain offenses; and others still gave prosecutors the discretion to determine on their own whether to file a case in juvenile or adult court.[63] As juvenile law scholars have noted, despite some legislative variety, the net result of this trend was to shift greater power to prosecutors away from juvenile judges and to make the juvenile transfer process simple and common.

Today, all states have transfer laws that permit adult criminal prosecution of some young defendants, even though these defendants would
otherwise qualify for adjudication in juvenile court because of their
age.[64] Most states have multiple mechanisms for transferring a child
out of the juvenile court's jurisdiction into adult criminal court.[65]
Forty-five states retain the traditional process of judicial waiver for
some kids, whereby the prosecutor bears the burden of proving why
the youth should be transferred to adult court.[66] However, 29 states
have statutes excluding certain youth from juvenile court based upon
the nature of the charged offense.[67] Murder is the most common charge
for automatic transfer to adult court under these statutes, but many of
the 29 states also include less serious offenses and offenses that can vary
widely by factual context, such as assault, robbery, and drug offenses.[68]
Laws in 15 states specify crimes for which both the juvenile court and
adult criminal court have jurisdiction, leaving the question of where to
process the child entirely to the prosecutor's discretion.[69] These prosecutorial discretion, or "direct file," statutes are typically silent regarding
the standards or protocols for whether to file charges in adult court, and
regardless of the criteria employed, there is no evidentiary hearing, no
record of the prosecutor's decision, and no basis upon which the juvenile defendant can challenge the judgment.[70] As a result, "it is possible
that prosecutorial discretion laws in some places operate like statutory
exclusions, sweeping whole categories into criminal court with little
or no individualized consideration."[71] Finally, 34 states have "once an
adult, always an adult" provisions, meaning that once a child has been
convicted in adult court, any future adjudications for that child will
take place in adult court.[72]

According to scholars and the Supreme Court alike, "direct file" laws
have been most problematic for youth.[73] Berkeley Law Professor Frank
Zimring, for example, has posited that get-tough transfer legislation
from the 1990s may have been "an attempt to push the allocation of
power in juvenile courts closer to the model of prosecutorial domina-
tion that has been characteristic of criminal courts in this United States
for a generation."[74] Moreover, whether intentional or not, direct file laws
certainly "[create] more power or less work for juvenile court prosecutors, or both."[75] In its recent *Miller v. Alabama* decision, the Supreme
Court noted the dangers of direct file laws for juveniles: "several States

at times lodge this decision exclusively in the hands of prosecutors, again with no statutory mechanism for judicial reevaluation. And those 'prosecutorial discretion laws are usually silent regarding standards, protocols, or appropriate considerations for decisionmaking.' "[76]

While state transfer laws vary in their scope and mechanism, they invariably result in many children being tried in adult court and exposed to generally applicable penalty provisions.

C. Determinate Sentencing Schemes: A Parallel Trend

Around the same time that states were amending their transfer laws, making it easier to prosecute children in adult court, the state and federal governments also implemented more punitive sentencing practices for adult offenders.[77] For context, it is important to understand the array of sentencing policy options. Sentencing guidelines range from mandatory to advisory. If a sentence is truly mandatory, it means that once the jury has convicted the defendant of a certain charge, the judge has no choice but to impose the sentence prescribed by the legislature for that crime.[78] A presumptive sentencing guideline, however, suggests a predetermined sentence for a crime, but permits the judge to impose a more lenient alternative sentence if the judge determines that there are mitigating circumstances. Typically, the legislature determines in advance what mitigating factors might justify a downward departure from the presumptive sentence.[79] Advisory guidelines are voluntary in that they provide a benchmark for the sentencing judge, but the judge may depart from the suggested sentence with or without explanation.[80]

For most of the 20th century, American judges enjoyed great sentencing discretion, and they could determine what aspects of a defendant's case and history were relevant to the sentencing determination. By the late 20th century, criminal sentencing laws shifted to a determinate nature—that is, the legislature specified in advance the sentencing range or sentence itself that attached to an offense, regardless of the particular offender's situation. Why the United States adopted a more punitive sentencing posture is a complex question and has been explored extensively, but there are a few known factors that are relevant here. After a period of relative stability, crime rates in the mid-1960's to 1970's increased as the Baby Boom generation entered its peak crime years and as urbanization occurred.[81] The public became concerned about crime, and politicians responded by making crime control a central feature of political rhetoric. Beginning in the 1970s, lawmakers and politicians embraced a tough-on-crime stance across the board, and by the 1980s, the War on Drugs was in full swing.[82] In 1984, Congress passed the Sentencing Reform Act as part of the Comprehensive Crime Control Act of 1984.[83] The Act created the United States Sentencing Commission, charged with creating federal sentencing guidelines and making federal criminal penalties more uniform.[84] At the same time, Congress enacted mandatory minimum sentences for certain federal offenses, most notably drug offenses.[85]

State legislatures did the same. "On the state level this trend began in New York in 1973, with California and Massachusetts following soon thereafter. While the trend toward mandatory minimums in the states was gradual, by 1983, 49 of the 50 states had passed such provisions."[86] At the same time, states increased the number of crimes on the books[87] and eliminated or narrowed parole provisions.[88] By the 1990s more than half of the states had three-strikes provisions on the books,[89] which sent repeat offenders, even nonviolent ones, away for long periods of time. Today, one in nine inmates in America is serving a life sentence;[90] life sentences have become a defining feature of American corrections even though there is good evidence to suggest that longer sentences are not an effective deterrent to criminal activity.[91] Because of these changes in sentencing practices, by the end of the 21st century, the United States had become the world's largest jailer, sending more people to prison than ever before for longer periods, oftentimes without any individual sentencing determination.

These two parallel trends—transferring juveniles to adult court and introducing determinate sentencing schemes—created the perfect storm for juveniles in the criminal justice system. State law often made it very easy for a child to be tried in adult court, and once that child was in adult court, he was exposed to generally applicable mandatory minimums. The two inmates whose cases were addressed by the Supreme Court in *Miller v. Alabama* provide a good illustration of this dynamic. Kuntrell Jackson was charged with capital felony murder, and Arkansas law permitted the prosecutor to charge him as an adult based on the nature of the charge itself.[92] Once in adult court, a jury convicted

Jackson of both capital murder and aggravated robbery.[93] As the judge noted in Jackson's case, Arkansas law permitted only one sentence: life without parole.[94] Similarly, Evan Miller was charged with murder in the course of arson.[95] Despite the fact that Miller was 14 at the time, the prosecutor successfully transferred his case to adult court, citing his "'mental maturity' and his prior juvenile offenses (truancy and 'criminal mischief')."[96] A jury found Miller guilty, and again, Alabama law permitted only one sentence: life without parole.[97]

The statutes at issue in *Miller* were not outliers. As the *Miller* Court noted, 28 states and the federal government imposed mandatory life without parole on some juveniles convicted of murder in adult court.[98] At the same time, the Court noted that many state transfer laws left no room for judicial discretion: "Of the [twenty-nine] relevant jurisdictions, about half place at least some juvenile homicide offenders in adult court automatically, with no apparent opportunity to seek transfer to juvenile court."[99] Moreover, even if one thought that a mandatory minimum was justifiable in the homicide context, mandatory minimums apply to juveniles prosecuted for much less serious crimes, such as nonviolent drug offenses or property crimes.[100] These two parallel trends—trying children in adult court and imposing mandatory minimums—converged to expose our nation's children to severe, unavoidable sentences.

Having explained the current state of affairs and how we got here, the next three chapters examine the machinery of juvenile justice: how certain kids are more likely than others to end up in the criminal justice system and what that bleak experience looks like for a juvenile inside the system.

2

Crime as a Child's Destiny

WHEN THE TRIAL COURT judge sentenced Terrence to life without parole in 2006, he seemed mystified why Terrence "threw [his] life away"[1] by violating the terms of his probation. The judge made statements suggesting that Terrence had been given every opportunity in life to be a productive member of society and to make good choices for himself. He said that Terrence had "quite a family structure" and "a lot of people who wanted to try and help [him] get [his] life turned around."[2]

In fact, nothing could have been further from the truth. Terrence was born into a world of poverty, drugs, and violence. Social science tells us that some children are virtually destined for criminal activity because of either immutable characteristics or environmental factors over which they have no control. And Terrence was one of those kids. This does not mean that Terrence, or other juveniles like him who violate the law, are absolved of responsibility for their actions. Rather, it tells us that social intervention is required far sooner and in a far different manner than what the criminal justice system metes out.

This chapter proceeds in two parts. Part A describes Terrence's childhood and the variables in his youth that made his criminal conduct readily understandable, if not virtually inescapable—contrary to what the sentencing judge said in 2006. Part B situates Terrence's experience in the larger context of social science research. This research demonstrates that certain children—namely, poor kids, minority kids, kids who have an incarcerated parent, and kids who witness violence in the home—are statistically more likely to end up in the adult criminal justice system. If we are to improve the odds for these kids, we must do more than tinker with that system when they finally get there.

A. Inheriting Crime

Unlike the initial trial court judge who sentenced Terrence, the judge who resentenced Terrence in 2012, after his Supreme Court victory, had the benefit of knowledge. The resentencing judge heard testimony both written and oral from a mitigation specialist who had done extensive research on Terrence's childhood, his education, his family, and the social context in which he was raised. The picture she paints is hard to stomach.[3]

Terrence was born into a family legacy of poverty, substance abuse, and violence. His mother, Mary Graham, grew up in a home much like the one she would later create for her own sons. Terrence's maternal grandmother, Mary Alice, was pregnant at 12 and went on to have five children—four sons and Mary Graham. Mary Alice abused her children physically and verbally. She regularly said to Mary as she beat her, "I'm gonna break your back open"; Mary Graham would later repeat that same threat while inflicting similar beatings on Terrence and his brothers. Mary Alice's four sons, Terrence's uncles, have all served time in the Florida Department of Corrections. Mary Alice died at the age of 44 addicted to drugs.

Terrence's mother, Mary Graham, and his father, Harry Jones, met when Mary was 22. Mary Graham has two sons with Harry Jones, Tarvus and Terrence. Mary's two younger sons, Michael and Deonte, each have different fathers—men whom Mary met after Harry moved out when Terrence was 6. Harry Jones, while he left home when Terrence was still young, is the only father figure Terrence ever had.

When they were first together, Harry introduced Mary to crack cocaine, and crack then dominated the balance of their life together. Mary denies having used crack during her pregnancy with Terrence, but family members recall her having done so. Social service records indicate that she had been addicted to drugs before Terrence's birth and that he exhibited symptoms of drug exposure at birth. In addition to crack cocaine, Mary also used marijuana and alcohol excessively during Terrence's childhood.

Terrence's mother and father allowed others to get high in their apartment in order to fund their own drug habits. Users who smoked crack in the home were required to "pay the house lady" by supplying Mary with drugs. Mary recalls that "whenever she was at home, she was high," and she has no recollection of what her children were doing then. Terrence and his older brother recall being sent out of the house when they were young boys because their mother and father, as well as other drug users, were getting high and didn't want to listen to the sound of children. The boys were also scared of their parents when they were high because they behaved in "strange and frightening ways" and looked like "two mutes with large bug eyes." Sometimes the boys played in parking lots until late at night—or until the drugs ran out. At times they would bang on the apartment door begging to come back home; other times they sought sanctuary in a neighbor's home. While Mary stopped using drugs when Terrence was still in grade school, Terrence's father remains addicted to this day.

Poverty was another central theme of Terrence's childhood. Terrence says he never saw someone go to work—that where he grew up "you either smoked crack or sold crack."[4] His mother and father did, at times, hold down low-skill jobs. Mary was a maid and a grocery store employee, while Harry was a trained carpenter but rarely employed. Harry received disability payments when Terrence was young, and he stopped working altogether in 1996.

Because of their drug addiction and underemployment, there was little money for basics, such as housing, food, clothing, and utilities. Mary's aunt, Jean, who functioned as a grandmother to Terrence, says that when Mary did have an income it was used to finance her drug habit, not support her children. By the time Terrence was 13, he and his family had lived in nine different homes, all of which were Section 8 subsidized housing. Hunger was a constant struggle. Terrence reports that he would sometimes call Jean when the hunger was unbearable. Mary was enraged when she found out the boys had done that, so they often went days without food before calling their "grandmother." They only called when "they got too hungry to wait another day."

Mary recalls having her utilities cut off for nonpayment. Sometimes, when that happened, Terrence's older brother, Tarvus, had to connect a garden hose to the neighbor's house so they could bathe, wash dishes, and have drinking water. Florida Department of Children and Families ("DCF") files from 1989 indicate that, at the time, when Terrence was three, Mary was on crack; there was no electricity in the apartment; and the children were poorly nourished. DCF contemplated removing the children from Mary's custody at that time because there was no food in the home, but no such action was taken.

In addition to addiction and poverty, abuse permeated Terrence's childhood. Terrence's mother repeatedly told him that she was sorry she'd ever given birth to him, that he was a motherfucker and a son of a bitch, and that he would amount to nothing. Mary also physically beat Terrence from the age of two, according to Jean. Jean says that Mary beat all of her sons, but that she was harsher with Terrence and Michael. She beat them with belts, and, as Terrence recalls, with "cords" or whatever was "handy at the moment" when her rage erupted. She beat them all over their bodies, including on their heads and genitals, leaving welts and bruises. Harry occasionally beat the children, but he was the less violent of the two parents. In fact, Harry sometimes fought with Mary trying to defend the children from her beatings. DCF files indicate that the agency was aware of this physical abuse, but again, no action was taken.

Terrence's educational experience was as chaotic and nomadic as the rest of his life. Because they moved homes so often, Terrence was switching schools just as frequently. By ninth grade, he had attended nine schools. Terrence was a quiet child, and he learned to internalize much of the physical and verbal abuse he suffered. Regarding his mother's beatings, he told Jean, "Let her beat me. I'll take myself out of my body." And perhaps he did, but he suffered the consequences of low self-esteem and chronic depression. By second grade, Terrence had been identified as a slow learner and was diagnosed with Attention Deficit Hyperactivity Disorder ("ADHD"). He was never treated with prescription medication because his mother did not allow it. Terrence was in special education classes throughout elementary school. He never completed high school, but he earned his GED in prison.

By the time he was in the 4th grade, Terrence ceded to the world of drugs and lawlessness into which he had been born. He began drinking alcohol that year and reports that he would get drunk at least four times a week. Starting at the age of 13, Terrence smoked marijuana and drank alcohol daily until he was incarcerated in 2004. In 2003, when he would have been in 10th grade, Terrence ran away from home, dropped out of school, and was living either in a car or with various friends. Those friends went on to become his codefendants in the barbeque restaurant robbery later that year.

DCF reports on Terrence and his brothers date back to when Terrence was three years old. Those reports document neglect, hunger, physical and verbal abuse, and an environment of drug abuse and abject poverty. The reports document that Mary sold her food stamps to buy drugs; that she left her sons unattended for extended periods of time; that she locked the children out of the house while she smoked crack; and that she physically beat her children with belt buckles. While Mary was required to participate in an outpatient drug rehabilitation program at one point, the records reveal no formal steps to remove Terrence and his brothers from her custody.

Sadly, as the next part of this chapter demonstrates, statistically speaking, Terrence was on a trajectory toward crime from almost birth.

B. The Research beyond Terrence

It is tempting to hear the horrific details of Terrence's childhood and conclude that his case is an outlier—that few children in this country endure the poverty, violence, and neglect that he did. Unfortunately, his childhood experience is far too common, and research tells us it is a toxic environment from which few kids can ever extricate themselves. In this part of the chapter, I address the ways in which race, poverty, exposure to violence in the home, and having an incarcerated parent affect the likelihood of criminal conduct.

Poverty

Eighty percent of adults prosecuted for a crime in this country are poor,[5] so it is no surprise that poverty is an equally damning reality for children and may ultimately usher them into the criminal justice system.

Poverty is an everyday reality for many children in America. Almost a quarter of all children in this country live in families with incomes below the poverty line,[6] defined as $24,000 for a family of four.[7] Among 35 industrialized countries, the United States has the second highest child poverty rate, despite the fact that we have the largest economy in the world.[8] Poverty threatens a child's well-being in a number of ways.

To begin, social scientists have demonstrated that childhood poverty hinders social, emotional, and physical development. Childhood poverty is linked with a host of interrelated dynamics, all of which make a healthy childhood nearly impossible: poor housing and homelessness; persistent hunger and malnutrition; inadequate health care; and a lack of quality child care and educational resources.[9] More specifically, children in poverty are more likely to have a low birth weight; to experience chronic health problems such as asthma, anemia, and pneumonia; to be exposed to environmental hazards, such as lead paint and toxic waste; and to have little access to healthy food and recreation space, often resulting in childhood obesity.[10] Children who are hungry; sleeping in cars; suffering from chronic, untreated asthma; and living amidst the ambient stress of poverty are hindered in their physical and emotional growth—this goes without saying.

The stress on development manifests itself on both a short- and long-term basis. Researchers at the Center for Poverty Studies at the University of California, Davis, recently demonstrated the risks associated with low maternal education, poverty, and maternal depression.[11] Specifically, mothers with lower household income and lower levels of education were more likely to be negative in their play interactions with their children; the children, in turn, were less capable of understanding emotions, both their own and others'.[12] And as the study demonstrates, emotional understanding in early childhood predicts later noncompliance with social norms and expectations.[13]

This study finds confirmation in statements of the American Psychological Association (APA).[14] APA research indicates that children in poverty are at increased risk for emotional and behavioral problems, such as impulsiveness, aggression, ADHD, and peer conflict.[15] At the same time, children in poverty have a higher risk for emotional problems, such as anxiety, depression, and low self-esteem.[16] More often than not, the adult parents living in poverty are experiencing similar emotional problems, and this can lead to poor parenting choices, which only exacerbate the child's emotional problems.

A child cannot thrive in a school setting when she is hungry, lacking consistent child care, potentially moving homes, and coping with parental stress. And research bears this out: low household income correlates with poor performance in school.[17] Once again, social science tells us that the instability and stress associated with poverty can hinder healthy childhood attachment and emotional growth.[18] A child who enters the school system with a host of emotional, social, and physical challenges faces an uphill academic battle. Educator Eric Jensen, author of *Teaching with Poverty in Mind*, explains that children raised in poverty are more likely than their non-impoverished peers to exhibit noncompliant behaviors, such as impatience, poor "manners," seemingly inappropriate emotional responses, and a lack of empathy and shame.[19] As he demonstrates, children raised in poverty are simply not taught the range of behavioral responses that more affluent children are taught, and thus they do not have the skills to respond to certain school scenarios. He gives the example of a child who, when reprimanded, smirks at the teacher, instead of expressing remorse. Since remorse is a taught concept, and the poor child is less likely to have been taught remorse for a host of complex reasons, the child simply cannot access that emotional response. The teacher, unaware of this dynamic, may label the child as "having an attitude," lacking in respect, or just a "problem kid."[20]

On top of a limited range of emotional skills, children raised in poverty endure chronic stress, and this stress can inhibit their learning capacity. As Jensen explains:

Exposure to chronic or acute stress is hardwired into children's developing brains, creating a devastating, cumulative effect. . . . Compared with a healthy neuron, a stressed neuron generates a weaker signal, handles less blood flow, processes less oxygen, and extends fewer connective branches to nearby cells. The prefrontal cortex and the hippocampus, crucial for learning, cognition, and working memory, are the areas of the brain most affected by *cortisol*, the so-called "stress hormone." Experiments have demonstrated that exposure to chronic or acute stress actually shrinks neurons in the brain's frontal lobes—an area that includes the prefrontal cortex and is responsible for such functions as making judgments, planning, and regulating impulsivity . . .—and can modify and impair the hippocampus in ways that reduce learning capacity.[21]

When one recognizes the way in which poverty impacts brain development and operation, it makes sense that childhood poverty correlates with poor learning outcomes, such as lower standardized test scores and grades, higher high school dropout rates, and lower college attendance rates. Decades of research document this correlation. In 1966, the U.S. Commissioner of Education asked Johns Hopkins Professor James Coleman to examine the question of what strategy was most likely to equalize educational opportunities for poor minority students. The Coleman Report, and various replications of its data since then, found that neither racial integration nor facility improvement were the optimal strategy—that, in fact, the best way to improve academic achievement for poor minority students was to increase family income.[22] More recently, Stanford Graduate School of Education Professor Sean Reardon has demonstrated that, as the income gap has widened in this country, so, too, has the education achievement gap. In fact, as Reardon's work shows, the educational achievement gap in this country is now more pronounced along class lines than along race lines.[23] More than half a century of social science research tells us that poverty hinders learning and educational outcomes.

Poverty also dramatically increases the likelihood of a child entering the juvenile justice system—even when controlling for other variables like race and ethnicity. As University of North Carolina Law Professor Tamar Birckhead explains, even well-intentioned state actors direct children to the juvenile court system, thinking that the system will meet their social welfare needs.[24] She calls this "needs-based delinquency," and describes how it is steeped into the very design of the juvenile court:

> The legislation that governs juvenile court practice in each state commonly contains provisions that explicitly call for consideration of the child's needs and the family's socioeconomic status. Court policies give decision-makers wide discretion to consider these factors at critical stages in the case. As a result, typical features of juvenile court laws and practices combine to shift the system's emphasis from

an evaluation of a child's culpability to an assessment of the family's class status. In this way, needs-based delinquency becomes the norm.[25]

Birckhead traces how this class-based delinquency determination proceeds from intake onward. At the intake stage, state law may require that the delinquency petition set forth the facts constituting the alleged crime but also a statement that the juvenile "requires supervision, treatment or confinement."[26] Thus, by definition, in some jurisdictions a petition alleging the same crime committed by two juveniles—one whose parents can afford to retain private treatment and one whose parents cannot—will result in two opposite outcomes. The low-income child's delinquency petition will move forward, while the more affluent child's will not. Once in the system, children living in poverty are less likely to be able to participate in diversion programs, again often for purely economic reasons. Juvenile court judges may be reluctant to, or by law incapable of, permitting a child to participate in a diversion program without certain provisions in place—like consistent parental supervision or access to a landline telephone for electronic monitoring. In these ways, "families without home phone lines or who have inconsistent access to transportation, unreliable child care, or inflexible work schedules will inevitably have difficulty complying with these policies."[27] Birckhead concludes that this needs-based delinquency model means something stark and terrifying: "Children from low-income homes do not have to be as 'guilty' as those from families of means to enter and remain in the juvenile system."[28]

Once adjudicated as a juvenile delinquent, a child faces a wide range of collateral consequences and may be more susceptible to future adult criminal charges. To begin, it is a common misperception that a juvenile adjudication is sealed and will not sully a child's record going forward. A child deemed delinquent may be suspended or expelled from school.[29] Depending on the nature of the juvenile adjudication, it can result in removal from public housing and exclusion from certain employment opportunities.[30] A juvenile adjudication can also serve as a sentencing enhancement factor in future criminal adjudications.[31] Moreover, just as adults who are arrested can be required to provide a DNA sample, so too can a juvenile in the system be required to provide a DNA sample and fingerprints.[32] This means that even if a juvenile seeks out and obtains expungement of his or her juvenile record, the mere fact of its occurrence can follow the child into adulthood. Thus, a juvenile court delinquency finding can leave an indelible mark on a child's record.

Finally, studies have demonstrated that a juvenile who is held in a detention facility suffers tremendous educational, emotional, and economic harm—and is more likely to engage in subsequent delinquent or criminal behavior.[33] Each year approximately 500,000 youth are sent to juvenile detention centers, and the bulk of them are placed in these centers on a pre-adjudication basis—that is, before they have been judged delinquent.[34] Juvenile detention centers are essentially jails for kids. Researchers estimate that up to two-thirds of the youth in detention centers meet the criteria for a mental disorder, and more than a third require consistent clinical care, which they are unlikely to receive in detention.[35] Moreover, studies have shown that the experience of being incarcerated amidst other troubled youth exacerbates existing mental health conditions, and it may introduce new ones.[36] Finally, study after study, from states across the nation, confirms that juvenile detention does not deter crime, but appears to enhance its likelihood.[37]

Thus, a child born into poverty is statistically more likely to have physical and mental health challenges, significant learning impediments, and contact with the juvenile justice system. In all of these ways, childhood poverty not only hinders healthy development but also paves the way for adult criminality.

Race

As Michelle Alexander posited in her groundbreaking book, *The New Jim Crow: Mass Incarceration in an Age of Colorblindness*,[38] our criminal justice system is anything but colorblind. Racial minorities, especially African Americans, are overrepresented at every juncture of the criminal justice system.

To begin, more than two million adults and children are incarcerated in this country, and African Americans make up nearly half of that population.[39] Together, African Americans and Hispanics comprise almost 60 percent of the nation's prisoners, despite the fact that these two groups make up only 25 percent of the population.[40] As of 2001, one in six black men had been incarcerated, and if current trends continue, one in three black males born today can expect to spend some time in prison.[41] As Professor Alexander explains in *The New Jim Crow*, America's criminal justice policies have decimated entire communities, and black men have paid the highest price.

How did this happen? Professor Alexander argues that we have replaced the system of slavery and its legacy of Jim Crow laws with a new method of social control of African Americans—incarceration. Whether one accepts her thesis or not, it is undeniable that, at every stage in the criminal justice system, race matters; blacks and Hispanics in this country are overrepresented at every juncture.

For many, their first disciplinary or law enforcement encounter happens in a school setting, and race matters in school. A new report by the Graduate School of Education at the University of Pennsylvania (the "Smith-Harper Report") found that black students are suspended and expelled at rates far higher than white students.[42] The Smith-Harper Report found that in the 2011–12 academic year, 1.2 million black students were suspended from K–12 public schools; 55 percent of those suspensions took place in 13 states in the South.[43] The Smith-Harper Report closely examined those 13 states and found that, while blacks were 24 percent of students in the school districts analyzed, they were suspended and expelled at disproportionately high rates across districts.[44] For example, in 743 districts in the South, black students were 50 percent or more of the students suspended from public schools;[45] in 84 districts, 100 percent of suspended students were black.[46] Similarly, in 484 districts, black students were 50 percent or more of the students who were expelled from school; in 181 districts, 100 percent of expelled students were black.[47] The report concludes that there is implicit racial bias in school discipline, just as others have found that there is implicit racial bias in criminal justice scenarios.[48] Not only do expelled and suspended students miss critical time in the classroom, but also studies have shown that those students "are more likely to have later contact with the juvenile justice system than similar students who are not removed from school."[49]

Blacks and Hispanics also experience disproportionately high rates of law enforcement encounters, whether or not those encounters result in arrests or criminal charges. A traffic stop is the most common reason a person interacts with a police officer, and studies have consistently shown that racial minorities, especially black males, are stopped for traffic infractions at a disproportionately high rate. It is hard to tease out racial bias or profiling in the work of law enforcement, but one recent compilation of data by the *New York Times* confirms that the bias is there, even if implicitly. In seven states required to report traffic stop information—Connecticut, Illinois, Maryland, Missouri, Nebraska, North Carolina, and Rhode Island—police are more likely to pull over black drivers than white ones as a function of the driving population.[50]

The *Times* focused on Greensboro, North Carolina, because of its robust data, and it analyzed tens of thousands of traffic stops made by hundreds of officers since 2010 in that city.[51] While blacks made up 39 percent of Greensboro's driving-age population, they constituted 54 percent of the drivers pulled over since 2010.[52] Even more troubling than the rate of stops is the encounter between police and black drivers once the stop happens. "[Police] used their discretion to search black drivers or their cars more than twice as often as white motorists—even though they found drugs and weapons significantly more often when the driver was white. Officers were more likely to stop black drivers for no discernible reason. And they were more likely to use force if the driver was black, even when they did not encounter physical resistance."[53] Federal government statistics confirm that—even when whites and blacks are stopped at approximately the same rate—black drivers are about three times as likely as white drivers and about two times as likely as Hispanic drivers to be searched during a traffic stop.[54] The danger of "Driving While Black" or "DWB" is so well documented that there is now "DWB—the App" so that black drivers can be quickly informed of their legal rights during a traffic stop and record the stop.

It can be equally risky to walk the streets while black in some parts of the country due to policing theories that gained traction in the late 20th century. In 1982, criminologists James Wilson and George Kelling described the "broken windows" theory of policing in *The Atlantic*.[55] They argued that allowing low-level crime, or social disorder, to go unregulated created a climate for more serious crime. As they explained, "disorder and crime are usually inextricably linked, in a kind of developmental sequence. Social psychologists and police officers tend to agree that if a window in a building is broken and is left unrepaired, all the rest of the windows will soon be broken."[56] Police departments across the country embraced this theory, resulting in much harsher enforcement of low-level offenses such as panhandling, being drunk in public, loitering, vagrancy, and prostitution.

One of the ways in which law enforcement implements the "broken windows approach" is by conducting "Terry stops"—a reference to the 1968 Supreme Court decision in *Terry v. Ohio* that authorizes such stops.[57] Under *Terry*, an officer may stop a person and briefly detain him if he has "reasonable suspicion" that crime is afoot.[58] The officer may also conduct a pat-down or frisk of the person's outer clothing to search for weapons if he suspects that the person is armed and dangerous. Reasonable suspicion is far less than probable cause, the standard that an officer must demonstrate in order to make a lawful arrest. Moreover, an officer is entitled to draw upon his personal experiences in law enforcement when determining if there is reasonable suspicion to make a stop.[59]

While mayor of New York City from 2002–2013, Michael Bloomberg pursued a dramatic increase in the use of stop and frisks in order to enhance public safety, and there were dire consequences for minority communities. New York City Police Department (NYPD) records indicate that stop and frisk encounters skyrocketed in number from 97,000 in 2002 to more than 500,000 in 2006.[60] In 2011, the NYPD conducted a record high number of stops—nearly 700,000.[61] City residents complained that the stops were harassing and without justification. The New York chapter of the American Civil Liberties Union (the NYCLU) sought from the NYPD its database of information regarding the stops, but the department refused. In 2007, the NYCLU sued the department and won access to the information.[62]

The NYCLU's independent analysis of the data was damning. The NYPD recorded more than five million stops between 2002 and 2013.[63] Approximately 86 percent of the people stopped were black or Latino,[64] and nearly 90 percent of stops resulted in no criminal sanction—the individuals stopped were found innocent and neither ticketed nor arrested.[65] The NYCLU and other organizations in companion lawsuits argued that this policy constituted unconstitutional discrimination on the basis of race.[66] In 2013, a federal judge agreed and held that the stop and frisk policy led to unreasonable searches and seizures and was racially discriminatory.[67] While Mayor Bloomberg initially appealed the ruling, his successor, Mayor Bill deBlasio, effectively put an end to the NYPD stop and frisk policy. In early 2014, the *New York Times* reported that stop and frisk "is all but gone from New York," noting that in the last half of 2013 there were only 33,699 stops and that violent crime was down across the city in 2014.[68] Over the course of a decade, though, black and Latino residents of the city had come to view police as the enemy, not the safekeepers.

New York City is not an isolated example of racially biased law enforcement practices. The Chicago Police Department recently entered into an agreement to avoid a lawsuit by the ACLU that similarly argued Chicago's stop and frisk practices were racially discriminatory.[69] According to an ACLU study, between May and August of 2014, Chicago police officers made more than 250,000 stops that did not lead to arrests.[70] Almost 75 percent of the people stopped were black.[71] A separate federal lawsuit is still pending in which six black Chicago residents allege that the city's stops are unconstitutional and involve excessive force.[72] And this problem is national in scale. Across the country, not just in Ferguson, there is tremendous racial disparity in rates of arrest; in some cities, black Americans are arrested at 10 times the rate of non-black citizens.[73]

Concern about racism in law enforcement practices has reached a fever pitch in recent years. Headline after headline suggests that black citizens are treated differently from their white counterparts by law enforcement. The death of Trayvon Martin, an unarmed black teenager in Florida, and the acquittal of his shooter, who argued self-defense. The deadly shooting of Michael Brown, an unarmed black teenager in Ferguson, Missouri, and the grand jury's decision not to charge the white officer who killed him. The death of Freddie Gray, a 25-year-old black man, while in Baltimore Police custody; and the acquittal of officers involved in his arrest. The reported suicide of Sandra Bland, a black woman in Texas who had a violent altercation with a police officer during a routine traffic stop. The statistics regarding law enforcement practices and these high-profile cases explain why the Black Lives Matter movement argues that "[b]lack lives are systematically and intentionally targeted for demise."[74]

Finally, when it comes to the most extreme form of punishment on the books in this country, capital punishment, blacks and Hispanics are still disproportionately impacted. According to the Bureau of Justice Statistics, almost 60 percent of the nation's male inmates are black and Hispanic, despite the fact that the black and Hispanic communities make up less than one-third of the U.S. population.[75] The numbers are equally disproportionate in the death penalty context. Blacks and Latinos comprise nearly 55 percent of the current death row population, whereas, again, those groups constitute less than one-third of the national population.[76] Criminal defendants have long argued that the death penalty is imposed in a racially discriminatory manner, and the Supreme Court squarely confronted that issue in *McCleskey v. Kemp*.[77]

The petitioner, McCleskey, argued that his sentence violated the 8th and 14th Amendments because it had been imposed in a racially discriminatory manner. Specifically, McCleskey's counsel relied upon a study of more than two thousand murder cases in Georgia during the 1970s.[78] The study demonstrated that, among other things, even after accounting for nonracial variables, black defendants who killed white victims were most likely to receive the death penalty.[79] Despite the rigor of the statistical evidence, the Supreme Court rejected McCleskey's challenge and held that he had failed to demonstrate a discriminatory *purpose* on the state's part.[80] To this day, the disparity in the death penalty is most pronounced in interracial murders. Since 1976, 31 white people have been executed for murdering a black victim, whereas 297 black citizens have been executed for murdering a white person.[81]

There is no denying that, at literally every point in the criminal justice system, racial minorities are negatively and disproportionately impacted. When a child like Terrence grows up experiencing police as terrifying occupiers, what impact does that have on his psyche? When a child like Terrence looks around and sees that almost every man he knows has had some interaction with the prison system, what message does that send? How does a child overcome that sense of defeat and hopelessness? Many do not.

Family History of Incarceration

Close to three million American children—1 in every 28 kids—have an incarcerated parent.[82] An even higher number of children have had a parent or family member in a local jail for some period of time. As with the prison population, the number of children with incarcerated parents has exploded in the last few decades. "In 1991, there were 452,500 parents in state and federal prisons, with 936,500 minor children. By 2000, the number of parents in prisons had nearly doubled to 737,400, and the number of children affected rose by over a third to 1,531,500."[83] Since 2000, the number of children touched by incarceration has nearly doubled again.[84] As with incarceration, this trend has had a disproportionate impact on minority children. While 1 in 57 white children has an incarcerated parent, 1 in 28 Hispanic children and *1 in 9* African American children have an incarcerated parent.[85]

Social scientists have documented the trauma and hardship of parental incarceration on children, and international human rights advocates have called parental incarceration "the greatest threat to child well-being in the United States."[86] The research does not clearly indicate *why* parental incarceration is so harmful, though. In the very short term, the arrest and removal of a parent can be emotionally traumatic. In 1998, a national study of arrested parents found that 67 percent of parents were arrested in front of their children and more than a quarter reported weapons drawn in front of their children.[87] Witnessing maternal arrest can cause nightmares and flashbacks related to the arrest.[88] In other cases, the child may not witness the arrest or even be told about it, as family members often engage in total or partial deception about the parent's incarceration. This "conspiracy of silence" can have its own set of deleterious effects on children.[89]

Once a parent is removed from the home and incarcerated, the children left behind suffer a number of longer-term consequences. First, a child's living situation most likely will be disrupted. If a child's father is incarcerated, the child is more likely to remain living with the mother; but if a child's mother is in prison, the child most likely resides with his or her grandmother.[90] While this arrangement is thought to be preferable to foster care, it is still a significant change and presents complex emotional challenges. At the same time, even if a child remains with her mother, the economic impact of incarceration may threaten stable housing.

Second, the child of an incarcerated parent loses the ability to have a sustained relationship with that parent. A 2010 study of incarcerated parents conducted by the federal government revealed that approximately 58 percent of parents in a state correctional facility and 45 percent of parents in a federal facility never had a personal visit from their children.[91] Many correctional facilities are located in remote spots, making it time consuming and expensive for a caregiver to enable visits with the incarcerated parent. The Prison Policy Initiative calculates that 63 percent of state prison inmates are confined more than 100 miles from their families, and thus families often need a full day in order to make even a brief visit.[92] In addition, prison regulations, such as limited phone call options and strict rules regarding in-person visits, can inhibit children from visiting. Harsh treatment by prison officials and the prison environment itself can cause great anxiety in children who are able to visit. Despite the fact that studies indicate the importance of maintaining the parent–child attachment, approximately half of incarcerated parents do not receive any visits from their children because of the challenges presented by such visits.[93]

Finally, children who have an incarcerated parent experience stigma, emotional disturbance, and related educational setbacks. Children of incarcerated parents have higher rates of attention deficit, behavioral problems, speech and language delays, and other developmental delays than children who have lost a parent through death or divorce.[94] Young children with incarcerated parents often exhibit anger, aggression, and hostility toward caregivers and siblings, according to a number of studies.[95] School-age children with incarcerated parents lag behind their peers who have non-incarcerated parents. Elementary-grade children of incarcerated parents were more likely to be held back at the end of the year.[96] In the long run, only 1 percent to 2 percent of students with incarcerated mothers and 13 percent to 25 percent of students with imprisoned fathers graduate from college.[97] While youth advocates resist the notion that children of incarcerated adults are more prone to criminal activity, one study suggests that such children are six times more likely to be incarcerated themselves one day.[98]

It is difficult to disentangle the various harms associated with parental incarceration, but it is clear that having a parent or caregiver incarcerated is a serious disadvantage for children. The experience of losing a parent to incarceration imposes significant economic, emotional, and educational costs, and it may even have a criminogenic effect on the child.

Violence in the Home

The American Academy of Child and Adolescent Psychiatry, citing hundreds of studies, reports that children who watch violence on television, particularly realistic depictions of violence, suffer a host of negative consequences. Specifically, children exposed to violence on television become immune to violence; they tend to resort to violence as a problem-solving technique; and they imitate the violence they see.[99] Extrapolate from that and consider the impact that witnessing violence firsthand in the home or neighborhood can have on a child.

Children can experience violence in a number of ways. First, a child can be the victim of violence. Each year in America nearly 700,000 children are abused or neglected—1 child every 45 seconds.[100] That abuse, in turn, enhances the likelihood that a child will end up in the criminal justice system. Studies have consistently shown that childhood abuse and neglect increase the likelihood of delinquency later in life.[101] Among those serving life without parole sentences in this country for a juvenile offense, approximately half were physically abused.[102]

Second, a child can witness violence by one family member against another family member, whether a caregiver or a sibling. Each year, approximately three to four million children may witness domestic violence.[103] By far the bulk of these cases involve a woman being battered by her male partner, and the woman's children often see the violence, recognize the symptoms and effects of the violent acts, and sense the tension in the home before and after the violence.[104] The impact of bearing witness to such violence can be devastating for a child. Children witnessing violence may experience shame, fear, isolation and abandonment, depression and anger.[105] They may have developmental delays and aggressive tendencies; they may engage in self-injury.[106] Children from violent homes are at an increased risk for juvenile delinquency. Among those serving life without parole sentences in this country for a juvenile offense, nearly 80 percent witnessed violence in their homes.[107]

Finally, a child can experience the trauma of violence in their neighborhood and suffer similarly dire consequences.[108] For example, researchers have examined the experience of the 300,000 children living in gang "hot zones" within Los Angeles.[109] Ninety percent of those minors have been victims of or witnesses to felony-level violence.[110] A third of the children have post-traumatic stress disorder and another fifth have clinical depression.[111] Moreover, the chronic stress associated with environmental violence can impede learning and cause long-term impulsive, aggressive behavior. More than half of the juveniles in this country sentenced to life without parole witnessed violence weekly in their neighborhoods.[112]

These variables—poverty, race, exposure to violence, and experience with familial incarceration—all increase a child's likelihood of contact with the criminal justice system. Moreover, these variables are not discrete. For example, black children in this country are more likely to be poor; they are more likely to have an incarcerated parent; they are more likely to live in a crime-ridden neighborhood because of their poverty; and thus they are more likely to witness violence.

Consider Terrence's childhood and social history. He is black; he grew up in the projects; he never saw an individual go to work. Terrence witnessed and experienced violence and abuse throughout his childhood. His parents were both drug addicts; four of his uncles have served time in Florida prisons; and two of his three brothers have criminal records. From a statistical standpoint, Terrence was on a path to prison long before he engaged in any unlawful activity.

Similarly, consider Evan Miller, whose case was heard by the Supreme Court in 2012. At 14, Evan killed a neighbor—his mother's drug dealer—with whom he had been drinking and smoking marijuana on the night of the crime.[113] By the age of 14, Evan had been in and out of foster care because his mother was an alcoholic and a drug addict and because his stepfather abused him.[114] Even at 14, Evan was regularly using drugs and alcohol, and he had already attempted suicide four times.[115] Evan was steeped in poverty, lawlessness, and violence from a young age, and as the statistics suggest, he later acted out violently himself.

Some variables, over which kids have no control, increase the likelihood of criminal activity. Further, most children who victimize others were victims themselves first. This does not mean that we "give kids a pass." If only the solution were that simple. Instead, it means that society has an obligation to intervene in these children's lives long before they commit criminal acts. At the end of the book, I return to discussing concrete steps that states can take to sever the path of crime as destiny.

If some demographic variables make crime feel like destiny for some children, certain legal and policy mechanisms turn that destiny into reality. The next chapter explores those mechanisms.

3

Legal and Policy Paths to Juvenile Incarceration

AT 17, ANDRE LYLE and a high school classmate in Des Moines, Iowa, fought over a bag of marijuana.[1] During the fight, Andre punched his schoolmate and seized the bag, for which Andre had paid $5 one day earlier.[2] As a result of the altercation, Andre was charged with and convicted of second-degree burglary, and sentenced to 25 years in prison—7 of which he was required to serve before he was eligible for parole.[3]

In 2014, the Iowa Supreme Court held that mandatory minimums like the one that sent Andre away have no legitimate application to children and that juvenile sentences must be tailored to the individual case.[4] Iowa, though, is the only state in the Union that has taken such a position, and mandatory minimums are the norm nationwide.[5] Equally common in this nation today are punitive school policies that render even offenses that we think of as "inane juvenile schoolyard conduct"[6] the basis for serious criminal charges.

This chapter explains that, if some sociodemographic factors make crime one's destiny, certain policies and laws make that destiny a reality. Specifically, this chapter identifies four fault lines that expose children to the criminal justice system and its harsh, often life-altering consequences: (1) the "school to prison pipeline"; (2) transfer laws that remove youth from the juvenile court's jurisdiction, often without judicial oversight; (3) ineffective assistance of counsel for juveniles accused of crime; and (4) the use of generally applicable mandatory minimums to sentence juveniles. Chapter 4 demonstrates the sobering fact that a juvenile's first interaction with the law, whether legitimate or permanent, may seal his or her their their fate as a "criminal."

A. School to Prison Pipeline

On October 26, 2015, at Spring Valley High School in Columbia, South Carolina, what should have been a typical, if frustrating, exchange between an adolescent student and a teacher turned into a violent assault by police officer Ben Fields on that 16-year-old student.[7] According to eyewitness accounts, the young female student had her cell phone out in the classroom, and the teacher told her to put it away. The student refused the teacher's instruction, and she also refused an administrator's direction to come to the office.[8] Officer Fields was then called into the classroom, and, after she refused the officer's order to leave the room, "Fields tipped the girl's chair and desk backward, lifting her out of her seat and slamming her to the floor, and then dragged her to the front of the classroom, where he cuffed her hands behind her back."[9]

A classmate recorded the episode on her cell phone, and the video went viral, prompting school officials and sheriff's department representatives to decry the incident. The county sheriff said the video "makes you sick to your stomach,"[10] and the superintendent's statement reported that the school district was "deeply concerned" about the incident.[11] The officer involved in the episode was ultimately fired,[12] and the Department of Justice launched a civil rights investigation.[13] But the practices that enabled the Spring Valley incident are endemic to modern American public education, and they often inflict more lasting harm on kids than the physical assault documented in the viral video. In fact, the practices that enabled the Spring Valley High School assault epitomize what social scientists call the "school to prison pipeline"—a metaphor to describe the concept "that excessive school punishment, rigid security, and the neglect of students' needs can increase the chances that youth go to prison."[14] This subsection of the chapter explains those practices, why they are so prevalent today, and the long-term damage they do to children.

As was discussed at the outset of the book, politicians of the late 20th century ushered in a series of tough on crime policies, the most significant of which was the War on Drugs. This shift in politics and practice trickled down to the level of school discipline, too. The concept of police in schools, or "school resource officers" (SROs), was first explored in the 1950s in Michigan in an effort to promote positive interaction between police and students.[15] At that time, there were fewer than 100 police officers in schools.[16] But high rates of community and school crime in the late 1980s and early 1990s, as well as the (later debunked) theory of the juvenile super-predator, generated a web of draconian school discipline and security protocols that remain in place today.[17]

In the 1990s, schools across the country began to introduce security measures that had been historically reserved for criminal justice efforts: surveillance cameras, metal detectors, drug-sniffing dogs, drug testing, and locked doors and gates became part of the public school experience.[18] The National Center for Education reports that in the 2009–10 school year, 60 percent of public high schools employed random searches with drug-detecting dogs, and 84 percent of public high schools relied upon electronic surveillance cameras.[19] In addition, nearly 70 percent of students surveyed between 12 and 18 years of age reported a security guard or police officer at their school.[20]

The most visible element of this trend is the presence of security personnel within school buildings. A recent Department of Education Survey found that 43 percent of public schools rely upon security staff, while 28 percent have "sworn law enforcement officers routinely carrying a firearm."[21] While SROs were initially introduced to promote good relations between students and law enforcement, in the wake of the 1999 Columbine shooting, the dynamic changed. The SRO model evolved to keep students safe from dangerous criminals, and the federal government invested heavily in the practice. Between 1999 and 2005, the Department of Justice's Office of Community Oriented Policing Services (COPS) poured over $750 million into more than 3,000 law enforcement agencies, resulting in more than 6,500 newly hired school resource officers.[22]

Similar programs exist at the state and local level.[23] The *New York Times* reported in 2009 that there were over 17,000 sworn officers in public schools that year.[24] The National Association of School Resource Officers (NASRO) estimates that today there are between 14,000 and

20,000 officers in schools nationwide.[25] School resource officers are currently the fastest-growing segment of law enforcement.[26]

At the same time that schools have increased security measures and reliance upon law enforcement, they have also adopted "zero-tolerance" policies for what many consider to be normal, age-appropriate behavior from children. These policies were first adopted as part of the War on Drugs in the 1990s as schools struggled to keep drugs out of schools.[27] Over time, though, the zero tolerance philosophy was embraced as a more widely applicable approach to school discipline. These policies "mandate[e] the application of predetermined consequences, most often severe and punitive in nature, that are intended to be applied regardless of the gravity of behavior, mitigating circumstances, or situational context."[28] The goal of such policies, as explained by James Alan Fox, professor of criminology at Northeastern University, is twofold: "deal with the small stuff so they won't go to the big stuff, and . . . sen[d] a strong message of deterrence."[29]

With this combination of zero tolerance rules and officers in the schools, "discipline" too often has morphed into law enforcement. For example, fistfights were once thought of as an "unfortunate but expected part of growing up,"[30] and they may have been dealt with in the past by a principal or other administrator meting out discretionary punishment in school. Today, fistfights regularly result in suspension and arrest.[31] In the 2006–7 school year, officers arrested 3,500 students across 11 Texas school districts, but only 20 percent of those incidents were violent or involved a weapon (and usually the weapon was a fist).[32] In St. Paul, Minnesota, a high school student, believed to be trespassing, was arrested for listening to music during class and refusing to obey an officer's instruction to leave the classroom; the officer used Mace on the student during the arrest.[33] In Jefferson Parish, Louisiana, a 15-year-old was charged with battery for throwing Skittles candy at another student on the bus.[34] In Jackson, Mississippi, kids are regularly arrested for minor infractions like walking in the hallway during class and fighting in the school cafeteria.[35] Mainstream media are replete with stories of age-appropriate behavior in school being treated as a law enforcement matter, and in part this is due to the mere presence of SROs. As Emily Owens, a criminology professor at the University of Pennsylvania, explains: "[O]f course, having an officer means that there will be an increased likelihood that law enforcement is involved in what would otherwise be a disciplinary event."[36]

Perhaps the most damaging feature of the zero tolerance approach to discipline is its reliance on exclusionary punishment—removing the student from his or her peers, whether through in-school suspension, suspension, or expulsion. Just as the American reliance on incarceration has exploded in recent decades, so too has its reliance on probation and suspension of students. There is some geographic disparity in the use of suspensions; Florida, which suspended nearly 20 percent of its secondary students in recent years, has the highest suspension rate, followed closely by Mississippi and Delaware.[37]

But the practice is common across the nation and across all age groups. In the 2011–12 school year, nearly 3.5 million children were suspended at least once, costing students nearly 18 million days of classroom instruction.[38] Surprisingly, even preschoolers are subject to expulsion and suspension.[39] According to federal data for the 2011–12 school year, more than 8,000 public preschoolers were suspended at least once[40]—a figure that U.S. Secretary of Education Arne Duncan called "mind-boggling."[41] Today's schools suspend and expel students at more than double the rate for such actions in 1974,[42] despite a nationwide decline in school violence and crime.[43]

In 2009, the issue of zero tolerance discipline and security came before the United States Supreme Court in *Safford Unified School District v. Redding*.[44] The case was based on the following facts.[45] In October 2003, the assistant principal of the Safford Middle School came to Savana Redding's math class and asked her to come to the office. Once in the office, the assistant principal reported that one of Savana's classmates had accused her of giving prescription-strength ibuprofen, a medication banned without advance permission, to a fellow student. Savana denied knowing about the pills and giving them to other students. She offered to let the assistant principal search her belongings, which he did. After finding nothing incriminating, Savana was sent to the school nurse's office where she was ultimately strip searched. No drugs were found on her, and because of her fear and humiliation, her parents sued the school district.

The Supreme Court held that the school had violated Savana's reasonable expectations of privacy with its strip search, especially given the minimal risk associated with the ibuprofen, lack of evidence against Savana, and her age and vulnerability.[46] While the Supreme Court drew a line in the sand in Savana Redding's case, finding that the strip search was unreasonable, similar security and disciplinary measures based on the zero tolerance philosophy are changing the experience of American public education.

Kids are not better off for these changes. To begin, social scientists have demonstrated that zero tolerance discipline is not even effective at achieving its stated goals of improved student behavior and safety. Russ Skiba, professor at Indiana University, examined the National Center for Education Statistics and its study of school violence. Skiba found that, after four years of implementation, schools that use zero tolerance discipline are still less safe than those without such policies.[47] Moreover, critics of zero tolerance point out that even "success stories" may be masking the real story. For example, some schools point to reduced expulsion rates in concurrent years as evidence of the success of zero tolerance. Often, the reduced rate of expulsion is attributable to students dropping out or being incarcerated—rather than returning to school as reformed citizens and community members.[48] Despite claims that students are "scared straight" by zero tolerance policies, there is no evidence to support the claim that these policies make schools safer.[49]

Moreover, the zero tolerance philosophy is affirmatively harmful in a number of ways. Students who are suspended or expelled are removed from the classroom and lose crucial instructional time. They may receive failing grades for each day of school missed; they rarely have adequate assignments to keep pace with missed school; and they may need to repeat the grade.[50] Despite the fact that "troublemakers" are often most in need of academic and social support, these kids, once excluded, fall even further behind academically.

At the same time, students who are suspended or excluded tend to experience a sense of community disenfranchisement that can last long beyond the exclusion itself. Leading psychologists explain that children need to develop strong bonds with adults and notions of fairness and justice, both of which are undermined by draconian school discipline procedures.[51] Most important, suspension increases a student's risk of dropping out of school and of coming into contact with the criminal justice system. More than 30 percent of sophomores who drop out have been suspended,[52] and there is a clear, pronounced link between drop-out rates and incarceration.[53] Approximately 1 in 10 young male high school dropouts is in jail or juvenile detention, as compared to 1 in 35 high school graduates.[54] A 2007 study similarly found that society could save more than $200,000 in prison and other costs for every potential dropout who completed high school.[55] Finally, if a student is arrested during school, even when those charges are dropped, the arrest record follows that student and can hinder their educational and economic opportunities. Draconian school discipline thus pushes students out of school and too often into the criminal justice system.

As civil rights advocates have noted, these myriad negative outcomes disproportionately impact society's most vulnerable children. School security measures are far more commonly employed in poor, minority neighborhoods than in white, affluent ones. The National Center for Education Statistics found that nationwide black students are five times more likely than their white peers to have metal detectors in their school, while Hispanic students are more than twice as likely.[56] At the same time, students from households with incomes below $15,000 a year are four times more likely to have metal detectors and searches at the school entrance than students from households earning $50,000 or more.[57]

Empirical research consistently indicates that black and Latino students are suspended and expelled at significantly higher rates than white students, and this differential treatment has only been widening over time. Since 1972, the suspension rate for white students increased only 2 percentage points—from 3 percent to 5 percent—while the suspension rate for black students nearly tripled from 6 percent to 16 percent.[58] As the NEW YORK TIMES reported in 2012, data from the Department of Education revealed tremendous racial disparity in school discipline: "Although black students made up only 18 percent of those enrolled in the schools sampled, they accounted for 35 percent of those suspended once, 46 percent of those suspended more than once and 39 percent of all expulsions."[59] Despite the fact that "misbehavior" is often an undiagnosed learning disability or mental health issue, poor, minority children are often punished while their white peers receive treatment in response to similar behavior.[60]

Mirroring the impact of mass incarceration, the shift toward severe and exclusionary discipline practices has had a disproportionate impact on poor children of color. As University of Delaware Professor of Sociology and Criminal Justice Aaron Kupchik explains, sadly, "rather than allowing a platform from which all youth can achieve success, students who arrive at school with the fewest social and academic opportunities for success are unfairly targeted and further marginalized."[61]

B. Transfer Laws

As with the school to prison pipeline, modern juvenile transfer laws have ushered kids into the adult criminal system who would not have been there a few decades ago. Chapter 1 addressed transfer laws and the role that they have played in exposing kids to steep mandatory sentences drafted with adults in mind. This section of Chapter 3 revisits transfer laws specifically to address the harms that current transfer provisions inflict on juveniles accused of crime today.

To recap, until the late 20th century, a juvenile accused of a crime was charged in juvenile court and appeared before a juvenile judge.[62] That judge enjoyed tremendous discretion to tailor the punishment or treatment to the individual and his or her surrounding circumstances. If the prosecutor believed that the juvenile's case should be transferred to adult criminal court, the juvenile court judge would hold a hearing and the prosecutor would have to convince the judge that the juvenile's alleged crime was too serious for the court to handle and/or required punishment that the court simply was not authorized to impose. At the same time, the judge would take into account age, the relative immaturity of the youth, and whether the youth had any prior record of criminal or delinquent conduct. For most of the 20th century, juvenile transfer was an uphill battle for prosecutors, and it was rare.

States and prosecutors' offices do not collect good data on the transfer decision, so there is a recognized dearth of information regarding the volume of youth transfer nationwide.[63] However, there is clear evidence regarding the direction of the trend toward adjudication in adult court. Before the 1970s, automatic transfer and prosecutorial discretionary transfer provisions were uncommon—only a handful of states had such laws.[64] By 2000, the exact opposite was true: 38 states had automatic transfer laws, while 15 had prosecutorial discretion transfer statutes.[65] Because of these transfer provisions, The Campaign for Youth Justice estimates that "250,000 youth are tried, sentenced, or incarcerated as adults every year across the United States," and most of these youth are charged with nonviolent offenses.[66] In sum, as described in Chapter 1, transfer to adult court is common today, and it is relatively easy.

The stakes are tremendously high at the transfer juncture, as the contrast between juvenile and adult court is stark. Historically, juvenile courts have been focused on discerning the reasons for youth misconduct and on rehabilitation.[67] In fact, the stated purpose of most juvenile laws begins with pursuing the best interests of the child.[68] Toward that end, the juvenile courts are relatively informal and less adversarial than adult court.[69] Juvenile judges tend to act in a paternalistic way, and they are more likely to impose probation or community service than incarceration.[70] While detention of any kind is harmful to youth, juvenile detention is safer and more successful than incarceration with adults. At the same time, individuals whose cases are adjudicated in juvenile court generally must be released at age 21.[71] Finally, juvenile court records are typically sealed in an attempt to safeguard the child's future educational and career prospects.[72]

On the other hand, adult criminal court does not formally ask about the best interests of the child; the applicable criminal code is the one drafted for adults with retribution and deterrence in mind. The adult criminal process is entirely adversarial, and incarceration is the common punishment. Even if the incarceration term is relatively short, the collateral consequences of an adult criminal conviction can be life-altering. A child convicted in adult court may be required to register as a sex offender for life; juvenile convictions in adult court can serve as prior convictions for purposes of adult recidivism statutes; and there is no expunging an adult criminal conviction, thus hindering long-term economic prospects for a youthful offender. In short, for a child accused of a crime, the threshold question of whether the case will be in juvenile or adult court is often outcome determinative.

There may be instances where a juvenile needs to be tried in adult court—for example, cases where an older adolescent has a lengthy record of delinquency, he has committed a very serious crime, and prior attempts at rehabilitation have proven unsuccessful. However, scholars studying juveniles agree that the trend toward adult prosecution of children is inappropriate and harmful in a number of ways for most youth. First, whether they are charged with a misdemeanor or a serious crime, juveniles are simply not developmentally equipped to deal with the adversarial process of adult criminal court. In particular, neurological, intellectual, emotional, and psychosocial development continues through late adolescence, and developmental immaturity on these fronts can hamper a juvenile's ability to comprehend the criminal process at every juncture.[73]

The MacArthur Juvenile Adjudicative Competence Study examined the empirical relationship between developmental immaturity and the abilities of young defendants to participate in their criminal trials.[74] The study revealed what every parent knows: that decision-making competence improves with age.[75] Participants were asked to consider hypothetical legal scenarios involving police interrogation and plea agreements.[76] The younger the participant, the more likely they were to waive their constitutional rights and admit wrongdoing, and the more likely they were to accept a plea agreement despite the adverse consequences of both choices.[77] The study concluded that, consistent with prior research, young adolescents are less capable of risk assessment and long-term planning and more susceptible to peer and authority figure influence.[78] These findings confirm that *by definition* juveniles are at a disadvantage in the adult criminal system—a disadvantage that only time and maturity can cure.

Second, juveniles charged in adult court are exposed to much harsher sentences and conditions of confinement than those in juvenile court. Again, juvenile courts are more likely to employ diversion programs, probation, and community service, whereas adult courts tend to impose incarceration. And while juveniles need educational, psychological, and vocational services given their critical stage in development, they are rarely able to obtain them in an adult prison context.[79] Moreover, studies have consistently shown that incarceration has a criminogenic effect on juveniles—that is, prison makes kids better criminals.[80] And it is easy to see why. Children are five times more likely to be sexually assaulted in adult facilities than in juvenile facilities,[81] and they are easy prey to violence at the hands of fellow inmates and staff.[82] As a result, juveniles housed in adult prisons are 36 times more likely to commit suicide than their peers who are housed apart from adults.[83]

By and large, transferring children to the adult criminal system is counterproductive and tragic. Precisely because children's brains are still in flux until late adolescence, they are more amenable to rehabilitation than adults. Studies have shown that probation and community service are more effective with juveniles than adults. This opportunity is lost when society exposes kids to harsh sentences rather than investing in their rehabilitation. At the same time, 80 percent of youth convicted as adults will be released from prison before their 21st birthday, and 95 percent will be released by their 25th birthday.[84] Youth detention not only reduces future productivity and earnings, but it also enhances the likelihood of future delinquency and recidivism. Society has a collective interest in ensuring that when those young adults rejoin its ranks, they have been improved rather than traumatized.

Unfortunately, despite these documented harms, the politically satisfying message of "adult crime, adult time" has generated laws enabling adult prosecution of kids, even very young ones. As of 2011, there were 21 states plus the District of Columbia that had at least one provision for transferring juveniles to criminal court with *no* minimum age requirement.[85] Three states set the minimum age for transfer at 10 years old, while another three states set the minimum age at 12 years.[86] Because more than half the jurisdictions in the United States set no minimum age for transfer to adult court, or set it at 12 and below, even very young children can be adjudicated in adult criminal court for serious crimes that the children themselves do not have the capacity to appreciate.

In 2001, Lionel Tate became one of the youngest children in America to be sentenced to life without parole when he was convicted of first-degree murder for killing his 6-year-old neighbor.[87] Tate, 12 at the time of the crime, never denied responsibility for the young girl's death, but instead claimed that he was imitating the pro wrestling moves he had seen on television when he accidentally killed her.[88] Tate's conviction and sentence drew international attention from human rights advocates and scholars who argued that there was simply no way for a 12-year-old child to be competent to face an adult criminal trial. In 2003, an appeals court overturned Tate's conviction and sentence, finding that his mental competency should have been evaluated,[89] but still the practice of charging kids in adult court continues.

In 2008, an 8-year-old boy in Arizona was charged with two counts of premeditated murder for shooting and killing his father and his father's friend.[90] Had his lawyer not accepted a plea deal that guaranteed the boy mental health treatment, the boy faced adult prosecution and a life sentence in prison even though critics argued that the child lacked the capacity to form criminal intent.[91] In 2015, an 11-year-old boy in Tennessee was charged with first-degree murder for killing his 8-year-old neighbor when she refused to let him play with her puppy.[92] That same year, a Wisconsin judge approved the adult prosecution of two 12-year old girls on first-degree attempted murder charges.[93] The two girls lured a third friend to the woods and stabbed her in order to appease "Slender Man," an Internet meme whom the girls claimed would harm them if they did not carry out the crime.[94]

All of these cases, and others like them, are tragic—for the victims, of course, but also for the children accused of the crimes and for their loved ones, as no healthy, well-adjusted child acts in such ways. But the remedy of adult prosecution and incarceration only compounds the underlying problems, as the statistics on abuse and suicide within prison reveal. In fact, these children are often lost entirely once they have been prosecuted as adults and sent away—whether or not they rejoin society at some point.

C. Ineffective Assistance of Counsel for Juveniles Accused of Crime

If arrested, whether in school or on the street, and if charged, whether in juvenile or adult court, a youth defendant is entitled to legal representation at the state's expense. As was discussed in Chapter 1, this has been true since 1967, when the Supreme Court held that the right to counsel for juvenile delinquents is central to the notion of fundamental fairness and due process. However, as is the case with poor adults accused of a crime—who are similarly entitled to legal representation per the Sixth Amendment—there is a great chasm between the right announced by the Supreme Court and the reality on the ground. Bryan Stevenson, who has successfully advocated before the Supreme Court

on behalf of poor criminal defendants, has said that the American criminal justice system "treats you better if you're rich and guilty than if
you're poor and innocent."[95]

This part of Chapter 3 explores another fault line that renders a brush
with the law life-altering for some youth in America: ineffective assistance of counsel for juvenile defendants. After briefly explaining the
nature of the right to counsel for a juvenile accused of crime, this part
then explores the problems that plague the system of representation for
poor kids and, finally, the ways in which these systemic problems harm
juvenile defendants—sometimes permanently.

Eighty percent of the people who are prosecuted for a crime in
America are poor.[96] In 1963, the Supreme Court held, in *Gideon v.
Wainwright*, that the Sixth Amendment requires states to provide legal
representation to indigent defendants who face a loss of liberty.[97] The
Gideon Court reasoned that it is an "obvious truth" that a person "too
poor to hire a lawyer cannot be assured a fair trial unless counsel is provided for him."[98] Over time, the Court has expanded upon this right,
requiring states to provide *zealous* representation, assistance for direct
appeals, and even expert assistance where necessary.[99] Thus, four out
of five criminal defendants are entitled to zealous representation at the
state's expense, but that legal entitlement has never translated into practice at the state and county level.

For the last half century, one report after another has documented
the states' collective failure to meet *Gideon's* mandate. Lawyers for
poor criminal defendants often operate with little to no training,
carry excessive caseloads that violate ethical norms of practice, and
merely process their clients through a "meet 'em and plead 'em" system of "McJustice."[100] On the 25th anniversary of the *Gideon* decision, Anthony Lewis reflected on its import and wrote, "Twenty-five
years later the *Gideon* case still has much to say to us—about the
Constitution, the Court, criminal justice. Rereading Justice Black's
opinion, one feels again a sense of wonder at the way the American system works. Yet we have to recognize that the premise of *Gideon* has not
really been fulfilled."[101] Sadly, on the landmark 50th anniversary, Paul
Butler wrote in the NEW YORK TIMES in exactly the same vein, lament-
ing prosecutorial overreach and excessive caseloads for poorly matched
public defenders: "The Supreme Court has famously stated that the

prosecutor's interest 'is not that it shall win a case, but that justice shall be done.' In our adversarial system, however, those are just words on paper. *Gideon*, meanwhile, is an underfunded mandate. Some public defenders are forced to juggle over 2,000 cases per year."[102] Because of the states' collective refusal to comply with *Gideon* for more than half a century now, professor and advocate Stephen Bright has noted that "[n]o constitutional right is celebrated so much in the abstract and observed so little in reality as the right to counsel."[103]

This is equally true in the context of juvenile representation. Under *Gideon, Gault,* and subsequent Supreme Court decisions, juveniles accused of a crime are entitled to counsel whenever they face a loss of liberty, but, as a practical matter, many young defendants do not have representation at critical junctures—let alone zealous representation. A 1995 report by the American Bar Association Juvenile Justice Center found that despite *Gault* and federal statutory law affirming *Gault*, "a large number of children in this country still appear in court without a lawyer."[104] Citing the work of juvenile law expert Professor Barry Feld, the report discussed a number of reasons for this lack of representation: inadequate public defender services; parents' reluctance to accept representation due to fear of fees; and judges encouraging kids to waive their right to counsel so as to expedite cases.[105] That 1995 report concluded that access to a lawyer was a nationwide serious problem, and that many children had no representation at critical stages in their cases.

Nearly a decade later, a 2003 survey by the Office of Juvenile Justice and Delinquency Prevention (OJJDP) found that only 42 percent of youth in custody reported having a lawyer.[106] In 2016, anticipating the 50th anniversary of the *Gault* decision, the National Juvenile Defender Center launched a campaign to publicize the failings of juvenile defense nationwide.[107] Kim Dvorchak, the center's executive director, said at the time that "[j]uveniles too often are questioned by police and enter guilty pleas in court without a lawyer and have no one to investigate their case or understand whether a plea disposition is appropriate.... That's not justice and it's certainly not representation. It's an assembly line process taking place across this country."[108] Thus, access to counsel as envisioned by the *Gault* and *Gideon* Courts has never existed in this country.

Even when a juvenile defendant has access to counsel, again, studies over time reveal nationwide deficiencies in the quality of that representation. The job of a juvenile defense attorney is "enormous":[109]

> In addition to all of the responsibilities involved in presenting the criminal case, juvenile defenders must also gather information regarding clients' individual histories, families, schooling, and community ties, in order to assist courts in diverting appropriate cases, preventing unnecessary pre-trial detention, avoiding unnecessary transfers to adult court, and ordering individualized dispositions.[110]

But most juvenile defenders cannot undertake this capacious vision of representation. To begin, the National Advisory Commission on Criminal Justice Standards and Goals (NAC) stipulates that a public defender should handle no more than 200 juvenile cases per year,[111] yet attorneys rarely can comply with this or other caseload standards set by NAC. A 2004 report by the American Bar Association (ABA) documented the nationwide problem of excessive workloads for public defenders,[112] and subsequently in 2009 two national studies confirmed that many public defenders have crushing caseloads and cannot effectively represent their clients as a result.[113] The American Bar Association's 1995 report found that, among surveyed offices, a public defender's average caseload often exceeded 500 cases per year and more than 300 were juvenile cases.[114] More recently, The Constitution Project conducted a case study of juvenile defender workloads in Clark County (Las Vegas), Nevada, from 1993 to 2001.[115] During that time period, juvenile defender assignments increased almost 400 percent—and by 2001 each attorney in the office was representing nearly 1,500 children, more than seven times the national standard.[116] With excessive caseloads, inevitably, attorneys are not well prepared and cannot adequately investigate their client's case. They are merely processing cases.

Moreover, juvenile defenders are often lacking in necessary, specialized training. The ABA has set standards for public defenders, but these standards are not binding and, in any event, resource constraints and excessive workloads often make the standards moot. For example, the ABA's Ten Principles of a Public Defense Delivery System state that defense counsel's training should match the complexity of the case and that defense counsel should be provided with mandatory continuing legal education.[117] In addition, the National Juvenile Defender Center updated its Ten Core Principles for representing juveniles in delinquency proceedings in 2008 and emphasized the specialized nature of juvenile defense work.[118] The principles recommend ongoing training in all areas of relevant law, but also in areas unique to working with kids, such as child and adolescent development, zero tolerance educational policies, and transfer to adult court.[119]

These articulated standards and principles remain aspirational. The 1995 American Bar Association report documented that more than half of surveyed offices had no manual devoted to delinquency court practice; two-thirds of the offices did not train attorneys regarding the critical issue of transfer into adult court; and more than half failed to address child development.[120] The Constitution Project's 2009 report, *Justice Denied*, cited instances where there was no public defender and juvenile cases were appointed to local members of the bar, some of whom had no expertise in juvenile law but rather had personal connections to the assigning judge.[121]

Finally, juvenile defense work is often perceived as low-status work merely required for promotion to adult court defense, and as a result, juvenile defenders have a high rate of turnover and thus a lack of concentrated knowledge.[122] This reality, in combination with excessive caseloads and a lack of training, leaves many juvenile defendants without effective representation.

That lack of effective representation, in turn, can have dire, life-changing consequences. First, an unrepresented child may feel pressured to waive his or her right to an attorney and thus accept a sentence on the state's terms that deprives the child of educational opportunities and, worse, exposes them to incarceration. Second, even if the child has an attorney, albeit an overworked and undertrained one, he or she may have little to no opportunity to meet with their attorney prior to adjudication of their case. Not only does this compromise the attorney's ability to investigate and prepare for adjudication and sentencing, but also the lack of communication hinders the child's ability to trust the attorney and comprehend the proceedings.[123] Third, an attorney who cannot meet with the client and generate a detailed profile of the client's social, psychological, and educational history cannot robustly argue against transfer to adult court. Finally, ineffective representation may result in the worst possible outcome for a child—secure detention, whether jail, juvenile detention, or prison. As discussed in depth in Chapter 4, incarceration for most youth entails a daily quest to survive and actually increases the child's likelihood of future criminal conduct.

Thus, in these ways, ineffective assistance of counsel for juvenile defendants is another social mechanism by which some children are shunted into the correctional system only to emerge in worse condition.

D. Mandatory Minimums—Drafted for Adults, Applied to Kids

As discussed in Chapter 1, if a child's case is adjudicated in adult court, he or she may be subject to mandatory minimums—statutory laws that require the judge to impose a predetermined sentence. This final section of Chapter 3 returns to the concept of mandatory minimums to explore how those sentences, often disproportionate for adult defendants, are especially unfair to juvenile defendants. To recap, kids can be charged with a crime even for age-appropriate actions in school; they can be transferred to adult court with ease; and they are unlikely to receive effective representation once there. For juveniles who experience that trajectory or some variation on it, the imposition of a mandatory minimum can be the final nail in the coffin.

Academics and practitioners have written about the ways in which mandatory minimums are dehumanizing for adult defendants, and this argument applies with equal, if not greater, force to minors. Molly M. Gill, of the advocacy group Families Against Mandatory Minimums (FAMM), has conceived of mandatory minimums, especially lengthy ones, as a human rights violation.[124] As she explains,

> Offenders go to sentencing hearings justifiably expecting to be treated like individuals. Mandatory minimums replace the individual in the sentencing equation with one or two factors—drug type and weight, or whether the crime is a third strike—that are poor substitutes for blameworthiness. They fail to account for the nature of the crime or the offender's mental state, criminal history, or role in the offense, essential factors in determining how much punishment is deserved.

The inevitable result is cruel, inhumane, degrading, and undeserved overpunishment.[125]

Moreover, as Gill explains, mandatory minimums often lead to sentences that are disproportionate to the crime committed. For example, sometimes a third felony offense indicates a dangerous criminal who should be removed from society for a lengthy period of time, but in other cases, a third felony is not indicative of a person who is past the point of redemption. Gill points to the case of Leandro Andrade, who stole $153 worth of videotapes and received a mandatory life sentence without the possibility of parole for 50 years because the crime was his third felony conviction.[126] Andrade had many mitigating factors in his case: he was an army veteran, a father of three, and a drug addict; his prior felonies were nonviolent property crimes.[127] Yet the mandatory sentencing scheme gave the judge no opportunity to distinguish Mr. Andrade from a hardened, violent criminal.

The case of Weldon Angelos also highlights the disproportionate nature of mandatory sentencing schemes. Angelos sold marijuana three times to an undercover officer, each time charging $350 for the drugs.[128] While Angelos lawfully owned a gun, and had the gun with him during two of the drug sales, he never brandished it or used it. Yet the relevant federal sentencing law, referred to as "gun stacking," required a 5- to 30-year mandatory minimum sentence for possessing, brandishing, or discharging a gun during a drug-trafficking crime, and for each subsequent gun conviction, there was a mandatory sentence of 25 years that had to be served consecutively.[129]

Once he had been convicted, Judge Paul Cassell, who presided over Angelos's case, had no choice but to impose a 55-year minimum for the three gun charges related to the drug sales.[130] The judge imposed one day for the marijuana sales, and he said at the time of sentencing that he knew the sentence was disproportionate and unfair. In his sentencing opinion, Judge Cassell highlighted the arbitrary and unpredictable nature of mandatory sentencing schemes, comparing Angelos's sentence of 738 months to the 188 months that a rapist of three 10-year-olds had received and the 235 months that a murderer of three had received.[131] Angelos was ultimately freed because of a deal orchestrated by the prosecutor who sent him away,[132] but the law that required his

55-year sentence is still on the books, and as Gill writes, "[m]andatory minimums make getting a proportionate sentence a matter of luck, not a matter of justice."[133]

If mandatory minimums are disproportionate and unfair to some adult offenders, they are particular irrational and cruel for juvenile defendants. Mandatory sentencing schemes were drafted with adults in mind. By and large, legislators were not considering the potential application of the mandatory sentences to minors,[134] and this oversight is crucial because the same sentence has a different impact on an offender depending on his age. Justice Kenendy explained this reality in *Graham*: "Life without parole is an especially harsh punishment for a juvenile. Under this sentence a juvenile offender will on average serve more years and a greater percentage of his life in prison than an adult offender. A 16-year-old and a 75-year-old each sentenced to life without parole receive the same punishment in name only."[135] Similarly, in Angelos's case, he was sentenced to 55 years at the age of 24. A 24-year-old man and a 65-year-old man each sentenced to 55 years are receiving different sentences, and the younger defendant receives the much harsher one. Thus, mandatory minimums tend to rob a juvenile defendant of a greater proportion of his or her life, and a more crucial stage of it, than an adult defendant.

Second, mandatory minimums deprive the court of the ability to take into account the mitigating aspects of youth. That is, everything that brain science tells us about kids—that they are less culpable than an adult offender; that they have greater capacity for change; that they are more susceptible and vulnerable within the system—applies whether a juvenile is sentenced to a mandatory term of 10 years or 75 years. Under a mandatory sentencing scheme, the judge simply cannot take into account youth and its attendant circumstances as a mitigating variable. According to the logic of the Supreme Court's recent juvenile sentencing decisions,[136] this is a grave injustice, and, as I discuss in the final chapter of this book, mandatory minimums should be abolished for juveniles.

This chapter began with a discussion of Andre Lyle's case, and it is worth returning to his case to see the impact of mandatory minimums on juveniles across the nation. The state charged Andre as an adult with second-degree robbery for punching a classmate who refused to turn over a bag of marijuana allegedly owed to Andre.[137] Under Iowa law, second-degree robbery is a Class C felony, requiring a sentence of no more than 10 years.[138] Because Andre was tried in adult court and because a mandatory sentencing scheme applied in that context, the sentencing judge had no choice but to impose on Andre a 10-year sentence, 7 of which he was required to serve before parole eligibility.[139]

In addition to his youth and the mitigating aspects of his age in its own right, the Iowa Supreme Court, overturning Andre's sentence, identified a number of other mitigating factors in his case.[140] Andre's grandmother raised him, as Andre's father was in prison and Andre's mother had threatened him with a knife.[141] His grandmother allowed Andre to smoke marijuana; his school attendance was sporadic under her care; and he entered the juvenile justice system at 12 years old.[142] During his teenage years, Andre was involved in many criminal acts.[143] The mandatory scheme under which Andre was sentenced gave no room for consideration of any of these variables. As the Iowa Supreme Court explained, any individualized consideration was obviated by the statute: "A forcible felony can be the product of inane juvenile schoolyard conduct just as it can be the product of the cold and calculated adult conduct most people typically associate with a forcible felony, such as robbery. Yet, our laws have been shaped over the years to eliminate any distinction."[144] As the Iowa Supreme Court recognized, meting out punishment to a juvenile without any consideration of youth and environmental factors is simply "an irrational exercise."[145]

In the wake of the Iowa Supreme Court's decision in *Lyle*, the state was required to provide a resentencing hearing for all inmates similarly situated with Andre Lyle—that is, all inmates who also had been convicted in adult court for crimes committed as a juvenile and who had been given a mandatory sentence.[146] Yet mandatory minimums for juveniles remain commonplace, and no other state supreme court has held that they violate the state or federal constitution. If there are roughly 100 inmates in Iowa alone serving a mandatory, adult sentence for a juvenile crime,[147] it is reasonable to conclude that there are thousands serving such a sentence nationwide, despite their dehumanizing and disproportionate impact.

This chapter, and those before it, explored how children in this country are swept up into the criminal justice system and exposed to harsh sentences, sometimes because of factors beyond their control and often without regard for their age. Having explained how a juvenile enters the system, the next chapter turns to the frightening reality of juvenile incarceration.

4

Life While Down

You asked me about my experience in prison, what my day to day life is like, and do I have access to education, training opportunities or work . . . I know you probably hear this a lot. But my day to day life in prison is hell.[1]

—LETTER FROM DE'ANDRE, incarcerated at age 15

PRISON IS A SCARY place—even for adults who know they are leaving its walls in a short while. The clanging of metal bars; the monotony of the routine; the sterile physical space; the pervasive sense of control and the looming violence that could be used to maintain that control at any time; the sheer weight of being in a cage—these are the defining features of incarceration. For young people, prison is a terrifying place, fraught with choice sets of victimization or violence and devoid of humanity. As De'Andre wrote, it's "hell."

Chapter 4 lays bare the reality of youth coming of age in prison, drawing upon corrections studies and upon the experiences of the inmates with whom I correspond. The chapter begins with a discussion of kids serving time in juvenile detention facilities. While superior to kids being housed with adult inmates, juvenile detention facilities have failed to rehabilitate kids since their inception. Instead, nationwide, juvenile detention facilities have been rife with abuse and neglect almost since they opened their doors.

Chapter 4 then turns to the experience of young people serving time in adult jails and prisons. Most of the inmates with whom I correspond were sentenced to lengthy term-of-year sentences in adult correctional facilities when they were adolescents. They represent a relatively small percentage of detained youth and for good reason: juvenile inmates housed with adults are the most vulnerable and typically the most abused within the system. The United States is virtually alone in the world in permitting the practice of incarcerating kids with adults, and it is considered by many to be a human rights violation.[2]

Chapter 4 closes with a discussion of coping techniques—the ways in which some young inmates navigate a path to survival amid the horrors of prison. Despite these coping mechanisms, the experience of youth incarceration suggests only one conclusion: youth incarceration should be a rare measure of last resort, and it should be age appropriate.

A. Juvenile Detention

On any given day in America, there are approximately 54,000 children confined in juvenile detention and correctional facilities.[3] Often referred to as camps, schools, or even charming names relating to nearby nature sites, these facilities are juvenile prisons.[4] About two-thirds of kids (approximately 36,000) in these facilities have had their day in court and have been committed to serve a term of months or years in a juvenile correctional facility.[5] The remaining third (approximately 18,000) are being detained temporarily, awaiting disposition of their case or permanent placement elsewhere.[6] Among all children in secure residential facilities, only about 25 percent of them have been charged with or convicted of one of the four most serious felonies—homicide, sexual assault, robbery, and aggravated assault.[7] Nearly a third are serving time based on a public order violation, a technical parole or probation violation, or a status offense.[8] Thus, juvenile detention is not being reserved for serious cases where the juvenile poses a risk to society; it is also being employed for school fights, truancy charges, and underage consumption of alcohol.

Fear-based policies about juvenile super-predators in the 1980s and 1990s fueled an enormous increase in juvenile detention during those

decades, but since then, there has been a steady decline in detention figures. For example, between 1985 and 1995 there was a 72 percent increase
in the population of youth held in secure detention nationwide.[9] After
peaking in 1999, though, the trend reversed and the number of juvenile
offenders in secure residential facilities has dropped nearly 50 percent.[10]

While the trend is positive, the overall number of youth in detention is still extraordinarily high compared to other developed nations.[11]
Moreover, as with all aspects of the criminal justice system, poor
minority children are overrepresented within the nation's juvenile corrections population. In 1985, almost 60 percent of youth in detention
centers were white, but by 1995 African American and Hispanic youth
comprised the majority of detained youth.[12] Today, this disparity in
detention persists even as overall detention numbers decline. In 2013,
minority youth made up 68 percent of the juvenile detention population, and black youth alone accounted for 40 percent of that majority.[13] In sum, overall youth detention numbers are declining, but white
youth are benefiting from this trend while minority youth are substantially overrepresented in secure detention centers.

In her groundbreaking book, *Burning Down the House*, in which
she called for the end to all juvenile prisons, Nell Bernstein describes
juvenile detention institutions as fraught from the very start.[14]
Nineteenth-century reformers sought to spare delinquent children
the harsh experience of adult prison and thus created separate facilities
for children. For example, the first private juvenile detention facility
was established in New York in 1825, and this "House of Refuge" was
designed "to provide wayward youth—whether delinquent or merely
destitute—with education and employment 'as in their judgement
will be most for the reformation and . . . future benefit and advantage of such children.'"[15] These institutions, in public and private
form, quickly spread across the nation, as did the recognition that
they could be moneymakers for the civic leaders who operated them.
Agents of these early juvenile facilities were free to roam the streets
and collect children whom they deemed delinquent or impoverished,
without any judicial oversight. Because the state was not regulating this activity, the children who were swept into the early juvenile
prisons were "'other people's children,'" at the time, mostly children
from poor immigrant families.[16]

While the narrative of early juvenile justice is one of paternalism, early juvenile detention facilities were not modeled around caretaking; many of the abuses rampant in today's juvenile prisons existed in the 19th century, too. For example, the concept of juvenile detention was premised on education, but cost constraints drove prison managers to require labor from the incarcerated youth. Boys ranging in age from 8 to 17 were required to perform manual labor during the bulk of their days, and they were managed with a strict disciplinary code that could result in the loss of meals, solitary confinement, and physical punishment.[17] By the end of the 19th century, every state had some form of a juvenile reformatory, though historians say they were "prisons, often brutal and disorderly ones."[18]

Fast-forward 100 years, and juvenile correctional facilities have not changed all that much. Today there are nearly 2,000 facilities nationwide housing juvenile offenders.[19] About half of these facilities are public facilities, while the other half are operated by private for-profit or non-profit groups.[20] Most juvenile correctional centers house youth convicted of violent offenses alongside those convicted of nonviolent offenses.[21] At the same time, 20 percent of kids charged with delinquency are detained prior to their trial and thus have not even been convicted of a crime.[22] Only about two-thirds of all juvenile detention centers offer onsite residential treatment such as mental health services and substance abuse treatment; among public facilities, only half offer such services.[23]

Extensive research has demonstrated that "[y]outh prisons harm kids."[24] And mainstream media headlines explain why.

- In December, 2015, federal and state law enforcement officers raided a Wisconsin facility for young offenders in order to investigate abuse of the minor inmates by staff and staff attempts to cover up the abuse.[25] At the same time, the Milwaukee County Juvenile Detention Center was so overcrowded that kids were forced to sleep on the floor with foam rubber mattresses and staff were required to work 12-hour shifts with no time off.[26]
- In 2015, the father of a detained 14-year-old sued San Mateo County after discovering that his son had been assaulted and raped twice by his 15-year-old cellmate. The victim had never been in the juvenile

correctional facility before, while the perpetrator had previously assaulted another inmate.[27]

- On April 5, 2015, a 14-year-old being held in solitary confinement hanged himself while neighboring inmates screamed for help; the correctional officer on duty told investigators that he was not able to do routine cell checks because he was the only officer on duty.[28]

These tragic headlines illustrate recurring problems with juvenile correctional facilities. To begin, one-quarter of youth detention centers are at or over their capacity,[29] and overcrowded facilities—whether adult or juvenile—create unsafe conditions for inmates and staff. "Crowding affects every aspect of institutional life, from the provision of basic services such as food and bathroom access to programming, recreation, and education. It stretches existing medical and mental health resources . . . and makes it more difficult to maintain cleaning, laundry, and meal preparation."[30] Moreover, as the Wisconsin example demonstrates, as youth inmate populations rise without a commensurate increase in staff, violence becomes more common, as do enhanced security measures such as lockdowns.

Second, the youth who enter juvenile correctional facilities are more likely to have disabilities, as well as emotional and behavioral problems, and they are not likely to receive the comprehensive services that they need.[31] While 10 percent of kids in the public school system are identified as having a disability and requiring special education, 30–50 percent of incarcerated youth have a disability; most perform four years below grade level.[32] Detained youth are entitled to educational programming by law,[33] and the Department of Justice has stated that education is the "foundation for programming in most juvenile institutions."[34] Yet because there is no centralized oversight of education in detention facilities, the result is a lack of programming, and a lack of consequences for detention facilities that fail to educate inmates.[35]

The youth in juvenile correctional facilities also have experienced great trauma and have the psychological scars to show it. Nearly a third of confined youth have attempted suicide at least once.[36] Seventy percent have witnessed someone being seriously injured or killed.[37] About two-thirds of confined youth have a diagnosable mental health condition, and by and large these mental health needs go unmet in secure detention facilities.[38]

Perhaps most troubling is that juvenile detention facilities now regularly employ correctional tactics that were once reserved for adults. Mechanical restraints, including hogtying, strip searches, and the use of solitary confinement, are commonplace in youth detention facilities.[39] While these harsh tactics are traumatic for any inmate, their use is especially damaging for adolescents, given their psychological immaturity and vulnerability.

Department of Justice data suggest that solitary confinement for youth in juvenile correctional facilities across the nation is commonplace.[40] Based on survey data from 2003, the department estimates that 35 percent of youth in custody had been held in isolation for any number of reasons—as a disciplinary tactic, as a medical precaution, or to protect the child from another young inmate.[41] This practice persists in the face of a mountain of evidence demonstrating the damage that isolation inflicts on incarcerated youth. Not only do youth held in isolation miss out on physical and mental developmental opportunities that other incarcerated youth may experience, they also suffer psychologically. Even adults who are held in solitary can decompensate from the experience and suffer anxiety, hallucinations, rage, depression, loss of appetite and weight, insomnia, and decreased brain function.[42] The American Academy of Child and Adolescent Psychiatry has concluded that all of these effects are amplified for adolescents, given their "developmental vulnerability."[43] Finally, juveniles held in isolation are at the greatest risk for suicide: more than half of juvenile detention suicides occurred when the youth was alone in their room, and more than 60 percent of detained youth who took their own life had a history of being held in isolation.[44]

For all the damage we are inflicting on kids in juvenile correctional facilities, as a society we have very little to show for it. Taxpayers spend about five billion dollars a year to confine youth in detention centers, and youth who are confined in these facilities leave with diminished education and employment prospects—and they are more likely to commit another crime.[45] Given the cruel realities of adult prison, as discussed later in this chapter, youth advocates consistently maintain that juvenile detention is preferable for any youth who must be in a secure detention facility. But that is not saying much. Over 100 years of studies on juvenile detention facilities reveal common themes: disproportionate reliance on juvenile prison for poor, minority children; a lack of educational resources and mental health treatment; and rampant abuse at the hands of fellow inmates and staff.[46] As set out in Chapter 7, juvenile incarceration should be a rare measure of last resort because the social science is clear: "[a]nything that can be done in a youth prison can be done in the community, only better."[47]

B. Kids in Adult Prison

Jonathan McClard was a rising high school senior, excited about the prospect of college, when his whole life changed in one night.[48] He and another teenage boy, Jeremy Voshage, had been fighting over Jonathan's ex-girlfriend for several weeks. By one account, the girl at the center of the love triangle had been calling Jonathan, reporting that she was pregnant, and that Voshage was forcing her to use cocaine; Voshage's mother counters that Jonathan was calling her son for weeks and threatening to harm him.[49] On the night of July 10, 2007, Jonathan described himself as "out of [his] head"; he popped some cold medicine pills, smoked some marijuana, asked Voshage to meet him at a local car wash, and packed his dad's .22-caliber rifle in his guitar case.[50] When Voshage arrived at the car wash, Jonathan shot him three times, leaving him badly injured and needing months of physical therapy.[51]

Jonathan confessed to the crime at the time and pleaded guilty to first-degree assault, which in his home state of Missouri carried a maximum penalty of 30 years.[52] Jonathan's attorney requested a dual jurisdiction sentence, which would have allowed Jonathan to remain in the custody of juvenile detention until his 21st birthday, at which point his case would be re-evaluated and a judge would determine if he needed more time in an adult facility. But Jonathan's judge rejected that request and imposed the maximum sentence of 30 years.[53] At 16, he began his sentence in a medium security adult prison, where he was kept in a separate unit until his 17th birthday. Upon turning 17, Jonathan was scheduled to be transferred to the Southeast Correctional Center in Charleston, Missouri, an adult prison that he described as "about the worst there is."[54] Jonathan and his family feared that his age would make him a target, and Jonathan had already been placed on suicide watch twice before his 17th birthday.[55] One week after turning 17 and a few days before his transfer, Jonathan used his bed sheets to fashion a rope, and he hanged himself in his cell.[56] Since his death, Jonathan's mother has become an advocate for juvenile justice reform, arguing that "kids don't belong in adult prisons."[57]

She's right, and yet, on any given day in America, 10,000 kids are housed in adult jails and prisons.[58] Over the course of a year, close to 100,000 youth will spend time in adult facilities.[59] The bulk of these youth are being held temporarily in adult jails while they await their trial.[60] A smaller number, between 2,000 and 3,000 youth, have been convicted and are serving a sentence in an adult prison.[61]

Given the presence of juvenile facilities, one may wonder how and why youth end up serving time in adult facilities at all. As discussed in Chapter 1, youth prosecution in adult court is a relatively recent phenomenon. Federal law creates financial incentives for states to keep youth separate from adults in correctional facilities, but that law does not apply to children who are charged as adults.[62] Once a child is transferred to adult court, only relevant state laws determine if he may be housed with adults, and state laws on that count vary widely.

Forty-eight states permit the practice of jailing youth accused of a crime with adults.[63] This means that in almost all states a child who is not old enough to buy cigarettes, get a body piercing, or vote, can be jailed with adult inmates, even violent ones. In 14 of those states, the use of adult jail is mandated under some circumstances, while in another 15 states some special finding or court order is required before a child can be held in adult jail pending trial.[64] Among the 48 states that permit children to be jailed with adults, only 18 require that juveniles be kept out of contact with adults in the jail.[65] As a practical matter, notwithstanding federal laws recognizing the dangers of adult confinement for kids, the practice regularly occurs nationwide.

Despite the limitations of juvenile detention just discussed, adult confinement for kids is exponentially worse, although exposing its hardships has proven difficult for researchers. Much of prison life is shrouded in secrecy; there is a code of silence. Inmates don't "rat" on other inmates; inmates fear retaliation if they "tell what's going on in the house,"[66] and there is great shame associated with an inmate admitting weakness or vulnerability. However, social scientists have consistently found that youth in adult facilities face a very high risk of physical and sexual assault, among other threats to their physical and psychological well-being. As one prison reform advocate in Arizona explained, prison is like "gladiator school"; "[i]t's a hardening of your soul and your mind and your body."[67] Inmates with whom I correspond confirm each of these dynamics.

Physical Danger

Physical violence, or at least the threat of it, permeates prison life. Approximately 20 percent of male inmates are physically assaulted within prison.[68] First, there is the violence between inmates. As social scientists have documented extensively, "[t]he inmate subculture equates manliness and status with displays of 'toughness' and aggression. . . . victimization itself and the fear thereof breed violence in the form of retaliation or preemptive attacks."[69] Second, violence can and does happen at the hands of correctional officers. For young people in prison, both kinds of violence are more common. According to a 2012 Human Rights Watch study, "adolescents who enter adult prison while they are still below the age of 18 are 'twice as likely to be beaten by staff and fifty percent more likely to be attacked with a weapon than minors in juvenile facilities.' "[70]

In some instances, the prison culture explicitly requires violence. According to a federal lawsuit filed in 2016, R.W., a 17-year old male, became an inmate at Sumter Correctional Institute in Florida in May 2013.[71] Soon after arriving at the prison, other inmates warned R.W. that he would need to pay for his safety in prison either by purchasing canteen items for other prisoners or by fighting another youth in a so-called Test of Heart. It was made clear to R.W. that if he did not do one or the other, he would be constantly subject to physical and sexual assault. R.W. had been living with his grandmother before his incarceration, and by the time he entered the Florida system, she had passed away, leaving him with no financial resources. The canteen purchases were beyond reach, and on July 24, 2013, the Test of Heart was initiated. Six other inmates quickly overwhelmed R.W., and when the attack ended 30 minutes later, he had been hit, choked, slammed against the floor and stabbed with "pokers" fashioned from barbed wire pieces of fencing. Inmates raped him with a broomstick.

The inmates with whom I correspond confirm this stark narrative of prison violence. As Terrence said to me on the day I met him, and as he repeats often in his letters, "I pray every day that I make it out of this place alive."[72] In 2014, 346 people died while incarcerated in Florida.[73] While the bulk of those deaths were attributed to HIV, cancer, cardiac arrest, and other medical issues, 21 of those deaths were homicides and suicides.[74] In another 24 cases the cause of death is still pending.[75] Terrence may not know these statistics, but he knows that the risk of dying in prison is real. Occasionally, if he is lucky, Terrence can visit the prison library, but for the most part, he is left to pass the hours with fellow inmates in the recreation pavilion where even a chess game can be a risky undertaking. As he explains, Terrence may think he's playing chess with another inmate to pass the time, but, as it turns out, that other inmate is "playing to win," and even when he is trying to "stay out of trouble, trouble can find [him]."[76]

While he puts on a brave face in most of his letters, occasionally he will confide his fear that "no one is safe [in prison]."[77] Terrence has watched inmates beat, stab, and rape one another "for no reason at all," and he has seen "officers beat inmates to death and get away scott [sic] free because they say the inmate assaulted them."[78] In one instance, he saw another young man stabbed to death by another inmate; "he came to prison at 16 and was sentence [sic] to 35 years and died at the age of 18 for standing up for himself." [79] With the threat of violence always looming, Terrence, like most young inmates, "wake[s] up scared every morning."[80]

Sexual Assault

Closely tied to the threat of violence is the threat of sexual assault. According to the most recent federal data, administrators of 10 percent of adult correctional facilities nationwide reported nearly 9,000 allegations of sexual victimization in 2011; that number has risen steadily since 2005.[81] About half of those allegations involved nonconsensual sexual acts and abusive sexual contact between inmates, while the other half (49 percent) were allegations of staff sexual misconduct and sexual harassment.[82] When sexual abuse occurs at the hands of a fellow inmate, there is also physical injury in nearly 20 percent of the cases; between inmates and staff there is almost never physical injury.[83] Thus, there is a close nexus between sexual abuse and either physical injury, the threat of injury, or some other power imbalance.

There is a "prototype" for a victim of prison rape, and a young inmate in an adult prison meets every aspect of it: they are young, physically diminutive, new to the facility, and immature. In a 1984 exposé about youth in adult prisons, a corrections officer stated that the chance of a young man avoiding rape in prison was "almost zero. . . . He'll get raped within the first twenty-four to forty-eight hours. That's almost standard."[84] Twenty years later, in 2005, author T. J. Parsell wrote in the NEW YORK TIMES about his own experience as a 17-year-old being sent to an adult prison in Michigan: on his first day there he was drugged and gang raped.[85] For the remainder of his five-year term, he was "the property of another inmate."[86]

The federal Prison Rape Elimination Act (PREA) was based on consistent findings: that prison rape was all too common nationwide, and specifically, that young inmates were five times more likely to be raped in adult facilities than in juvenile ones—often within 48 hours of incarceration.[87] The 2003 law established the National Prison Rape Elimination Commission and charged the commission with crafting standards for eliminating sexual assault in correctional facilities nationwide.[88] Those standards went into effect in 2012, and now states must submit audit evidence demonstrating compliance with PREA standards.[89]

However, in reality, PREA has been more bark than bite. States who are not in compliance are subject to losing 5 percent of their federal prison grant funding, and while that's something, it's not a lot.[90] Most states aspire to PREA compliance, including measures such as training staff to report rape and providing rape kits for all inmates who report sexual assault. Even so, as of summer 2015, only 11 states certified to the Department of Justice that they were in compliance with PREA's standards for eradicating prison rape.[91] While a majority of states have filed letters of assurance with the department, indicating steps toward compliance, a handful of states have yet to do so, citing administrative burdens.[92]

There has always been a concern about the underreporting of prison rape. To admit that one has been the victim of sexual assault not only is humiliating, but it also can make one even more vulnerable to future assaults. Not surprisingly, then, the inmates with whom I correspond mention sexual assault infrequently—and when they do it is presented as a fact of life. Terrence told me that soon after he arrived in prison another inmate calmly told him not to go in the shower room because an inmate was being raped.[93]

Jackson, Terrence's friend and mentor from prison, who is also seeking relief under the *Miller* decision, describes "gangs and homosexuality" as part of the experience.[94] Jackson writes that he tries to mentor younger inmates coming in, now that he has been "down" for nearly 20 years, but he says that many inmates "give up" and become "gangbangers" or "homosexuals."[95] "Guys, try you every day . . . you either have to fight or you know, and I'm not going that route, so we try to stay to ourselves . . . Just pray for us."[96]

Disciplinary Double Bind

Young people coming of age in adult facilities are caught in a double bind. They are uniquely vulnerable to physical and sexual assault, and yet, if they act out, they risk violating the intricate web of rules that govern prison life. Many choose misconduct over abuse. Across the board, younger inmates, especially those under 18, have higher rates of disciplinary violations.[97] According to New York's Department of Corrections, the most common infraction for adolescents is fighting.[98] Not only are young inmates more impulsive and susceptible to peer pressure, but also they quickly realize that they must acclimate to a culture of violence. As one young inmate in Pennsylvania told researchers:

> If someone puts their hands on you, you must defend yourself. They want to know that you will defend yourself. I seen [*sic*] people get hit and now everyone hits them. You have to deal with it. Once you set the record straight you can stay out of trouble.[99]

Similarly, Ramon Mendoza, who was imprisoned at age 14 for burglary in Arizona, assaulted another inmate soon after arriving at prison. He did it so that other inmates would know "that I don't mess around."[100]

While an inmate may be disciplined for fighting, he also may be "written up," "receive a ticket," or get an "incident report" for far less serious prison misconduct.[101] Upon admission, inmates are notified of prohibited acts. While such acts vary by state, there are categories of acts prohibited across correctional institutions. The most serious prohibited acts are no surprise: killing, assaulting, rioting, the possession of weapons, and similarly dangerous actions.[102] Then there are mid-level infractions: fighting with another person, making sexual proposals, stealing, and indecent exposure.[103] In addition, though, inmates can be sanctioned for engaging in any number of ill-defined or less threatening actions, such as insolence toward a staff member, participating in an unauthorized meeting or gathering, failing to stand count, being unsanitary or untidy, feigning illness, and disrupting the orderly running of the institution.[104] At the end of the day, it is easy for an inmate to get a ticket, especially a young inmate who is scared, impulsive, and trying to find his way in a new, threatening environment.

Accordingly, inmates ages 18–24 have approximately 10 times as many disciplinary reports per year as inmates ages 45 and older.[105] Those who write to me consistently share disciplinary records that track this trend. Upon entering prison, they accumulate a lot of tickets; as they age and establish themselves and a routine, their number of tickets declines and often drops off altogether. Jaime, who was incarcerated at the age of 17 for his participation in a felony murder with three adult codefendants, writes that during his first 10 years, he "stayed in trouble," but now, he hasn't been in any trouble for nearly a decade.[106] Similarly, Jackson, who's been incarcerated for nearly 20 years, writes that he hasn't had any trouble in the last 2 years, and in the last 8 years he has had only two disciplinary reports.[107] But try as they may to stay out of trouble, inmates report that tickets can be arbitrary and hard to avoid. Terrence writes in frustration that he's navigating two sets of rules: "We have rules and guidelines that we are suppose [*sic*] to follow but there are 2 types of rules and guidelines. The one's [*sic*] inmates enforce and live by and the one's [*sic*] the officers enforce and live by, but like all rules they only imply [*sic*] when one want them to."[108]

Time in the Hole

When an inmate violates a prison rule, any number of consequences may follow depending upon the severity of the infraction and the discretion of the correctional officer on hand. For example, the inmate may lose visiting or commissary privileges; he may be given extra work or lose the opportunity to participate in recreational activities; and he may lose any reduction in his sentence that had been earned through good behavior.[109] In nearly a third of rule violation instances, inmates are sent to solitary confinement.[110]

Ironically, even though solitary confinement is the worst kind of punishment for the reasons discussed earlier in this chapter, it is not doled out just as punishment. Jails and prisons typically have at least two forms of solitary confinement, and they use solitary for youth and adult inmates alike.[111] When an inmate is sent to isolation as a form of punishment for misbehavior, it is referred to as disciplinary segregation and it can range from a few days to many months.[112] Sometimes, though, an inmate is sent to isolation because he is in danger of being harmed by another inmate or inmates; this is referred to as administrative segregation and it may continue indefinitely.[113]

Whether a person is sent to solitary for punishment or protection, the experience is equally harmful. As discussed previously, solitary confinement is psychologically traumatic even for an adult who enters "the box" mentally intact. Few people can tolerate being in a cell of approximately 80 square feet alone—all day, for many days.[114] For young inmates, common responses to solitary confinement include self-harm, such as cutting, suicidal thoughts, and hallucinations.[115]

During a recent stint in solitary, Terrence wrote to me about his experience in the small space and the arbitrariness of the disciplinary process. He was charged with inappropriate interaction with a female corrections officer; Terrence disputed the charge, as did two other eyewitness inmates. "There were two other inmates right there who wrote witness statements on my behalf, but like always inmates [*sic*] words mean nothing . . . And now I'm in the box for 60 days. I'm on the same wing as the guys who are on death row! And I don't see how they wake up in this cell. It's almost like been [*sic*] outside with bars around you. Kind of hard to describe."[116]

Between physical and sexual assault, the no-win scenario of victimize or be victimized, and the specter of time in the hole—it is no surprise that youth in adult prison have an incredibly high risk of suicide. A 1980 study funded by the federal government found that the suicide rate of youth in adult jails was nearly eight times that of youth in juvenile detention centers.[117] More recently, in 2012, Human Rights Watch and the American Civil Liberties Union reported that it is "uncontroversial that suicide and solitary confinement are correlated" for youth in prison.[118]

Monotony and Dehumanization

When violence and fear abate, inmates still struggle with the numbing monotony and the slow dehumanization of incarceration. It starts with the loss of a name. Inmates are referred to by their Department of Corrections number—not by their name. Even when the state uses an inmate's name, it is often spelled incorrectly. Terrence Graham's case made it all the way to the United States Supreme Court with his name spelled incorrectly on every document. When I asked him about it—because he signed his letters with a different spelling from the court documents—he said, "Yes, I spell my name with an 'E' but the courts never ask me how to spell it they just put it with an 'A.'"[119] Years later, when I spoke with and then met Terrence's mother, who has three sons in Florida's prisons, she echoed the same sense of resignation: "Your voice inside don't matter; they've lost their name." As for the numbers they do go by, she says, "the state gave them that name."[120]

Beyond names, there is the language of prison. Inmates speak of how much time a person has served by "how long they have been down." This phrase makes sense in a number of ways; there is something underground and dark about the whole prison environment. It is hidden from the world for the most part, and it is inherently depressing. Similarly, when inmates describe meals they do not speak of breakfast, lunch or dinner; they refer to feedings, as in "they wake us and the feeding process begins."[121] The caging, shackling, and feeding of prison life suggest the warehousing of animals, not human beings.

By and large inmates share that they have very little to do to pass the time, and yet there is a rigid structure to the day. Correctional officers wake inmates at dawn, and the first formal count of inmates occurs to ensure that all inmates are accounted for and in their specified location.[122] Inmates typically have a predetermined schedule for the day from 5 or 6 a.m. to 11 p.m. when lights are turned off; mostly, the day consists of meals, work, and recreation (if permitted). "Correctional staff count and recount inmates over and over,"[123] and these counts mark the passage of time.

As part of the tough on crime movement of the 1980s and 1990s, education and rehabilitation services were largely stripped from prisons.[124] As a result, few inmates serving lengthy sentences have access to such programming, and many inmates write about the sense that time is standing still. De'Andre writes that he has been trying to take a GED class since he entered prison at 17, four years ago. Because he is serving an 80-year sentence for a homicide he committed at 15, he also cannot work, as he is deemed too dangerous.[125] Alex, serving 62 years for a robbery during which his codefendant shot and killed someone, notices the irony of where his prison is located. Though it is situated on "Reformatory Road," he writes: "there is no true attempts [*sic*] from the prison to reform. Some people spend 22 hours a day in a cell and that's general population. There's no programs. Just people growing old waiting for their out date."[126]

Jaime, like many inmates, speaks of trying to "carve out [his] own routine."[127] But for most that routine involves a lot of monotony: waiting for mail call and hoping for a letter from someone on the outside; "the slamming of doors, count time, and the yelling of [the] authorities."[128] Terrence writes that he feels "dead to the outside world," and wonders if there is a difference between being dead and locked up.[129]

C. Survival Skills

Given the harsh realities of prison, one wonders how anyone survives the experience, let alone comes of age inside such a facility. While certainly not representative of all young men aging in prison, many of the inmates with whom I correspond appear to share some common coping techniques.

First, I hear a lot of gratitude in the letters of inmates. Many inmates are grateful to their family members who make a long trip to see them in person; they are grateful for the chance to see their child, whom they have not seen in a decade; and they are grateful for the opportunity to see the grandmother who raised them one last time before her death. Inmates are thankful for a response to their letter, for a phone call to their loved one on their behalf, and for someone telling them that they have not been forgotten. For many, faith in God and gratitude for these small gestures are the key coping strategies.

Second, those who survive incarceration tend to find something on which to focus their energy. Even those who cannot work may be able to take advantage of recreational time, and small goals in that realm can be a motivator. Many inmates write about their sports activities, perhaps their desire to remain undefeated in flag football. Others focus their time and energy on reading, writing, and artwork.

Men who have been inside for some time often speak of their mentoring activities. For example, Jackson writes about the privilege of being able to organize football, basketball, softball, and track at various facilities.[130] He keeps a record of sporting achievements and posts names and accomplishments in what he calls his "Sporting News Flash." He'll buy the younger men sandwiches and sodas—"little incentives"—that motivate the younger inmates and that also help Jackson from "falling back in that mind state of hopelessness."[131] Similarly, Jaime writes about listening to NPR for book ideas, how he just finished reading about the beatification of Oscar Romero, and how he "tries to challenge the younger guys to read and think."[132]

Not surprisingly, many inmates spend a great deal of time considering the legal issues of their cases. Many write and ask sophisticated legal questions—ones that judges themselves are grappling with today. Is an 80-year sentence that was partially a function of a mandatory sentencing scheme within the purview of *Miller*? Is a life without parole (LWOP) sentence permissible for a juvenile who participated in a felony murder but was not the triggerman? Justice Breyer would say no,[133] and inmates ask why that position has not taken hold. What about resentencing hearings in light of *Miller*? Should an inmate be able to put on evidence regarding his intellectual and social capacity at the time of the crime? Who will prepare that kind of mitigation report? *How* after many years? And at whose expense? Even those inmates who cannot articulate precise legal questions have a very keen sense of the animating principles of the

Miller trilogy. Alex wrote, "I never understood how at 17 I could get a life bid, at 18 I could get death, but can't get a beer til I'm 21 . . . go figure that one out."[134]

While these coping mechanisms may make day-to-day existence more tolerable for an inmate, they do not necessarily translate into life skills for the free world. In fact, many of the skills that inmates must acquire in order to survive prison are precisely the opposite of those they need to exist in free society: a physically and psychologically threatening posture; readiness to attack preemptively so as to ward off a sexual or physical assault; comfort with monotony and boredom; and fear, or at least suspicion, of authority. In a world where youth who come of age in prison are simply warehoused for the rest of their lives, perhaps these are grim realities that most people can just set aside.

However, as discussed in Chapter 3, most young people who enter prison will rejoin the ranks of society. Eighty percent of youth convicted as adults will be released from prison before their 21st birthday, and 95 percent will be released by their 25th birthday.[135] After *Graham* and *Miller*, even those who were sentenced to life or its functional equivalent now have a shot at release, and as discussed in Chapter 6, some inmates have already been released pursuant to those cases. Given this reality, we cannot afford to persist in our current juvenile incarceration practices. We must take a stance against incarceration, reserving it for the rare juvenile who poses a danger to society and ensuring that the arrangement is age appropriate as discussed in the final chapter of this book.

5

Progress and Hope from the Nation's High Court

THE LAST FEW CHAPTERS have exposed the harsh reality of juvenile justice in America today—how vulnerable children, typically in need of social services, are too easily swept into the system and the dire consequences they suffer once they are inside that system. Beginning with this chapter, the book pivots to look at the future of juvenile justice. This chapter examines recent Supreme Court decisions in the area of juvenile sentencing at a granular level, highlighting the ways in which these cases lay the foundation for radical reforms to come. Chapter 6 demonstrates, through the lens of three individuals, the idiosyncratic and bumpy road to implementing these decisions. Finally, Chapter 7 maps out the important, and achievable, work that remains for juvenile justice advocates.

This chapter proceeds in three parts. Part A discusses recent Eighth Amendment Supreme Court decisions that have significantly curbed extreme juvenile sentences at the state level and that have provided moral leadership on this front generally. Part B identifies promising legislative and judicial developments in the wake of the Supreme Court's recent juvenile sentencing decisions. Finally, Part C explains why, even with these recent developments, American juvenile justice is still in desperate need of reform.

A. The *Miller* Trilogy

In its 2012 decision, *Miller v. Alabama*, the Supreme Court held that mandatory LWOP sentences for juveniles violate the Eighth

Amendment's ban on cruel and unusual punishment. The Court had begun to lay the foundation for its *Miller* decision in two earlier cases, *Roper v. Simmons* (2005) and *Graham v. Florida* (2010). Scholars have come to refer to these cases as the *Miller* trilogy. This part of Chapter 5 unpacks these three critical decisions and explains why they are so powerful for proponents of juvenile justice reform.

The road to *Miller* began with *Roper v. Simmons* in 2005.[1] In *Roper*, the Supreme Court held that the practice of executing those who had committed their crimes prior to the age of 18 was unconstitutional.[2] The *Roper* Court employed long-standing Eighth Amendment analysis for the capital setting: it examined juveniles as a group and asked whether the use of execution was proportionate given the diminished culpability of youthful offenders.[3] Further, in assessing proportionality, the Court looked at the "objective indicia of consensus, as expressed in particular by the enactments of legislatures that have addressed the question" and then exercised its own "independent judgment" as to "whether the death penalty is a disproportionate punishment for juveniles."[4] In that process, the *Roper* Court found that a majority of states forbid the practice of juvenile capital punishment; that it was rarely employed in the states that permitted it; and that the national trend was moving away from subjecting juveniles to the death penalty.[5] On this basis, the Court held that the Eighth Amendment forbids juvenile execution.

Having demonstrated that the practice was inconsistent with "evolving standards of decency," the *Roper* Court proceeded to render its own judgment regarding the penalty as it applied to juveniles.[6] The Court focused on three reasons why juveniles are categorically different from adults and thus should not be exposed to capital punishment: they lack maturity; they are far more susceptible to external pressures; and their moral character is still fluid.[7] Finally, the Court held that, in light of juveniles' diminished culpability, neither stated rationale for the death penalty, deterrence or retribution, was adequate justification.[8]

Two aspects of the *Roper* decision are noteworthy in the context of *Miller* and its aftermath. First, the *Roper* Court drew upon science and the proven fact that children are not just small adults. The Court's discussion of the unique attributes of children was anchored in social science work, documenting the inchoate nature of the adolescent brain.[9]

The scientific bent to the *Roper* Court's decision laid important foundation for both the *Graham* and *Miller* decisions.

Second, the *Roper* Court noted that the United States was out of sync with the rest of the world in its use of juvenile capital punishment. While the Court explained that its decision rested on an analysis of legislative trends coupled with its own independent judgment, the Court said, "Our determination that the death penalty is disproportionate punishment for offenders under 18 finds confirmation in the stark reality that the United States is the only country in the world that continues to give official sanction to the juvenile death penalty."[10] The *Roper* Court's reference to American sentencing practices relative to the international arena was also important to the *Graham* and *Miller* decisions, as those cases, too, examined a sentencing practice foreign to most other developed countries.

Five years after *Roper*, in *Graham v. Florida*, the Court took up the question whether LWOP was permissible for a non-homicide juvenile offender.[11] Writing for the majority, Justice Kennedy held that the Constitution categorically forbids such a sentence.[12] First, he explained that the Eighth Amendment bars both "barbaric" punishments and punishments that are disproportionate to the crime committed.[13] Within the latter category, the Court explained that its cases fell into one of two classifications: (1) cases challenging the length of term-of-years sentences, given all the circumstances in a particular case; and (2) cases where the Court has considered categorical restrictions on the death penalty.[14] Because Graham's case challenged "a particular type of sentence" and its application to "an entire class of offenders who have committed a range of crimes," the Court found the categorical approach appropriate and relied upon its recent death penalty case law for guidance.[15]

Just as the Court had done in *Roper*, the *Graham* Court looked to objective indicia of national consensus, beginning with relevant legislation regarding juvenile LWOP. Justice Kennedy explained that, while 37 states, the District of Columbia, and the federal government permitted life without parole sentences for non-homicide juvenile offenders, the actual sentencing practices of these jurisdictions told another story. Based on the evidence before it, the Court determined that, at the time of the decision, there were 123 non-homicide juvenile offenders serving a LWOP sentence nationwide and 77 of them were in Florida prisons.[16] Given the "exceedingly rare" incidence of the punishment in question, the Court held that there was a national consensus against LWOP for non-homicide juvenile offenders.[17]

Again, consistent with the *Roper* approach, the *Graham* Court acknowledged that "community consensus" was "entitled to great weight," but it proceeded to render its own judgment regarding the constitutionality of Graham's sentence.[18] In this regard, the Court focused on two aspects of the case: first, the uniqueness of juvenile offenders— specifically their lessened culpability and their greater capacity for reform—and second, the historical treatment of non-homicide crimes as less severe than crimes where a victim is killed.[19] Looking at these two features, the Court reasoned: "It follows that, when compared to an adult murderer, a juvenile offender who did not kill or intend to kill has a twice diminished moral culpability."[20] At the same time, when the Court examined the various justifications for any criminal sanction, it determined that none could justify LWOP for defendants like Graham. Accordingly, the Court held the following:

A State is not required to guarantee eventual freedom to a juvenile offender convicted of a nonhomicide crime. What the State must do, however, is give defendants like Graham some meaningful opportunity to obtain release based on demonstrated maturity and rehabilitation.... The Eighth Amendment does not foreclose the possibility that persons convicted of nonhomicide crimes committed before adulthood will remain behind bars for life. It does forbid States from making the judgment at the outset that those offenders never will be fit to reenter society.[21]

Thus, the U.S. Supreme Court found LWOP sentences unconstitutional for juvenile non-homicide offenders and, with its decision, entitled Terrence Graham and those similarly situated to a new sentence.

As the Supreme Court itself had acknowledged in *Graham*, its decision applied to a small number of inmates nationwide.[22] At the same time, more than 2,000 inmates nationwide were serving LWOP on the basis of a juvenile *homicide* conviction. In this sense, the *Graham* decision avoided the question whether the Eighth Amendment also precluded LWOP for juveniles convicted of homicide offenses. Only two years later, the Court took up that question in *Miller v. Alabama*. In an opinion authored by Justice Kagan, the majority held that the Eighth Amendment bars mandatory LWOP for juveniles—even those convicted of a homicide offense.[23]

The *Miller* Court explained that its decision rested on two relevant strands of precedent: (1) its line of cases adopting categorical bans on certain sentencing practices, and (2) its line of cases requiring certain procedural safeguards in the capital sentencing context.[24] As to the first line of cases, the Court viewed its ban on mandatory LWOP for juveniles as analogous to its ban on the death penalty for the intellectually disabled or its ban on LWOP for non-homicide juvenile offenders. In both cases, the Court had determined that the sentence at issue was disproportionate in light of the mitigating attributes of the defendant.[25] As to the second line of cases, the *Miller* Court explained that, for juveniles, LWOP is analogous to the death penalty: "[Life without parole] is an 'especially harsh punishment for a juvenile,' because he will almost inevitably serve 'more years and a greater percentage of his life in prison than an adult offender. . . . The penalty when imposed on a teenager, as compared with an older person, is therefore 'the same . . . in name only.' "[26] In light of these two lines of precedent—those finding certain punishments excessive for classes of offenders and those dealing with procedural safeguards required in the capital context—the *Miller* Court forbade the states from sentencing juveniles to LWOP under a *mandatory* sentencing scheme.[27]

These three decisions—the *Miller* trilogy—together stand for the proposition that children are different in the eyes of the law, and they provide much-needed moral leadership in the juvenile justice arena. The importance of this line of cases cannot be overstated. To begin, the four dissenting Justices in *Miller* recognized the decision for what it was—nothing short of revolutionary. Chief Justice Roberts posited that "[t]he principle behind today's decision seems to be *only* that because juveniles are different from adults, they must be sentenced differently,"[28] and that such a principle and the process the majority employed in applying it "has no discernible end point."[29] Similarly, Justice Thomas wrote that *Miller* "lays the groundwork for future incursions on the States' authority to sentence criminals."[30] The dissenting Justices are absolutely right. *Miller* has laid the foundation for future reforms far beyond the scope of the decision itself.

In addition, the *Miller* Court (and the work that the *Graham* Court had done in laying the foundation for *Miller*) was an enormous break with Eighth Amendment precedent dealing with non-death, term of years, or life sentences, and the Court made this break because it was dealing with children. Prior to *Graham*, the Court had not invalidated a custodial sentence since its 1983 decision in *Solem v. Helm*.[31] Helm had been convicted of writing a check from a fictitious account, and that conviction exposed him to a possible five-year sentence. Helm's check fraud was his seventh felony, though, and under South Dakota's recidivism statute, Helm was sentenced to life without parole. The Supreme Court found this sentence disproportionate under the Eighth Amendment, given the relatively minor nature of his seven convictions and the severity of life without parole. However, in the three decades between *Solem* and the culmination of the *Miller* trilogy, the Court examined other proportionality challenges to equally draconian custodial sentences—and rejected the inmate's challenge in every instance.[32] Thus, the mere fact that the Court agreed with a defendant's proportionality challenge outside the death penalty context in the *Graham* and *Miller* decisions renders the decisions monumental in their own right.

Further, the *Miller* opinion insists that a child's developmental environment must inform the sentencing process, and thus state actors cannot comply with the decision in a perfunctory manner. The *Miller* Court explained that mandatory life without parole prevents a sentencer from considering precisely those factors most relevant to a juvenile's culpability: "[It] precludes consideration of his chronological age and its hallmark features—among them, immaturity, impetuosity, and failure to appreciate risks and consequences. It prevents taking into account the family and home environment that surrounds him—and from which he cannot usually extricate himself—no matter how brutal or dysfunctional."[33] At the same time, mandatory LWOP precludes the sentencer from considering the role that the juvenile played in the crime and whether he might have been charged with a lesser crime but for his immaturity and incompetency in navigating the criminal justice process.[34] Thus, according to the *Miller* Court, context matters—both life context and crime context—and the sentencer must take both into account before imposing the harshest sentence upon a juvenile.

Related, the *Miller* Court made clear that in order to appreciate the context in which the juvenile has committed a homicide crime (or at least been convicted of one), states must employ a process that allows the defendant to explain his life context. The majority explained: "the mandatory penalty schemes at issue here prevent the sentencer from taking account of these central considerations."[35] Further, it noted that, since the early 1980s, the Court had recognized youth itself as a relevant mitigating factor at sentencing, and that " '[Just as the chronological age of a minor is itself a relevant mitigating factor of great weight, so must the background and mental and emotional development of a youthful defendant be duly considered' in assessing his culpability.' "[36] Thus, *Miller* demands an expansive reading because the decision is so heavily focused on the juvenile's developmental context and procedural safeguards that can illuminate that context.

The *Miller* Court also continued to emphasize—as the *Roper* and *Graham* Courts had done—science as it relates to juveniles, and that brain science suggests that children should be treated differently from adults in the criminal justice process. Referring to its earlier decisions in *Roper* and *Graham*, the *Miller* Court explained that "[o]ur decisions rested not only on common sense—on what 'any parent knows'—but on science and social science as well."[37] And the *Miller* Court then went on to reiterate how that science informs legal decisions. It tells us that only a relatively small percentage of juvenile offenders later " 'develop entrenched patterns of problem behavior.' "[38] The same body of science tells us that juvenile brains have not developed fully, especially in the areas that relate to behavior control.[39] And it tells us that, because adolescence is "transient" by definition, we can expect juveniles to possess greater capacity for reform and rehabilitation than their adult counterparts.[40]

Finally, in dicta, the *Miller* Court suggested that it was concerned with juvenile justice practices beyond the juvenile LWOP schemes at issue in the case. For example, the Court spent a significant amount of time responding to the states' claim that youth was already taken into account at the transfer stage and thus need not also be taken into account at the final sentencing stage.[41] The Court explained that many states use mandatory transfer systems, and that even in states where the transfer system has some discretion, it is often "lodged exclusively in the hands of prosecutors . . . [a]nd those 'prosecutorial discretion laws are usually silent regarding standards, protocols, or appropriate considerations for decisionmaking.' "[42] The majority went on to explain that even where *judges* enjoy some discretion regarding the transfer decision, the system is poorly designed to protect the interests of the child. Not only does the judge have limited information at the transfer juncture, but also the judge often faces extreme choices between a lenient sentence in juvenile court and an extreme one in adult court.[43] The *Miller* majority stated that, in light of its reasoning in the *Miller* trilogy, juvenile LWOP should be a rare sentence—even for juveniles who commit homicide.[44] Thus, the *Miller* majority made clear in dicta that its opinion was an indictment of broader juvenile justice practices and not simply a decision requiring a certain process before states could impose LWOP.

For all of these reasons, the *Miller* trilogy portends monumental juvenile justice reform.

B. Judicial and Legislative Responses to *Miller*

In the wake of the Court's *Miller* decision, there have been numerous positive developments, further suggesting that the time is right for rethinking juvenile justice. The first question post-*Miller* was that of who stood to benefit from the Court's decision. In general, the Supreme Court's decisions apply prospectively so as not to disturb the states' interest in finality of criminal cases.[45] However, when the Supreme Court announces a new substantive rule, rather than one that is merely procedural, its rule applies retroactively—to all similarly situated inmates. In addition, when the Supreme Court announces a "watershed" rule of criminal procedure—one that implicates fundamental notions of fairness—that kind of rule also applies retroactively.

Immediately after the Court's *Miller* decision, the question whether it applied retroactively loomed large. If it did, then all 2,500 inmates nationwide currently serving a mandatory LWOP sentence for a juvenile homicide offense would be entitled to a resentencing hearing and potentially a new, reduced sentence. If it did not, then the Court's

Miller decision would forbid mandatory LWOP in cases post-2012, but it would afford no relief to those inmates across the country currently serving mandatory LWOP for a juvenile homicide offense. Those inmates would die in prison serving a now-unconstitutional sentence.

Inmates across the country serving mandatory LWOP for a juvenile homicide offense rushed to court seeking relief under *Miller*. The majority of state supreme courts that looked at the issue held that *Miller* should apply retroactively,[46] but supreme courts in a few states, including those that housed the majority of JLWOP inmates, refused to apply the decision retroactively.[47]

In *Montgomery v. Louisiana*,[48] the Supreme Court held that, in fact, its decision in *Miller* was retroactively applicable, and all inmates serving a mandatory JLWOP sentence would be entitled to a second look at their sentences. Henry Montgomery was 17 when he killed a deputy sheriff and was convicted in state court.[49] Initially sentenced to die, Montgomery was retried at 23 because of racial hostility at the time of his first trial.[50] His second jury also convicted him, but found him "guilty without capital punishment," meaning he would serve a mandatory life without parole sentence.[51] Before the Supreme Court in 2015, Montgomery argued that his criminal actions were the product of his immaturity and impetuosity and that in his five decades in prison he had rehabilitated himself. In other words, he argued that he was precisely the kind of defendant the *Miller* Court had in mind when it spoke of a child's diminished culpability and greater capacity for rehabilitation. Moreover, he urged the Court to find *Miller* retroactively applicable so that inmates like him might be given a second chance. Despite an oral argument that suggested the Court might not even reach the merits of his case,[52] ultimately the Supreme Court agreed with Montgomery and held *Miller* retroactively applicable.[53] In fact, the Court went one step further and said that states need not resentence inmates like Montgomery, but instead could make them parole eligible immediately.[54] *Montgomery v. Louisiana* was a huge victory for the more than 2,500 inmates nationwide serving LWOP for a juvenile offense.

Beyond the Supreme Court's own expansion of the *Miller* ruling, some states have heeded the call of the *Miller* Court and have comprehensively reconsidered LWOP and extreme custodial sentences as they apply to children. Recall that the Supreme Court first addressed the unconstitutionality of JLWOP in 2010, and in 2011 only five states banned JLWOP.[55] As the Court has continued to take a stance against JLWOP and as society has embraced the science that tells us children can change in positive ways, the trend away from JLWOP has been dramatic. Since 2011, the number of states that ban JLWOP has more than tripled; today 17 states ban the practice of JLWOP altogether.[56] Five additional jurisdictions ban JLWOP in nearly all cases, and 3 states that technically have JLWOP on the books have never imposed it.[57] In a very short period of time, the nation has reached a point where nearly half its jurisdictions have said no to JLWOP. Perhaps most remarkable, some of the states that have banned or narrowed JLWOP have been historically tough on crime states, like Texas, Kansas, Florida, and California.[58] Nationwide abolition of JLWOP is achievable and on the horizon because of the Supreme Court's work in this area.

At the same time, some states have enacted model legislation that reflects the animating principles of the *Miller* trilogy. West Virginia and Delaware have enacted legislation that abolished juvenile LWOP and provides for ongoing, periodic review of lengthy custodial sentences for children.[59] Under West Virginia's new law, a juvenile convicted of an offense that would otherwise permit an LWOP sentence is eligible for parole review after serving 15 years. At the same time, the West Virginia law requires the sentencing court to consider a comprehensive list of mitigating factors, drawn from the *Miller* Court's language, before imposing any sentence on a juvenile transferred to adult criminal court.[60] Similarly, Delaware's new law precludes LWOP for juveniles and instructs the sentencing judge to exercise discretion when imposing a juvenile homicide sentence in light of the mitigating aspects of youth addressed in *Miller*.[61] The new legislation also applies retroactively, thereby entitling Delaware inmates currently serving an LWOP sentence for a juvenile crime to a resentencing hearing.[62]

Some state supreme courts have read *Miller* broadly to justify juvenile sentencing protocols beyond what the *Miller* Court squarely considered. The Massachusetts high court held that *Miller* applies retroactively and precludes juvenile LWOP under any circumstance.[63] That same Court held that juveniles being resentenced under *Miller* have a right to representation during the resentencing hearing.[64] The

Iowa State Supreme Court held that *Miller* precludes mandatory minimums for juveniles *across the board*.[65] The Supreme Court of Florida, considered to be among the most punitive of all states, recently decided a handful of juvenile sentencing cases and held in favor of the juvenile petitioner in each instance, based on *Miller*.[66] These legislative and judicial responses reflect a holistic interpretation of the *Miller* decision and its motivating rationales, and they signify a promising degree of receptiveness to juvenile justice reform.

C. Still a Time of Urgency

Yet juvenile justice advocates must remain vigilant in their efforts to seek reform. First, the Supreme Court's recent juvenile sentencing decisions have addressed only the two harshest sentences available under American law: the death penalty and LWOP. The Court has yet to address the procedural mechanisms that expose kids to long sentences in the first place or juvenile conditions of confinement. These unresolved questions are just as threatening to children's welfare and need to be pursued in the courts. The final chapter of this book returns to those and other reform measures.

Second, some state legislators have missed the mark by replacing mandatory juvenile LWOP with another mandatory juvenile sentence, and, in some cases, still leaving juveniles exposed to an LWOP sentence.[67] For example, Pennsylvania, which houses the most juvenile LWOP inmates nationwide, enacted post-*Miller* legislation that permits an LWOP sentence and simply adds less punitive alternatives for juveniles convicted of first- and second-degree murder.[68] Similarly, Louisiana's revised law requires juveniles convicted of murder to serve a mandatory minimum of 35 years before parole eligibility, and it too permits juvenile LWOP.[69] Of the 13 states that have passed legislation in response to *Miller*, 9 still permit juvenile LWOP, and none set an alternative minimum sentence at less than 25 years.[70] State legislation that replaces mandatory juvenile LWOP with an alternative, steep sentence and that fails to account for the mitigating qualities of youth at sentencing does not do justice to the *Miller* decision.

And then there are the individuals whose sentences seem incredibly harsh, especially after the *Miller* trilogy, but who are not legally entitled to any relief under those decisions. Take De'Andre, for example. At 15 he was convicted of murder. Under state law, because of his age and the offense, De'Andre was tried and sentenced as an adult, with no account for his youth and its mitigating circumstances. The court sentenced him to 80 years: 55 years for the homicide offense and a mandatory sentencing enhancement of 25 years because of his use of a firearm; the terms must be served on a consecutive basis and he is not entitled to any credit for good conduct. By any estimate, De'Andre will die in prison.

The same is likely true for Alex. At 16, Alex was addicted to drugs. In the course of stealing to support his drug habit, Alex's codefendant shot and killed their victim. The felony murder doctrine says that a defendant is responsible for the death of a victim that occurs during the commission of the felony, even if the death is accidental, and even if, as in Alex's case, one's codefendant actually causes the death. Alex was facing an LWOP sentence, so he entered into an "open plea" where a defendant admits his role in the crime and essentially asks for mercy from the court. Unlike a traditional plea bargain, where the defendant enters a guilty plea in exchange for an agreed-upon sentence, Alex's open plea meant that he was exposed to a range of 45 to 65 years for homicide. The judge imposed 62 years.

Just as Evan Miller was sentenced to die when he was given LWOP, so too have Alex and De'Andre been sentenced to die in prison. By any actuarial estimate, neither of them will survive into their 70s and beyond. But unlike those who have some hope in the retroactive application of *Miller*, Alex and De'Andre do not necessarily stand to benefit from the *Miller* trilogy. The *Miller* decision dealt with one case or controversy, as the Supreme Court is required to do. It answered the question whether mandatory LWOP sentences for juveniles convicted of homicide are unconstitutional. It did not address whether a 62- or 80-year sentence is tantamount to an LWOP sentence, nor did it deal with discretionary sentences or open plea deals.

At some point, the Supreme Court may reconsider those tangential questions, but it will take years, if not decades, for the many variations on *Miller* and its implementation to trickle back up to the Supreme Court. It is for the states to resolve these issues as a matter of fairness. While the foundation has been laid by the Court, and while some states have begun to move in the right direction, the nation still needs to rethink its treatment of kids in the adult criminal system altogether. The final chapter of this book turns to those broader reform questions.

Before exploring the reform agenda, though, the next chapter examines the implementation of the *Miller* trilogy. The Supreme Court has established new constitutional principles regarding juvenile sentencing, but, as is often the case, the devil is in the details. Chapter 6 examines the inconsistent and often messy task of implementing new constitutional law.

6

The Uneven and Unpredictable
Path of Implementation

IN 1984, WHEN HE WAS 17 years old, George Toca lost his closest childhood friend, Eric Batiste.[1] Eric had been involved in a botched attempt
at carjacking and his friend and partner in crime accidentally shot and
killed him. When Eric was killed, George was no stranger to crime and
violence. George's own father was killed when he was a baby; he grew
up with a single mother to seven children; he dropped out of the seventh grade; and he spent his childhood in a "drug-infested" housing
development.[2] But the loss of Eric was different from George's prior
devastations. Because of George's close friendship with Eric, the police
quickly focused on George as the prime suspect in Eric's death. While
George insisted from the get-go that he had been at a hotel with his
girlfriend the night of the shooting, and while he looked nothing like
the man described by the robbery victims, George was charged and
convicted of second-degree murder. At 18 he was sentenced to die in
prison.[3]

Today, in the wake of the Supreme Court's recent juvenile sentencing decisions, George Toca is a free man. After serving more
than 30 years in Louisiana's Angola state penitentiary, one of the
worst in the nation, George is seeking to build a life for himself at
the age of 48 in his hometown of New Orleans. It is not an easy path,
but it is one filled with hope and aspiration. George is not alone. In
this moment of courts and legislatures reconsidering the legitimacy
of extreme sentences for juveniles, hundreds of individuals have

been released after coming of age in prison while serving lengthy terms.[4] At the same time, hundreds more are seeking relief under the *Miller* line of cases only to find that relief is elusive and unpredictable. Chapter 6 examines early implementation efforts in the wake of these recent Supreme Court decisions, looking specifically at three individuals who have been impacted by those decisions. The three cases demonstrate the ways in which implementation of new laws can be painfully unpredictable and uneven—as well as the persistent ways in which our criminal justice system is deeply flawed.

The three men discussed in this chapter—George Toca, Greg Diatchenko, and Louis Costa—were all sentenced to die in prison for a juvenile crime. George maintained his innocence from the day of his arrest, and yet it took three decades and recent Supreme Court decisions to prompt serious consideration of that claim. Greg's case is more common in the world of JLWOP. He found himself addicted to drugs and alcohol as a young teenager, and while under the influence of both, he killed a man who propositioned him. He, too, served more than 30 years of a life sentence before the Supreme Court's *Miller* decision provided him an opportunity for release. Like George, Greg is attempting to reintegrate into a society that has changed dramatically while he aged in prison. Finally, Louis's case represents the most difficult aspect of implementing *Miller*: not all individuals who seem objectively ready for a second chance in society will get it. Recruited by his adult codefendants, at age 16 Louis participated in a murder, and he was sentenced to life without parole for his involvement in that crime. By the time the *Miller* decision came down 30 years later, Louis had transformed himself into a thoughtful and remorseful college-educated adult. Despite his being "the poster child of demonstrated and indisputable maturity and rehabilitation,"[5] Louis remains in prison today after being denied parole.

These three cases demonstrate the power of the Court's recent juvenile sentencing decisions, and they offer concrete examples of how some individuals have made it out of prison after decades of incarceration and what that experience is like. Most important, though, these cases reveal that the road to implementing *Miller* is already proving to be slow and unpredictable.

A. George Toca

Like many children who come into contact with the criminal justice system, George grew up in a world steeped in poverty, drugs, and violence.[6] George was the third of seven children his mother raised on her own. He never met his father, who was killed when George was a baby. As a young man in Angola, George would hear bits and pieces about his father from other inmates who had known him. George recalls that growing up they didn't have much to eat, and they barely had money for clothes.

As discussed in Chapter 2, poverty hinders a child's educational potential in a number of ways, and this was certainly true for George. His experience of school was that some teachers "passed him on," while others "put him out."[7] He had no sense of self-worth and was convinced by adolescence that he "was not smart enough to be in school."[8] At age 14, he dropped out and turned to the streets.

George had been a street-smart kid from a young age. Not only had he been surrounded by crime for most of his childhood, but when he was 11 years old, Big Leroy, his stepfather, entered the picture and brought drug dealing right into the family room. Big Leroy was a mixed blessing at first. George recalls that they were so poor and regularly hungry, and Leroy brought consistent money and food, not to mention new furniture and a drum set for George. For a while there was some family structure, and George had a glimpse of what it would be like to have a father, something he'd always wanted.

But things took a turn for the worse over time. Leroy starting using drugs, and he was physically abusive with the whole family. George recalls fleeing to the home of his grandmother, whom he describes as "a godly woman" and their "champion."[9] His grandmother made sure they had clean underwear and food; she was an escape from their "drug-infested" home. George knew that Leroy's life was a dangerous one—he watched from behind a sofa as Leroy sold the family TV to pay for drugs—but he also learned from Leroy that drugs were a way to make quick money.

Eventually, the law caught up with Leroy. George was there the day police came to the home, search warrant and weapons in hand, as Leroy attempted to flee on the roof. When Leroy was hauled off by law enforcement, George and his family were "poor and hungry," but they breathed a "sigh of relief."[10] George did not see his stepfather again until they were both inmates at Angola.

The events of April 23, 1984, changed George's life forever. According to George's own testimony and that of many others, George, 17; Eric, 16; and several other friends went to a dance at the Superdome on the night of April 22, 1984.[11] The dance ended around 2 a.m., when George and his girlfriend, Danielle Bernard, left the Superdome and rented a room at the MRV motel.[12] George never saw Eric again. Danielle eventually went home in the early morning of April 23, while George stayed in the motel room until around 10 a.m.[13]

Eric was killed by his accomplice in a botched carjacking at around 6 a.m.[14] The two victims of that crime, Anne Marie Collins and Todd Struttman, testified at George's trial that around 6.a.m. on the morning of April 23, 1984, they stopped at a Timesaver convenience store in New Orleans. A black teenager, later identified as Eric, approached their car window and asked for change for a dollar; a "taller, older boy" then walked up to their car window, put a gun in Ms. Collins's face, and demanded the keys to her car. She refused, got out of her car, and began fighting with the gunman. At the same time, Mr. Struttman got out of the front passenger seat and began struggling with the younger boy, Eric. During this brief struggle, the gunman fired one shot and hit Eric, who later died at the scene.[15]

When a homicide detective sent out word of Eric's shooting, Officer Marlon Defillo responded to the alert and suggested to the detective that George Toca might be a suspect in the killing; he knew Eric and George were best friends from his beat in the Lafitte public housing development where both boys had grown up.[16] Based on this tip, the detective put together a photo array including a picture of George, and, when it was shown to the witnesses three days after the crime, they both picked George as the shooter.[17] George was arrested and charged with second-degree murder. When the police came to arrest him, his mother urged him to flee, but, remembering Big Leroy's attempted rooftop escape, George refused. He recalls, "I despised him so much . . . he was so repugnant, so I said no."[18]

George was incredulous that he was the defendant in the case. He maintained his innocence from day one, and he presented an alibi defense at trial. Both George and his girlfriend, Danielle, testified that they had been at the MRV motel during the early morning of April 23, 1984.[19] The victims of the attempted robbery described the shooter as between 5´10´´ and 6´ and weighing about 140 pounds.[20] George was 5´5´´ and weighed less than 125 pounds.[21] A friend from Angola remembers him back then as a "little bitty fella"[22]—far from the description given by the victims of the crime who said the shooter was older, taller, and heavier than Eric. Another noticeable distinction: the eyewitness accounts mentioned nothing about distinguishing facial features,[23] and George was known for having four gold teeth.[24] The state presented evidence to discredit George's alibi. Specifically, the MRV owner and one of its employees testified that they would not have rented a room to George because of its policy against renting rooms to minors. George was convicted of second-degree murder on April 16, 1985, and one week later he was sentenced to life without parole.[25]

Today, the innocence movement has proven that the criminal justice system consistently generates wrongful convictions,[26] but in the mid-1980s, when George was convicted, it was a different era. Violent crime had been on the rise since the 1960s,[27] and the War on Drugs was in full swing.[28] Lawyer and Professor Barry Scheck founded the Innocence Project in 1992, but initially its efforts were focused on the exoneration of prisoners whose wrongful convictions could be proven with DNA evidence.[29] Over time, his organization set in motion a movement that examined wrongful convictions based on faulty science, as well as systemic failures of the criminal justice system.

The University of Michigan's National Registry of Exonerations, established in 2012, collects and analyzes information about all known exonerations in the United States since 1989.[30] To date, the Registry has documented nearly 2,000 cases where a person was wrongly convicted of a crime and later cleared of those charges based on new evidence.[31] Those cases are not only about junk science or missing evidence; they also reveal chronic ineffective assistance of counsel for the poor, misconduct by state officials, and false confessions from accused individuals.[32] While annual exonerations based on DNA evidence have been fairly constant over the last 25 years, the number of non-DNA exonerations has nearly quadrupled in the same time frame.[33]

Which brings us back to the issue of eyewitness identification in George's case. When people think of wrongful convictions they often think of sexual assault cases or homicide cases where there is DNA evidence at the heart of the case, and either the state's forensic evidence was flawed or defense counsel was not able to prove its faultiness in court. In fact, of the 1,884 exonerations identified by the National Registry since 1989, only 428 were DNA exoneration cases.[34] Mistaken identification was present in 572 of those cases—more than a quarter of them.[35] Social scientists have confirmed what the Registry reveals: that eyewitness identifications, like the one that implicated George, can be inherently flawed.

Human memory is complex, and the last three decades have demonstrated that eyewitness identifications are unreliable in many cases—even if there is no improper suggestion introduced by the state.[36] To begin, memory fades quickly, and when it does, the brain has a tendency to fill in the gaps. While moderate stress may enhance skills of observation, high stress situations, like crime victimization, can lead to misidentification.[37] At the same time, human beings are especially prone to error when asked to identify a suspect from a different race.[38] Finally, once a witness has identified a suspect, the brain becomes committed to that identification, and yet certainty is not tied to accuracy, as studies have shown.[39] According to the American Psychological Association, the rate of incorrect identifications is approximately 33 percent.[40]

Despite the documented infirmities of human memory, jurors continue to place high value on eyewitness identification and its perceived reliability.[41] Because of this, defense counsel have argued that their clients should be able to call expert witnesses who can explain to jurors the flaws of eyewitness identification. Even today, though, courts are split on the question whether this is permissible.[42] Some courts have held that social scientists offer genuine expertise that the average juror does not have, while other courts have held that such testimony interferes with the jury's core function of assessing witness credibility.[43] At the time of George's trial in 1985, this legal issue was not on the horizon, and the Innocence Project was still years away from its first case. It would be years before George would have a chance to argue for his exoneration using these tools.

During those years, George came of age within the walls of Angola. The Louisiana State Penitentiary, known as Angola, was once a plantation named for the country from which its slaves had been brought. Today Angola is the nation's largest maximum-security prison.[44] More than 6,000 men are incarcerated there, and nearly 80 percent of them are African American.[45] The bulk of Angola's prisoners—75 percent— are serving life without parole, and among the remaining population, the average sentence is 90.9 years.[46] Upon arrival at Angola, a doctor performs a medical assessment and healthy inmates are assigned to a "job" that pays them pennies per hour, if at all.[47] Inmates work in the vast fields of the 18,000-acre complex, picking vegetables and cotton, while armed correctional officers on horseback preside over " the Farm."

Historically, Angola has had a notorious reputation. In addition to its legacy of slavery on the same fields cultivated by inmates today, the facility has been rife with violence from the time the state took over its operations in 1901.[48] In the 1960s Angola was labeled "the bloodiest prison in the south" because of its high number of inmate assaults.[49] A decade later, in 1973, four Angola prisoners sued the state in federal court, arguing that the conditions at the prison constituted cruel and unusual punishment.[50] As part of the litigation, the court found that the facility was "terribly overcrowded"; inmates were not classified according to danger, thus exposing vulnerable inmates to attack; insufficient staffing led to widespread weapons possession by inmates; forcible rape was common; and within a three-year time span alone, there were 270 inmate stabbings, 20 of which resulted in death.[51] The trial judge found that Angola's conditions of confinement "shock the conscience of any right thinking person" and "flagrantly violate basic constitutional requirements as well as applicable State laws."[52] The court ordered remedial measures, and years of federal monitoring ensued.

In recent decades, Angola has garnered mixed reviews from inmates and criminal justice reform advocates. From 1995–2016, Warden Burl Cain ran the facility with an emphasis on "moral rehabilitation."[53] For the most part, Cain pursued this goal through the widespread introduction of Christianity. Under his leadership, the prison opened a branch of the New Orleans Baptist Theological Seminary, and prisoners can now earn a two-year associate's degree in pastoral ministry and a four-year bachelor's degree in theology.[54] Churches are peppered across the prison complex, and services happen regularly throughout the day.[55] At the same time, Cain expanded the kinds of education and employment offered at a time when the federal government was cutting back on inmate resources. Some prisoners are tending to dying inmates as hospice care workers, while others serving life sentences are training inmates close to a release date to be mechanics, electricians, welders, and horticulturists.[56] Whether directly attributable to Cain's efforts or not, violence is down: in 1990 there were more than 1,100 inmate-on-inmate assaults, and by 2012 that number was just over 300.[57]

To be sure, there are still Angola (and Cain) critics. In recent years, prisoners have prevailed in federal lawsuits over conditions of confinement. One suit demonstrated that the prison's new death row housing unit lacked any air conditioning, and that prisoners' health conditions were compromised by the soaring heat and humidity during Louisiana's summers.[58] Critics argue that the prison still relies far too heavily on solitary confinement as a disciplinary tool; that its prisoner labor practices smack of racism and slavery; and that the reliance upon Christianity at the facility is a form of social control exerted over—literally—captive minds.

Regardless, it is hard to dispute the rehabilitative effect that Angola had on George. George spent two of his three decades in Angola under Cain's leadership, and he took advantage of every growth opportunity Cain brought to the facility. George entered prison with a seventh grade education, thinking that he would "never . . . work a day in [his] life."[59] Like most young men arriving at Angola, his first work assignment was picking vegetables and cotton in the fields. Over time, he worked his way out of the fields. Behind bars, George earned a high school diploma, a diploma in carpentry from the Louisiana Technical College, horticultural certificates, and an associate and bachelor's degree in Christian Ministry from the New Orleans Baptist Theological Seminary.[60] He also learned the value of routine and work, and it was this process that George credits with "preparing [him] for society."[61]

In 1989, George heard of the Innocence Project's first DNA exoneration case, and he began more than a decade of persistent effort to have a lawyer champion his claim of innocence.[62] At that time, the Project was barely off the ground in New York, and the nation's understanding of wrongful convictions was still nascent. But George kept at it. In 2001,

Innocence Project New Orleans (IPNO) opened its doors, and in 2002, George made it to the top of a waitlist; IPNO began investigating his case.[63] The lawyers at IPNO quickly discovered a wealth of new evidence that demonstrated George's innocence and implicated another mutual friend in Eric's shooting death.

Two new developments, in particular, came out of this investigation that were key to exonerating George. First, lawyers at IPNO discovered several witnesses who saw Eric Batiste leave the Superdome dance the night before his death with a group of friends.[64] That group, according to witnesses, did not include George, who had left earlier, as he had testified, but did include two other friends—Edison Learson and Sean Jackson.[65] Second, Edison Learson, with whom Eric was last seen alive, *did* match the description provided by the eyewitnesses to Eric's shooting.[66] Recall that those eyewitnesses described Eric's shooter as an older youth between 5'10'' and 6', approximately 140 pounds. While George was smaller than this profile, Edison Learson was 5'8'', 135 pounds, and had been wearing clothes identical to those described by the eyewitnesses.[67] IPNO lawyers successfully demonstrated that George's trial lawyer never knew about these exculpatory facts—in fact, he had never investigated the issue of who else may have been with Eric that night. On the basis of this new evidence, George won the opportunity to demonstrate his innocence at a new hearing.

While that issue was pending, though, the United States Supreme Court decided *Miller v. Alabama*, and George's lawyers now had two avenues for seeking relief. In addition to his claim of actual innocence, George had been sentenced to mandatory life without parole for a juvenile homicide crime, a sentence now unconstitutional according to *Miller*. Relying upon *Miller*, George's lawyers at IPNO filed a motion to correct his illegal sentence. Recall from Chapter 5 that one of the initial questions post-*Miller* was that of retroactivity—who was entitled to benefit from the ruling. The State of Louisiana argued that *Miller* was merely a procedural rule, applicable only to *future* juveniles convicted of homicide, and thus it did not afford inmates like George any relief.

George's lawyers from IPNO argued that not only should *Miller* be deemed retroactively applicable, but also that George's case was the ideal vehicle for such a ruling.[68] As discussed earlier in this chapter, George demonstrated exactly what the *Miller* Court had contemplated: that youth can mature and outgrow their impetuous behavior. Even setting aside the doubts about his guilt, George had entered Angola as a middle school dropout, and he had transformed himself into an educated, thoughtful, and considerate person over three decades.[69] In addition to his college education and technical certifications, George was a model prisoner from a disciplinary standpoint. His only physical instances of misconduct occurred during his first few months in prison when he was a very young man, and for more than two decades George's only disciplinary infractions were for status offenses—things that are impermissible only because of one's status as an inmate, such as walking too close to a fence or being late for a visitor.[70] Perhaps most impressive: when George engaged in all of these rehabilitative efforts, he had no hope of release, as he was serving a life without parole sentence. Needing to resolve a split among lower courts on the question of *Miller*'s retroactivity, the United States Supreme Court granted certiorari in George's case on December 12, 2014.[71]

Juvenile justice advocates were eager for the Court to resolve the retroactivity question and cautiously optimistic that it would come to a favorable decision for inmates like George. And then a strange series of events followed. Despite the fact that George had always maintained his innocence to no avail in prior years, early in 2015, the Orleans Parish District Attorney's office agreed to vacate his murder conviction.[72] The prosecutor offered him the opportunity to plead guilty to two counts of attempted armed robbery and one count of manslaughter, and in exchange, he would be released immediately.[73]

George faced an agonizing decision. If he took the District Attorney's offer, he would be home with his family, a free man, immediately—something he had been dreaming about for over 30 years. He also knew that if he persisted in his claim of actual innocence, it was not clear he would prevail. And even though the Supreme Court was poised to review George's case, there was no telling whether the Court would rule in his favor and determine that he was entitled to a new sentence under *Miller*. Finally, even if he won at the Supreme Court on the *Miller* issue, there was no predicting what kind of resentencing hearing George would receive in the Louisiana courts and when he might have a chance again at freedom. On the other hand, hundreds of prisoners at Angola—people just like George who had been sentenced to die in prison when they were kids—were holding out hope that George's case before the Supreme Court would bring them relief, too. If the Court held in George's case that *Miller* applied retroactively, then George and close to 250 prisoners at Angola serving a mandatory JLWOP sentence would get a new hearing and potentially a second chance at life in the free world.[74] These 250 prisoners were not just statistics; many of them had become George's friends during his three decades of incarceration.

Ultimately, on January 29, 2015, George appeared in a New Orleans criminal court and accepted the District Attorney's offer.[75] He entered into what is called an "Alford Plea," under which the defendant maintains his innocence but concedes that the state has sufficient evidence to convict him.[76] Eric Batiste's 76-year-old aunt, one of Eric's many family members who had lobbied for George's release, was there in court for the plea and noticed that George wept as he signed the agreement.[77] George says that "it was the worst thing in [his] life to admit something [he] didn't do"; "I'm not a murderer . . . I never shot no one."[78] And the tearful court appearance was only the beginning of an emotional day. Quickly after the plea was entered, George returned to Angola for one last time where he was "processed out," which included a medical examination and a chance to gather and give away some of his belongings.[79] George recalls holding his head down, standing in line and saying goodbye to many others with juvenile life sentences. One of those goodbyes was to Henry Montgomery, another juvenile lifer who had become a good friend to George and with whom George shared a love of gardening. George gave Henry some vegetable seeds to plant in the small plot that other horticulture students maintained.[80] And then he left Angola—and the life he had come to know for three decades.

Without an actual controversy to resolve in George's case, the Supreme Court declared the *Miller* retroactivity question moot and dismissed *Toca v. Louisiana.*[81] Because of the suit's dismissal, nearly 2,500 inmates nationwide serving a JLWOP sentence, 250 of whom were at Angola, were left in limbo, wondering if and when the Supreme Court would revisit the question. One has to wonder why the District Attorney's office in New Orleans Parish settled George's case after so many years, on the eve of his case going to the Supreme Court. The District Attorney's office attributed it to warming relations with IPNO and to George's rehabilitation over time; the office insisted that the plea deal had nothing to do with George's pending case before the nation's high court.[82] Skeptics wondered if the move was obstructionism—an attempt to hinder the Court's effort to extend *Miller*'s ruling to older cases, like George's. In any event, the Supreme Court quickly agreed to hear the retroactivity issue in another case of a juvenile lifer in Louisiana: Henry Montgomery, the man to whom George had given the vegetable seeds weeks earlier.[83] As discussed in Chapter 5, in *Montgomery v. Louisiana*, the Court found *Miller* to be retroactively applicable, opening the door to resentencing hearings for more than 2,500 prisoners like George across the country.

George lives now with his sister in New Orleans once again as a free man. While he notices a lot that has remained the same in his hometown, he also senses major changes. He says there is more fear than when he was growing up, that the streets seem deserted at night; everything is locked up.[84] He is working hard to make a life for himself, and he describes the three biggest challenges in building that life: housing, transportation, and steady work.[85] He has a car, a cell phone, and a résumé, outlining his technical certifications, his education, and the work experience he has had since he was released in 2015. He is adapting to the modern world in which he now lives, despite missing three decades of change. He texts with me to exchange information, to arrange phone calls, and to plan interview times. He manages his potential landscaping clients in the same polite way. He takes whatever jobs he can find in the greater New Orleans area, and he goes to job sites to give estimates in hope of getting longer-term landscaping projects. He tells me that he would like to save up for a nicer car so that he can earn extra money as an Uber driver.

More than anything, George celebrates the simple things in his life that bring him tremendous joy. His freedom. Being able to be a brother and to help his family members. A Big Mac. The sound of his niece and nephew playing. The buzz of traffic.[86] At the same time, he has bigger goals. He would like to own his own successful landscaping company. He would like to help other at-risk youth stay out of prison. And he looks forward to reuniting with his childhood girlfriend, Danielle, with whom he spent the night at the motel when Eric was killed. After serving more than 23 years in federal prison for a drug offense, Danielle was released in 2016 as part of President Obama's clemency program to reduce sentences for nonviolent drug offenders.[87]

George will never get the time he lost in Angola back, but he relies on the same mantra today that he used in prison: "put yourself in a position to be blessed."[88] George's release—and his successful transition back into a world that has changed tremendously since his last days of freedom—is reason for hope. George's experience demonstrates that young people can grow and mature even under the harshest of circumstances in prison. Just as important, his story reveals that it is never too late to remedy the failings of the criminal justice system.

B. Greg Diatchenko

George Toca is an important part of the story of the war on kids in America, and in some ways his case illustrates variables discussed throughout this book. Certain factors beyond his control made him more likely to come into contact with the criminal justice system, as discussed in Chapter 2: race, poverty, violence, parental incarceration, and exposure to substance abuse. At the same time, policy and legal mechanisms discussed in Chapter 3 made that probability a reality: a school system that failed him; ineffective assistance of counsel; and a mandatory sentencing scheme that required LWOP in his case. Most important, George is a testament to the fact that juveniles can mature and successfully rejoin society even after a long period of incarceration.

Having said that, there are some ways in which George's story is unusual. The United States Supreme Court accepts for appellate review less than 2 percent of the cases in which the parties petition the Court.[89] So most people serving an extreme sentence for a juvenile crime will never have their case accepted for review by the highest court in the land. Likewise, the majority of individuals serving life sentences (or their equivalent) for a juvenile offense in this country are not arguing actual innocence. Instead, they recognize that their actions were grave and life altering for their victims and themselves. Yet they are asking for a second chance.

Greg Diatchenko is one of a relatively small pool of people who have been given that second chance. At 17, Greg fatally stabbed a 55 year-old man, Thomas Wharf.[90] Greg was convicted of first-degree murder, and at the time, Massachusetts law required him to serve a mandatory sentence of life without the possibility of parole.[91] Greg had been arrested in the past, but he had never been convicted of a crime, and at 17 he was sentenced to die in prison. His story reveals some critical junctures at which kids tend to commit criminal acts, but it also, again, demonstrates that young people often outgrow risky, impetuous behavior and can rehabilitate themselves.

Greg's family life growing up was "dysfunctional."[92] His parents, Benita and Vladimir, had "terrible fights,"[93] and they ultimately divorced when he was a young child. Greg said that witnessing those fights changed his life,[94] and the same was true for his older sister, Iveta. While she was only 12 or 13 at the time, Iveta developed a serious heroin problem, began running away from home, and was in and out of the Department of Youth Services' custody.[95] By 13, Greg was on his own downward spiral.[96] He began skipping school, drinking, getting high, and engaging in low-level crime, like vandalism.[97] He was arrested for the first time at 16, and at 17 Greg was charged with a series of offenses, including assault and battery, larceny, and possessing alcohol, all of which were dismissed.[98] In 1981, when he was 17, Greg was a high school dropout; he was bouncing back and forth between his parents' homes, and he was regularly "drinking and drugging."[99] He was barely hanging on.

May 9, 1981, the night of Greg's homicide crime, started out like another one of those days of drinking and hanging out with friends. As he described to the Parole Board at his hearing, in the afternoon of May 19, he "got buzzed drinking beer and Southern Comfort."[100] Later that day, he met up with friends in Brookline and stole red spray paint from a store. Greg bought more beer and drank by the river in Brookline before leaving for Copley Square; Boston's Copley Square was Greg's normal spot "to hang out, drink and smoke marijuana."[101] When Greg's friends decided to leave Copley Square and head for Mission Hill, Greg was spray-painting his name on a wall; he missed the bus his friends caught to Mission Hill. Greg sat down on the steps of the library in Copley Square to wait for the next bus so that he could catch up with them.

Before long, Thomas Wharf drove by Greg in his automobile once— and then a second time. It was Greg's experience that adult men were often cruising that street "trying to pick up kids."[102] Greg decided to rob Wharf and to demand a ride to Mission Hill.[103] According to Greg, when Wharf stopped his car, he said "You're a good-looking kid; do you want to fool around?" He offered to pay Greg $25 in exchange for oral sex.[104] Greg got into Wharf's car, and soon thereafter he pulled out a buck knife he had been carrying, intending to rob Wharf.[105] When Wharf pulled his car over into an alley and shut off the engine, Greg cursed at him and demanded his money. But the plan "[didn't] go right."[106] Wharf grabbed Greg and slammed on the car horn. Greg struggled to get away, yelling "get off me." He couldn't find the car door handle; he "panicked" and started stabbing Wharf.[107] Before fleeing on foot, Greg took Wharf's wallet. Greg stabbed Wharf nine times; the paramedic on the scene described Wharf's body as "filleted."[108]

It did not take police long to identify Greg as the perpetrator in Wharf's murder because two witnesses saw him that night. First, Lori Pearlman, whose living room overlooked the alley where Wharf was killed, heard shouting and the car horn.[109] She called the police, assuming it was a robbery, and reported that, when the horn stopped, she saw a young man with blond hair and a leather jacket (as Greg had been wearing) fleeing the scene.[110] Second, James Ryan reported that he was waiting for a streetcar in Brookline near the scene of the murder when a young man approached and sat down next to him.[111] The young man asked Ryan for a match, and his hands were covered in blood. Mr. Ryan asked the young man if he had cut himself, to which he responded that he had been in a fight and had stabbed someone about 20 times. They then talked for a bit and the young man identified himself as "Greg."[112] The next day, Mr. Ryan read an account of the murder in the newspaper, and he reported his interactions with Greg at the streetcar station to police.[113] When police showed the witness a photo array, he picked out Greg. A search of Greg's apartment later turned up a brown leather jacket described by the witnesses and a knife.[114] Greg's fingerprints were also found in and on Wharf's car.[115]

Greg was charged with first-degree murder. After being jailed for about a month, Greg was released on bail pending his trial[116]—an unusual scenario for someone facing first-degree murder charges. In the weeks leading up to his trial, Greg persisted in self-destructive behavior, fighting in Copley Square and drinking daily.[117] Even with the Commonwealth's compelling evidence against him, Greg refused to accept a guilty plea on second-degree murder charges. As Greg realized later, this was a crucial mistake and just another example of his youth-ful valuing of short-term gains over long-term solutions. He recalled, "I didn't want to plead and go into prison. I didn't realize the magnitude of the harm or the severity of what I was facing. I was at a point in my life that I was blind to everything."[118]

In November 1981, a jury convicted Greg of first-degree murder, and at 17 he was sentenced to a mandatory term of life without parole. Initially, he was sent to the state's only maximum-security prison facility, in Walpole, Massachusetts. Greg recalls vividly his arrival at MCI-Walpole on the Wednesday before Thanksgiving in 1981.[119] It was evening as his transport car pulled into the prison complex, and Greg was overwhelmed: lights illuminated the 20-foot walls surrounding the facility.

Greg was scared, and he had good reason to be. In the 1970s and 1980s Walpole was known as one of the most dangerous prisons in the nation,[120] and its prisoners were the state's most violent offenders. When Greg entered Walpole, three-quarters of its prisoners were serv-ing time for a crime against a person, including rape, homicide, and assault; nearly a quarter were serving a life sentence; and 66 percent of its inmates had served a term in a correctional facility in the past.[121] Greg had heard stories about the prison on the news, and he knew that he was entering a dangerous place.

He recalls being placed in a single cell on a row of eight cells—the newcomers unit—his first night.[122] He'd been crying most of the day, and his eyes were swollen. The man in the cell across from him asked, "how old are you, kid?," and when Greg answered that he was 17 the man said "you don't look 14." Greg was whimpering, and the man across from him offered him a joint to smoke so he could calm down. Greg was relieved by the offer and learned that night how easily inmates could obtain and use drugs at Walpole. Across from him in another cell was a more menacing newcomer, who paced his cell while muttering to Greg "under the bunk, punk." Greg didn't know that bunk punk is prison slang for a sexual slave, but he knew that the man was making some kind of threat—and the threat was real.

Later that night, the older man across from Greg, concerned about Greg's safety in the general population, asked him if he knew someone "upstairs." In fact, he did. Greg had grown up as family friends with a well-known New England Mafia boss, who was in prison at the time. Greg hoped that this connection would help keep him safe.

Unbeknownst to Greg, the plan for his protection had already been set in motion.[123] As soon as Greg had been sentenced, the mob boss learned of Greg's impending arrival at Walpole and he put in motion some measures to protect Greg. Within hours, through the prison network, officers and inmates at Walpole learned that Greg was to be "left alone." By the time Greg woke the next morning, as he ate powdered scrambled eggs, an inmate came to his cell to deliver a package. Wary of what strings were attached to the package, initially Greg refused the goods. The inmate explained that Greg *had* to take the package—that it was from this Mafia kingpin and that he would need its contents: food, cigarettes, and toiletries. He also gave Greg some key survival tips. First, he told Greg, when officers come to do to an intake risk assessment, they are going to want to put you in protective custody (PC) because of your age; don't let them. "PC is for rats and rapists," and Greg was warned that he wouldn't survive starting out with that reputation. He needed to insist on going into the general population. Second, when he got there, as soon as he went to the "chow hall," he needed to find a guy named Bobby.[124] Bobby would help him survive.

Two weeks later, Greg was released into the general population of the Walpole State Prison. When he entered the chow hall for the first time, Greg felt hundreds of eyes on him, and a hush fell over the room as the other inmates took in the shock of his youth. Greg carried his tray from empty table to empty table, looking for a place to sit, only to be told to move on. He didn't realize that "there are separate tables where Latin Kings, Boston and Springfield gangs, Muslims, and sex offenders, among others, segregate themselves";[125] each table belonged to a group even when it was empty. Finally he found a table of "nerdy" looking guys who seemed as scared as Greg. He placed his tray down and began scanning the room for the man who fit the description he'd been given of Bobby.

Spotting Bobby at the "gangsters" table, Greg cautiously approached. Bobby stood up, shook Greg's hand and embraced him. The other men at the table did the same, as the hundreds of men in the hall watched. Without saying a word, the gangster crew sent a message to all: don't touch this kid or there will be hell to pay.

Even with this protection, Greg's early years at Walpole were rough. Greg admits that he was angry and disrespectful at the time; he feared being taken advantage of early on so "he was mouthy toward corrections officers in front of other inmates."[126] If a guard asked him to do something, he'd refuse and say, "I was sentenced to life, not to labor."[127] At the same time, Greg was still sporadically using drugs—which were everywhere in Walpole at the time. As a result, most of his early citations were for insolence, but he was also cited for possessing a weapon, disobeying orders, threatening staff members, and possession of a controlled substance.[128]

Greg's disciplinary record is typical of a young man who came of age in prison: most of his infractions occurred in his first few years and then tapered off as he matured and established his own routine in prison. Greg credits one correctional officer, in particular, with prompting him to change his ways.[129] Three years into his sentence at MCI-Walpole, Officer Thomas Baroni, a well-respected officer in his 30s, confronted Greg. He asked him: "When are you getting out of Walpole?" At first Greg didn't even understand the question; he thought the answer was "never," because of his life sentence. Officer Baroni explained to Greg that if he settled down and improved his attitude and behavior he could be reclassified to a medium-security facility, and that someday he could learn a trade and enjoy greater freedom of movement. Greg recalls that Officer Baroni made him take responsibility for himself. "He told me I was a better person than I was portraying. He said, 'Only one person put you in prison and that was you.'" For Greg, the fact that an officer "cared about [him] even though [he] was a punk" was a game-changer. Soon thereafter, Greg earned his GED; he joined Alcoholics Anonymous; and he began working with Project Reach Out, meeting with young people to demonstrate the consequences of crime.[130]

In March 1985, Greg was transferred to MCI Norfolk, a medium-security facility where he remained for almost the next three decades. In the mid-1980s, Greg still had not fully processed that he was serving a life sentence.[131] As is true with many young inmates sentenced to LWOP, Greg simply could not wrap his head around what that sentence actually meant: that he would die in prison. Moreover, in Massachusetts in the early 1980s, inmates serving life sentences were getting furloughed, and Greg had the illusion that someday he would enjoy that same privilege.

And then the Willie Horton tragedy occurred.[132] Horton was serving a life sentence for murder in 1986 when he was released on a weekend furlough program designed to rehabilitate inmates. During his weekend release, Horton fled to Maryland, where he raped a woman twice after binding, gagging, and beating her fiancé. Massachusetts Governor Michael Dukakis, the Democratic candidate for president in 1988, had supported the furlough program, and his position destroyed his prospects for the White House. Soon thereafter, Massachusetts abandoned the furlough program. Inmates sentenced to life, like Greg, were going to serve life.

Over time, Greg accepted this reality and embarked on a path of self-improvement.[133] He was trained as a plumber and eventually became the on-call plumber for the entire MCI Norfolk facility, a role that brought him great pride and satisfaction. He took college courses through Boston University's Prison Education Program and ultimately earned his bachelor's degree in liberal arts. Greg also cofounded a program in which inmates made wooden toys for the Toys for Tots charity. He did extensive programming, including Anger Management, Alternatives to Violence, and Jericho Circle, a program dedicated to helping incarcerated men become emotionally literate and repair broken relationships. Eventually, Greg converted to Buddhism, and he attributes his sobriety for more than two decades to his practice.

Greg's efforts toward rehabilitation had been undertaken without any hope of release. In 2010, Greg's family had helped him retain the services of a private attorney to revisit the argument of diminished capacity—that Greg had been a child at the time of his crime and that his youth should have mitigated the harshness of his sentence.[134] Having unsuccessfully made the legal claim in 1982 that LWOP was unconstitutional for juveniles, and having spent nearly 30 years in prison, Greg was realistic about his prospects in court. Despite some bouts of depression and even suicidal thoughts over the years, Greg had reached a place of acceptance for the most part. He recalls being at the "Lifers Group" in prison and once a year reading the names of other "lifers" who had passed away each year inside a Massachusetts prison.[135] After reading the names, during the moment of silence, Greg recalls thinking, "One day I'll be on that list."

Instead, though, Greg experienced a "blessing," he never saw coming.[136] While a private attorney, Jeff Beckerman, was working with Greg on the diminished capacity argument, *Miller v. Alabama* was decided and breathed new life into the claims of juveniles like Greg serving mandatory LWOP sentences for a homicide crime. Recall that Greg had already raised the argument in the Massachusetts courts back in 1982 that JLWOP was unconstitutional in its severity. While he lost the claim, he had gone on record as raising it—30 years before the United States Supreme Court even confronted the question.

On March 19, 2013, Greg filed a petition in the Supreme Judicial Court for Suffolk County arguing that, post-*Miller*, the Massachusetts sentencing scheme as applied to juveniles convicted of homicide was unconstitutional.[137] *Miller* had held that states could not impose mandatory LWOP on juveniles convicted of homicide, but recall that the Supreme Court had not yet addressed the question of who benefited from that ruling. In 2013, state supreme courts were still resolving that issue on an ad hoc basis. Greg argued that *Miller* was a substantive rule that applied retroactively to him and all other individuals in the state similarly situated, and the Massachusetts Supreme Judicial Court agreed.

First, the Massachusetts high court found that *Miller* announced a new rule. "At the time Diatchenko's conviction became final, there was no suggestion in existing Federal or State law that the imposition of a mandatory sentence of life in prison without the possibility of parole on an offender who was under the age of eighteen at the time he committed murder was constitutionally suspect."[138] In fact, as the Court noted, it had rejected Diatchenko's claim to that effect in his own 1982 appeal. Second, the Court went on to hold that the *Miller* decision was retroactively applicable to prisoners like Greg: "we conclude that the 'new' constitutional rule announced in *Miller* is substantive and, therefore, has retroactive application to cases on collateral review, including Diatchenko's case. The rule explicitly forecloses the imposition of a certain category of punishment—mandatory life in prison without the possibility of parole—on a specific class of defendants: those individuals under the age of eighteen when they commit the crime of murder. Its retroactive application ensures that juvenile homicide offenders do not face a punishment that our criminal law cannot constitutionally impose on them."[139] Finally, the state supreme court went one step further than the *Miller* Court and held that, as a matter of state constitutional law, all sentences of JLWOP were unconstitutional. "Simply put, because the brain of a juvenile is not fully developed, either structurally or functionally, by the age of eighteen, a judge cannot find with confidence that a particular offender, at that point in time, is irretrievably depraved."[140] With its decision, the Massachusetts high court made Greg—and all other Massachusetts prisoners serving a JLWOP sentence—eligible for a parole hearing, and it outlawed JLWOP sentences going forward.

Less than one year after the state supreme court decision in his favor, Greg appeared before the Parole Board for his initial hearing represented by counsel from the state's public defender office. The Parole Board reviewed Greg's criminal history, the facts of his homicide crime, his institutional history and his "long path to rehabilitation."[141] The Board noted that Greg had made "incremental but steady improvements in his character and conduct."[142] Importantly, Greg received his last disciplinary report in 1998 for destroying a food tray and fighting with another inmate.[143] He was 34 at that time, and he never received another write-up during his remaining 17 years in prison. The Board also emphasized the program work that Greg had done to address his anger, violence, and substance abuse. In sum, the Board unanimously found that Greg was "rehabilitated and present[ed] no current risk for violence."[144] He was transferred to a minimum-security facility for 12 months and then paroled to his mother's home.[145]

Today Greg seems incredibly grateful for his freedom while appropriately somber about his life circumstances.[146] He was able to move into a finished basement apartment in his mother's home in Roslindale, so, unlike many recent parolees, Greg avoided time in a halfway house. With a family introduction, Greg secured a job working as a custodian for a parking garage in Cambridge. Greg works hard, and the company has been good to him. When he developed pneumonia and was hospitalized, the management sent him an Edible Arrangement from his "work family." Later, when he thought he would have to quit because of incredible pain from plantar fasciitis, his manager offered him a desk job working overnights at the parking garage office booth; this allowed Greg to be off his feet and recuperate. In these ways, Greg is incredibly fortunate, and he knows it.

At the same time, Greg was released from prison at 51 years old, having missed more than three decades of his life, and that presents unique challenges. Even though he earned a college degree in prison, Greg has a 30-year gap on his résumé. Employers know that there are few explanations for that kind of gap, and none of them are good. Greg's plumbing training was informal, and while he was invaluable at MCI Norfolk, in the free world he is competing with certified, union-member plumbers. As a result, he earns $14 an hour as a custodian, barely a livable wage. He would like to have a home independent of his mother, and that would probably be good for both of them, but he cannot afford even a room rental in the greater Boston area on his current salary. Greg never learned to drive because he entered prison as a child. Despite studying hard for the driver's permit test, when he took it at the DMV, all of the questions related to "junior" drivers, something for which he was not prepared. He failed twice and has been too dejected to go back even though he knows that, without a license and car, his employment options are limited. Even the basics have proven to be an uphill battle.

Aside from the challenges of securing a home and a job, Greg, like most individuals paroled after a long period of incarceration, is dealing with a fair amount of emotional loss. While he was incarcerated, both of Greg's siblings passed away. His younger brother, Andrejs, died in a house fire in 1992. His older sister, Iveta, who had been addicted to heroin for many years, became sober in her 20s, but died from HIV-AIDS in 2001. Greg's "stepfather"—his mother's boyfriend of 36 years—died of cancer very soon after his release. Time did not stand still while Greg was incarcerated, and part of his punishment was the loss of time with family members.

Moreover, while Greg is grateful to be free, parole itself can be an anxiety-producing condition of life. Greg is on lifetime parole, which means he must meet certain conditions in perpetuity. Upon release on December 7, 2015, he was given two weeks to secure employment. It is challenging for anyone to find a job within two weeks during the holidays, but nearly impossible for a recent parolee. That challenge caused

Greg tremendous stress because he knew that he could be sent back to prison if he did not find work. Each month he needs to visit his parole officer at her office, provide a urine sample, and take a breathalyzer test. She also comes to his home approximately once a month on short notice simply to check in. As a condition of parole, Greg cannot be in touch with anyone who is incarcerated—and in Greg's case, that rules out even birthday and Christmas cards for most of his closest friends. He also fears a simple disagreement; raised voices, shouting, anything that may prompt a call to the police, even if it is a fleeting event, could mean Greg's return to prison. Despite the fact that he is very clearly a man walking on eggshells, Greg remains steadfast in his gratitude for his freedom.

C. Louis Costa

Notwithstanding the challenges of living under lifetime parole constraints, Louis Costa would gladly swap places with Greg Diatchenko. Louis is one of the hundreds of individuals serving JLWOP who are still hoping to be released under the *Miller* line of cases. Like Greg, Louis was sentenced to LWOP as a juvenile in Massachusetts nearly three decades ago. Unlike Greg, though, Louis appeared before the Massachusetts Parole Board in 2016 and was denied parole based on the Board's assertion that he was "not yet rehabilitated, and his release [was] not compatible with the welfare of society."[147] When one tracks the parallel paths that Greg and Louis have traveled over the last 30 years, it is hard to make sense of the Parole Board's decision in Louis's case. At bottom, Louis's case highlights the ways in which *Miller's* implementation is proving to be uneven, unpredictable, and arguably unfair.

Louis grew up in the North End, Boston's traditionally Italian neighborhood. His mother, Lois Pagliuca, married Ricky Costa when she was still a teenager, and they quickly had two sons, Louis and Jason.[148] Even before Lois married Ricky, the Pagliuca family was worried; Ricky was wild and lived a life of lawlessness. He was a "gangster."[149] By the time Louis was a toddler and Jason was an infant, Ricky was in prison, leaving his young wife, Lois, to raise their two sons. She struggled to do this, as Lois suffers from schizophrenia and has spent much of her adult life in and out of institutions. Despite witnessing the ravaging effects of her mental illness, what he calls "an evil disease," Louis describes his mother as a "beautiful, caring and loving person."[150] Still, Lois was fragile and Ricky was absent; as children, Louis and Jason relied on their extensive, close-knit family. Louis's maternal grandparents supported Lois in raising her two boys, living with or near them at all times and sending the boys to St. John's Catholic school in the North End.

As a child, Louis barely knew his father, and yet the notion of Ricky Costa, the respected and feared gangster, loomed large. Although surrounded by a loving family, Louis witnessed significant violence beginning around the age of 7 or 8.[151] He saw people in his neighborhood get beaten and stabbed, and he knew men who were murdered.[152] Louis remembers visiting his father in prison when he was about 5 years old, and, on some level, he knew that his father was involved in the violence he witnessed on the streets of the North End. Louis only saw his father one more time as a child—when he was 12 and his father was briefly out on parole before being sent back to Walpole State Prison.[153] As an adolescent, Louis felt a great deal of social pressure to be like his father, and "he became 'more infatuated with the street life,' distancing himself from his family and hanging out with his friends while they sold drugs."[154] Louis acknowledges that, while he did not know his father, he wanted to be like him "based on his reputation in the street."[155]

It was during this impressionable stage of his adolescence that Louis was caught up in a criminal act that would forever change the lives of at least three families. About two weeks before his crime, Louis became aware of a drug territory dispute.[156] At the time, two of his friends, both of whom were older by several years, Paul Tanso and Frank DiBenedetto, were selling drugs in the North End.[157] Joseph Bottari and Frank Chiuchiolo made it clear to Tanso and DiBenedetto that, if they were going to sell drugs in the neighborhood, they would have to pay them.[158] In the weeks prior to the shooting, Joseph Bottari and Frank Chiuchiolo threatened DiBenedetto and beat up Tanso.[159] Intent on selling drugs in the neighborhood without threat of interference from Bottari and Chiuchiolo, Tanso and DiBenedetto began to discuss killing the two men.

On February 19, 1986, Louis was at a friend's house when Tanso and DiBenedetto came over and explained that the murder was going to take place that night.[160] Tanso gave Louis a loaded gun and showed him how to use it.[161] They explained to Louis that a third friend would be picking up Bottari and Chiuchiolo and bringing them to Slye Park for a meeting. Within the hour, the men walked to Slye Park, and shortly after meeting up with the victims, DiBenedetto shot Chiuchiolo and Louis shot Bottari.[162] Louis also shot at Chiuchiolo as he attempted to flee the park.[163] When Chiuchiolo fell to the ground, Louis ran out of the park and threw the gun that he had fired into the harbor.[164] Louis had never been involved in any crime before that night; he had no prior arrests and no juvenile record.[165]

Louis, Tanso, and DiBenedetto were arrested on February 23, 1986—four days after the murders.[166] Three months later, the Suffolk County Grand Jury returned two indictments against Louis, charging him with the murders. Louis's case was transferred to adult court, but because of his age, he remained in the custody of the Department of Youth Services (DYS) until he turned 18. On April 11, 1988, a jury found Louis guilty on two counts of murder in the first degree, and he was sentenced to LWOP.[167] Four years later, his original conviction was overturned because Louis had been unable to confront one of the witnesses against him at trial.[168] Pending his second trial in 1994, Louis was out on bail and working for approximately 14 months.[169] In 1994, the state retried Louis for the double homicide and once again convicted him.[170] At 25, Louis was sent back to Walpole State Prison to serve two consecutive LWOP sentences.

In the years following his second trial, Louis had somewhat of a convoluted appeals process in court. There was a direct appeal of his second conviction; a collateral attack on his conviction, arguing ineffective assistance of counsel; and a later motion for a new trial based on newly discovered evidence.[171] As with many juveniles convicted of life without parole, Louis had not been a ringleader in the homicides; he had not played a role in planning the crime, nor did he know how to shoot a gun prior to that night. Louis was drawn into the crime at the last minute, and he recalls that he participated, not because he wanted to see the two men dead, but because he felt pressure—he "had been taught to always be loyal to [his] friends."[172] Over the years, Louis's family and lawyer worked tirelessly to make this case of diminished responsibility in court, but, for the most part, the courts—both state and federal—were not amenable to his argument.

However, after the United States Supreme Court decided *Miller v. Alabama*, abolishing mandatory JLWOP sentences, Louis and his family had new reason to be hopeful. Recall that the Massachusetts high court quickly expanded the scope of *Miller* as a matter of state law. As discussed in the context of Greg Diatchenko, the Massachusetts Supreme Judicial Court held in *Diatchenko* that the Supreme Court's decision in *Miller* was a substantive rule, which applied retroactively to all juveniles who had been sentenced to mandatory LWOP in the past.[173] Further, the *Diatchenko* Court held that juveniles serving LWOP in Massachusetts would be eligible for parole after serving 15 years.[174]

But the *Diatchenko* Court had been dealing with a defendant convicted of one count of homicide; Louis had been convicted of two counts and was serving two consecutive LWOP sentences. At the time of his sentence in 1994, the distinction between concurrent and consecutive sentences was purely symbolic, as Louis would never be parole eligible under even one of the sentences.[175] In the wake of the *Diatchenko* decision, though, the issue was of great practical import. If Louis was serving concurrent life sentences, he would be parole eligible after 15 years, whereas if his sentences remained consecutive he would not become parole eligible until he had served 30 years.[176] Having already served 28 years, Louis was anxious to appear before a Parole Board immediately.

In 2015, Louis argued that he was entitled to a resentencing hearing on the question of whether his life sentences should be concurrent or consecutive.[177] Specifically, Louis argued that (1) the original trial court judge who imposed consecutive sentences could not have predicted the significance that would later attach to the difference between consecutive and concurrent sentences in a post-*Miller* world, and (2) the original sentencing judge did not have at his disposal the wealth of contemporary scientific evidence demonstrating the diminished culpability of juvenile offenders.[178] The Massachusetts high court agreed with his position: "[T]he defendant merely argues that, because his sentence of life with parole eligibility after thirty years derives from the judge's decision to impose consecutive sentences, and because the sentencing judge could not have understood that his decision would have that effect, resentencing is appropriate. We agree with that reasoning."[179] Further, the Supreme Judicial Court held that the nature of the resentencing proceeding at the trial court level should reflect the fact that Louis was a juvenile at the time of his conviction, drawing upon the social science embodied in the *Miller* and *Diatchenko* decisions.[180] On October 9, 2015, Louis was resentenced to serve two concurrent life sentences with the possibility of parole, and with that new sentence, he became immediately eligible for a parole hearing.[181]

A little more than a year later, on February 25, 2016, Louis appeared before the Massachusetts Parole Board to ask for a chance to live again in the free world. He and his lawyer presented a mountain of evidence indicating that he was, in fact, the model for why juveniles convicted of even a homicide crime deserve a second chance. To begin, Louis presented evidence that he had been a nearly perfectly compliant inmate. He had not received a disciplinary report since 1989—meaning he had navigated a maze of prison regulations for nearly 30 years without incurring an infraction. As his lawyer brought to the Board's attention, Louis's record of not receiving a single disciplinary report for 27 years "may be the longest and most impressive in the history of the Massachusetts Department of Correction."[182]

In addition to staying out of trouble, Louis demonstrated that he had made affirmatively good use of his time while incarcerated. He maintained steady employment during his years of incarceration, but education became his central focus over time. When he was arrested, Louis had been sporadically attending 10th grade, and his performance in school was "mediocre at best."[183] While in prison, though, he obtained his GED and later enrolled in Boston University's Metropolitan College, taking courses with the goal of earning his bachelor's degree. Over a seven-year period, Louis took college courses, making the Dean's List consistently, and in 2011, he graduated cum laude from Boston University with a degree in History.[184] Several of his college professors submitted testimony for the Board to consider regarding Louis's performance. One professor, with whom Louis studied the American Presidency, remarked that "Louis's desire to learn, apply what he learned into everyday practices, and his level of respect for me as the professor and his classmates exhibits an individual exercising the characteristics one would want in a member of civil society."[185] Another professor reiterated that sentiment, saying, "Louis has devoted himself to self-improvement. His transformation and growth in the time I have known him are remarkable."[186] Furthermore, Louis undertook all of this education at a time when he had no hope of release; he did it simply out of a "love of learning" and a desire to improve himself.[187] As his lawyer made clear to the Board, Louis has continued his education even though he receives no credit for the course work he does.[188] He audits classes, and he acts as a tutor or teaching assistant in college courses, helping other inmates find the satisfaction that he gained through education.

Beyond his educational efforts, Louis took advantage of nearly every program the Department of Corrections offered to inmates, the most significant of which was the Restorative Justice Program.[189] The Program employs annual "retreats" to bring together homicide and other offenders, victims' families, prosecutors, judges, correctional administrators, elected officials, mental health professionals and academics "in an attempt to bridge gaps and heal wounds."[190] In addition to the retreats, Louis and other inmates participated in a series of programs called the "Victim Offender Education Group" (VOEG).[191] Through the VOEG sessions Louis and the other inmates met with survivors of crime to better understand the harms they had inflicted, to accept responsibility, and to become more self-aware about the history that drove them to crime. Not only did Louis complete the VOEG classes, but he then went on to become a VOEG facilitator.[192]

Louis also presented the findings of two forensic psychologists who independently established his incredible journey of maturation and his low risk of recidivism if paroled.[193] To begin, both psychologists concluded that Louis's involvement in the homicide crime had been a function of his youth and immaturity, rather than an underlying mental problem or character defect.[194] At the same time, both found that Louis had been rehabilitated.[195] In fact, one of the two doctors had also evaluated Louis at the time of his first trial, so he had the benefit of assessing the same man over a 30-year time period. He noted that Louis had "matured into mid-adulthood as a person who is very different than the adolescent I evaluated in 1986. The adolescent bravado has been replaced by a capacity for adult engagement, his perspective of the world has been broadened by life experience and higher education, his decisions are driven by goals he has set for himself and not the approval of others whom he insecurely aspires to be like."[196] That same doctor concluded that Louis "would be likely to contribute positively to society,"[197] while the second evaluator described Louis's commendable prison career as "a living testament to his maturation and growth."[198]

In addition to the testimony of these two psychologists, the Board also heard from Louis himself, his aunt, a friend, and a representative from a support group for former prisoners—all of whom spoke in support of Louis being paroled. The judge who had resentenced Louis to concurrent life terms in 2015 had remarked upon Louis's record of achievements, saying: "You cannot feign decency for over two decades."[199] At the parole hearing, Louis's lawyer, David Apfel, echoed that sentiment, driving home the message that Louis was rehabilitated, that he presented little to no risk of recidivism, and that there was no theory of punishment that would counsel for his further incarceration. Given his broad network of family support and his impeccable record in prison, Mr. Apfel asked the Board to grant Louis parole and permit him to move in with family immediately rather than engaging in a "step-down" transition process.

Six months later, in an opaque decision, the Parole Board concluded that Louis was "not a suitable candidate for parole."[200] The Board recounted the facts of the homicide, Louis's family history, his commendable prison record, and the testimony of those who had spoken on Louis's behalf. And then with no explanation, the Board stated that it "believe[d] a longer period of positive institutional adjustment and programming would be beneficial to Mr. Costa's rehabilitation."[201] The Board set another parole hearing for Louis two years from the date of the initial hearing—February 2018—and it "encourage[d] Mr. Costa to continue working toward his full rehabilitation."[202]

When one compares Louis's case with those of other juvenile "lifers" who have been granted parole in the post-*Diatchenko* era, the Board's decision seems nothing short of incomprehensible. While each case is unique, there are some consistent variables that the Board examines. The Board employs the standard that its members shall grant parole only "if they are of the opinion that there is a reasonable probability that, if such offender is released, the offender will live and remain at liberty without violating the law and that release is not incompatible with the welfare of society."[203] In addition, when considering cases of juveniles convicted of murder, the Board takes into account "the attributes of youth that distinguish juvenile homicide offenders from similarly situated adult offenders."[204] When looking at JLWOP cases the Board has considered in recent years, it is apparent that some variables argue against parole—such as acts of violence, gang activity, and substance abuse—while others count favorably in the parole decision, such as good behavior in prison, educational attainment, and rehabilitative programming.[205]

As Louis's attorney demonstrated in his supporting materials before the Board, Louis's case compared favorably to every single JLWOP case in which the Board had previously granted parole. In some instances, the comparison was stunning. For example, in one case the Board granted parole to an inmate who had been the ringleader in a first-degree murder case and who had spent years in a disciplinary unit during his incarceration.[206] Louis, in contrast, was a last-minute addition to a murder planned by two adults, and he came before the Parole Board free of disciplinary tickets for nearly three decades. In another favorable Parole Board decision, the Board described the inmate's record in prison, which was spotless for 20 years, as "remarkable."[207] One wonders how Louis's record is not even more remarkable, considering that he had been engaged in even more programming and had been discipline free for almost a decade longer.

On the other end of the spectrum, Louis's case looks starkly different from those cases where the Board has *denied* parole. Generally, those cases are marked by years of disciplinary infractions, a refusal to accept responsibility and show remorse for criminal conduct, and a failure to engage in rehabilitative programming.[208] In contrast, Louis, again, has a nearly perfect record of prison behavior; he has publicly acknowledged his criminal act, and has spent years reflecting on that act; and he has spent decades educating and improving himself.

This is not to say that the Board was wrong in its prior decisions, but it does make one wonder why Louis was denied parole when he compares so favorably to the other inmates granted parole—let alone to those denied parole. Even more troubling, one is left wondering: what did the Board have in mind when it urged Louis to "continue working toward his full rehabilitation"? If three decades of a perfect institutional record, exhaustion of programming available, and demonstrated remorse are not sufficient to merit parole, what is?

Despite his parole denial, Louis remains unbelievably upbeat and optimistic. His family and his lawyer are equally resolute in continuing to seek his release as soon as possible. Louis was recently approved for a transfer to a minimum-security prison facility in Massachusetts, and this is a positive development. Even in favorable decisions, the Parole Board typically requires an inmate to spend some period of time—often a year—in a minimum-security facility before being released to the public. If Louis were to receive a favorable Parole Board decision in the future, it is possible that the time he begins serving now in a minimum-security facility could count toward that transition requirement, expediting his release to family. At the same time, day-to-day life for an inmate within a minimum-security facility affords greater freedom and flexibility. While Louis's transfer to a lower-level facility is not parole, it's an improvement. He is staying focused on his goal to someday see the horizon instead of the walls of a prison.

D. Lessons

When the Supreme Court announces a new rule—even after it clarifies for lower courts what that new rule means—it can take years for state actors to implement that new rule. The road to implementation, as these three cases demonstrate, can be messy, unpredictable, and unfair. At the same time, the road to implementation can raise as many, if not more, questions than the case before the Supreme Court originally presented.

This is no more evident than in the wake of *Miller*, as lower courts, state legislatures, and executive actors like Parole Boards seek to implement the Court's new rules regarding extreme sentences for youth. To begin, there is the question of what standard Parole Boards should be using post-*Miller*. Even in Massachusetts, a state whose high court has articulated youth-specific parole considerations and whose Parole Board has adopted those considerations in theory, the standard is not clear. If it were clear, there would be greater consistency to the Board's decisions. Moreover, while the law makes it clear that parole is a privilege—a gift that the state does not owe a prisoner—once the state engages in the process of granting parole, it should do so in an even-handed manner, taking great measures to avoid even the appearance of arbitrariness.

This is one early implementation question: does *Miller* demand a new parole standard and criteria for its application?

A second implementation question relates to conditions of parole. That is, of course, it is reasonable for a state to impose certain conditions on an individual who has been incarcerated for a long period of time. Such individuals need to be monitored, for their own sake and for the safety of the general public. However, if the state makes the determination after *Miller* that an individual is serving a now-unconstitutional sentence, that he has rehabilitated himself, and that he no longer poses a threat to society, the state should set parole conditions that encourage successful reentry. Current procedures for parole and reentry do not necessarily do that.

Consider, for example, the work dilemma. Parolees are told they must find gainful employment within a certain time from their release date. This is easier said than done, especially for someone who entered prison as a juvenile. A recently released parolee who entered prison as a teenager may not have his Social Security card, and he likely did not have a driver's license. Even obtaining the requisite identification to apply for a job can be time consuming. Moreover, inmates like the three profiled in this chapter entered prison at a time when a job seeker read the Help Wanted section of a newspaper. Today, they need to be proficient with Monster.com and other online job searching tools—and have a smartphone or computer on which to do that searching. Finally, there is great stigma associated with having a felony conviction, and even employers who do not explicitly filter out those with a criminal record in the application process are skeptical of decade-long employment gaps. That hesitation is understandable, but it does set a trap for even the most earnest, job-seeking person on parole.

Parole conditions should be a map for success—for the parolee and for society—rather than a complex maze for individuals to navigate. Some people may feign homelessness to avoid being supervised by a parole officer; some people may pretend they are seeking work when they are, in fact, just passing time with friends. But those stereotypes do not apply to all individuals newly released from prison—especially not those who entered prison for a juvenile crime and have been traveling a long path to rehabilitation. Most formerly incarcerated youth want a chance to be industrious and independent.

Parole policy needs to be flexible enough to distinguish between the earnest job seeker confronting discrimination and the person who has returned to crime; it needs to separate the person who claims a lack of residence as a way to dodge parole visits and the individual who cannot afford a place to call home. The policy design needs to recognize that charging a monthly parole fee—which most states do—may be the financial breaking point for someone who is barely able to afford housing and food.

Parole protocols also need to recognize that there is great stress associated with parole and reentry—even though any individual paroled feels blessed to have that chance at freedom. People released after serving a lengthy term have missed out on central, basic life skills: how to file an income tax return; how to apply for a credit card, and then manage its balance. At the same time, some paroled individuals are experiencing residual trauma from their years of incarceration while also feeling guilty that they left behind others who became close friends and a family of sorts. Parolees worry: should I risk having a girlfriend? What if we have a fight and she calls the police? Can I attend a family reunion where I may run into an estranged cousin? What if we have a heated disagreement and a neighbor calls the police? Parolees are tip-toeing all the time, and they know it. For some people, like George and Greg, that precarious state never ends, as they are on lifetime parole.

Finally, the length of parole terms needs to be weighed carefully. Is lifetime parole necessary in all cases where it is used, given the emotional toll it takes on individuals and the fiscal cost of oversight? Might it be possible for someone who has been on parole without a hiccup for 5 years—or 10 years—to be put on administrative parole so that his or her freedom is still conditional but the monitoring provisions become less burdensome? Whatever its details, the parole system should be premised on the goal of successful reentry rather than catching someone in a technical violation.

Third, early implementation efforts after *Miller* drive home the close connection between conditions of confinement and successful reentry. For example, family, even under less than ideal circumstances, is key to reentry. Family can provide housing, transportation, a financial safety net, consistency, and much-needed emotional support to someone navigating a changed world. As I discuss in Chapter 7, the mode of juvenile incarceration needs to be reconsidered altogether, but a piece of that rethinking must entail making family contact a priority and a viable option during custodial detention. Otherwise there may be no family for inmates to come home to, and, as discussed in earlier chapters, most incarcerated youth do eventually rejoin society.

Equally important is access to programming and rehabilitative services during periods of incarceration. The *Graham* and *Miller* Courts contemplated youth having an opportunity to demonstrate maturity and growth over time.[209] In *Graham*, Justice Kennedy wrote that "[t]he juvenile should not be deprived of the opportunity to achieve maturity of judgment and self-recognition of human worth and potential."[210] In *Miller*, the Court made it clear that one of the constitutional infirmities of mandatory JLWOP was the fact that it "disregards the possibility of rehabilitation even when the circumstances most suggest it."[211] Under both decisions, a juvenile enjoys the *prospect* of eventual release—so long as he or she is able to demonstrate maturity and rehabilitation. Fortunately, the three individuals profiled in this chapter were able to take advantage of resources that enabled them to experience and then demonstrate self-awareness, education, and maturity. In some states, though, there are no Restorative Justice programs; there are no correspondence college courses. Many inmates write that they spend their days in their cells simply waiting for time to pass. In such cases, how does a juvenile offender, even one given the chance to appear before a Parole Board, demonstrate maturity and rehabilitation? As they implement the mandates of *Miller*, state actors need to be mindful of this double bind that can hamstring the efforts of youth serving extreme sentences.

Finally, early efforts in the wake of *Miller* demonstrate just how uneven—and maybe unfair—the implementation of new constitutional rules can be. As discussed earlier in this chapter, it is hard to understand why Louis Costa was denied parole when others with seemingly inferior petitions before the Board have been granted parole. At the same time, at least Louis is in the pipeline to be considered for parole. Of the three named petitioners whose extreme juvenile sentences were considered—and rejected—by the Supreme Court in recent years, not a single one is free today. Terrence Graham, as discussed in earlier chapters, was resentenced in the Florida courts after his victory before the Supreme Court. After a resentencing hearing, he received a 25-year sentence for his involvement in an attempted armed robbery—a non-homicide crime. Compare that to a state like Massachusetts, where juveniles serving life terms for *homicide* convictions are now eligible for parole after 15 years. Similarly, Evan Miller, whose case set in motion the abolition of JLWOP for homicide crimes across the country, has yet to be resentenced—4 years after his victory before the United States Supreme Court.[212] Without new legislation in Alabama, the state courts may be waiting for guidance on how to resentence an inmate like Miller.[213] And Henry Montgomery, whose case before the Supreme Court in 2016 resulted in *Miller* being held retroactive, is also waiting for a new sentence.[214] He is 70 years old and has spent more than 50 years in the Louisiana prison system.[215] Not only do the wheels of justice turn slowly, but also, as a function of federalism, they turn differently depending upon where an inmate is incarcerated.

As the individuals in this chapter demonstrate, youth can mature and outgrow criminal tendencies and impetuous decision-making. Some jurisdictions are recognizing that and are making good faith efforts to implement the promise of *Graham* and *Miller*; in other states, the prospect of release under those decisions remains elusive. Even as implementation efforts continue, juvenile justice advocates can push states to return to the rehabilitative ideal that motivated the creation of the juvenile court a little more than a century ago. The final chapter of this book turns to that juvenile justice frontier.

7

The War for Kids

IN THE LAST DECADE, the United States Supreme Court has championed the cause of kids in the criminal justice system. The Court has held that the most serious punishment on the books, the death penalty, is never permissible punishment for a child—no matter how heinous the crime. At the same time, the Court has significantly narrowed the circumstances under which states may sentence children to life without parole—the second-most-serious sanction in our system. In its recent juvenile sentencing decisions, the Court has relied extensively on modern neuroscience and what it tells us about children: that they are less culpable by definition; that their moral character is fluid; and that they are more amenable to rehabilitation than adult offenders. While the Court's opinions dealt only with the two most severe punishments at law, they were a stark indictment of broader juvenile justice practices, including automatic transfer provisions and one-size-fits-all sentencing schemes. In sum, the Court has heralded the message that children are different for constitutional purposes and state laws must reflect that fact.

States are now in the process of implementing the Court's recent juvenile sentencing decisions, a process that will take years. For example, there are approximately 2,500 inmates nationwide serving a life without parole sentence for a juvenile homicide crime, and most of them received that punishment because of a mandatory sentencing scheme. Now that the Court has held that (1) a juvenile may not be sentenced to LWOP on a mandatory basis, and (2) that its decision on that count applies retroactively—to all currently serving that sentence—states across the nation are conducting resentencing hearings and parole hearings for these 2,500 inmates. As discussed in Chapter 6, in some instances, individuals who, as children, were sentenced to die in prison are now free because of the Court's recent juvenile cases.

Some states have heeded the Court's call to treat children differently and have enacted more comprehensive reform measures than the Court's decisions technically required. As discussed in Chapters 5 and 6, states legislatures in West Virginia, Delaware, and California have passed laws that reflect the spirit of the Court's sentencing decisions. These laws ban juvenile life without parole, or significantly narrow it, while creating opportunities for incarcerated juveniles to get a second look once they have served a portion of their initial sentence. This is progress.

And yet, there is still a war on kids in America. Many states continue to treat age-appropriate misconduct in school as the basis for criminal charges. Children are still easily moved from juvenile to adult criminal court on a regular basis. Once in adult court, children too often go without effective representation and face sentencing schemes that were drafted with adults in mind.

Moreover, as prior chapters have demonstrated, this war on kids is unfair in the way most wars are: the poor, the uneducated, and the vulnerable constitute the bulk of its casualties. This war is also irrational, as studies consistently show most kids will outgrow criminal inclinations, and incarceration itself tends to increase the likelihood of future criminal behavior. The Supreme Court has provided moral leadership, and that leadership has provided the impetus for modified state juvenile sentencing laws. But so far, what we have seen is tinkering at the margins.

If we take seriously the claim that states have instituted a war on kids in the last half century, and if we intend to generate lasting juvenile justice reform, there is only one path forward. We must launch a war *for* kids. This war for kids will need to be fought on both legal and policy fronts. In this chapter, I map out a blueprint of reform measures that a war for kids must entail.

A. Secure the Implementation of the *Miller* Trilogy

The Supreme Court has laid the foundation for a juvenile justice revolution, but the long-term value of its opinions hinges on their implementation. States like Nevada and West Virginia offer examples for other states to follow.[1] Since the *Miller* decision, both states have enacted legislation that bans the use of LWOP for children. Moreover, both states now require judges sentencing kids in adult court to consider the mitigating aspects of youth, and in both states a child becomes parole eligible after 15 or 20 years. These are model pieces of legislation in that they reflect the science and logic of the Supreme Court's decisions.

Not all states are on this path of robust implementation, though. In fact, some states are flouting the Supreme Court's recent juvenile sentencing directives. For example, Michigan incarcerates 363 of the roughly 2,500 inmates nationwide serving JLWOP.[2] Under the *Miller* ruling, these individuals should receive a new sentencing hearing that takes into account their youth and its mitigating circumstances at the time of their crime. Moreover, the *Miller* Court explicitly said that, given what we know about children's brain development, "appropriate occasions for sentencing juveniles to this harshest possible penalty will be uncommon."[3] And yet, prosecutors in Michigan are seeking to resentence more than half of these individuals to LWOP.[4] While Michigan prosecutors may argue that they are technically complying with the Court's decisions, they are doing so in a way that eviscerates the Court's rationale that children are different and must be sentenced in an age-appropriate way.

Other state supreme courts have dodged the implementation of *Miller* by labeling their sentencing schemes "discretionary" and declaring them outside the *Miller* Court's ruling. Recall that *Miller* banned *mandatory* LWOP for juveniles and held that, before imposing LWOP on a juvenile defendant, the sentencer must engage in an individualized hearing where youth and all of its mitigating circumstances are evaluated. That is, the court left open the possibility of a juvenile defendant receiving an LWOP sentence—albeit rarely—on a *discretionary* basis.

A few states have seized upon this loophole as a way to avoid granting each juvenile defendant an individualized "Miller" hearing before imposing LWOP. For example, the Virginia state supreme court took the position that, because judges had statutory authority to suspend a sentence in whole or part, JLWOP sentences in Virginia were "discretionary," and thus *Miller* would never apply to juvenile homicide cases in the state.[5] Similarly, state supreme courts in Georgia and West Virginia have held that, because the state homicide code permits two sentences for juveniles convicted of first-degree murder—life in prison or life without parole—JLWOP is "discretionary" and thus outside the purview of *Miller*.[6]

These courts are using semantics to avoid the implementation of the *Miller* ruling.[7] The *Miller* Court relied upon extensive social science that tells us children are less culpable and more amenable to rehabilitation, and as a result, "imposition of a State's most severe penalties on juvenile offenders cannot proceed as though they were not children."[8] Further, according to the *Miller* Court, states run afoul of the Constitution unless they engage in an individualized sentencing hearing at which no fewer than six factors related to youth have been considered before imposing JLWOP.[9] *That* is the kind of discretion that the Supreme Court envisioned. That discretion, that process, is not satisfied simply because there is the binary sentencing option of life with or life without parole. Nor is a JLWOP sentence "discretionary" because there is the theoretical possibility that a judge would invoke her own statutory authority to set it aside. So far, the Supreme Court has declined to take up this question of what "discretionary" means for *Miller* purposes,[10] and advocates will need to continue pressing for review of this issue in the years to come.

Another issue percolating in the courts is the question of "de facto life sentences" for juveniles. While the Court only dealt with life without parole sentences in *Graham* and *Miller*, its reasoning applies with equal force to all custodial sentences that are the functional equivalent of LWOP—whether or not the sentence has that label. If a child is sentenced to a term of years that in all likelihood will exceed his natural life expectancy, surely the *Graham/Miller* rulings apply, as those Courts were concerned with sentences that "foreswea[r] . . . the rehabilitative ideal."[11] Some courts have recognized this reality and have struck down 45-year,[12] 50-year,[13] 52.5-year,[14] and 110-year[15] sentences as triggering the protections afforded by *Graham* and *Miller* even though they were not "technically . . . life-without-parole sentence[s]."[16] Other federal and state courts, though, have held that extreme term-of-year sentences are not governed by *Miller* and *Graham*. By factually distinguishing the cases from *Miller* and *Graham*, courts have upheld juvenile sentences of

89[17] and 315 years.[18] These decisions are not consistent with the fundamental principle that children have diminished culpability as compared to adults and equally greater capacity for rehabilitation.

Even for those individuals whose cases fall squarely within the purview of the *Graham* and *Miller* decisions, there is the question of remedy. That is, the Court has declared that the Eighth Amendment prohibits JLWOP in non-homicide cases and that it bars mandatory JLWOP even when the defendant is convicted of homicide. But the Court did not craft– nor is it the Court's job to craft—a method for the states' compliance with its decisions. The *Graham* Court required states to provide juvenile non-homicide offenders with a "meaningful opportunity to obtain release based on demonstrated maturity and rehabilitation."[19] What exactly does that "meaningful opportunity" standard demand from the states? The Supreme Court has not squarely addressed this question, but there is some indication of what does *not* satisfy the standard.

A federal appeals court recently addressed the question whether a geriatric release program satisfied the "meaningful opportunity" standard and concluded that it did not.[20] Dennis LeBlanc was convicted of rape and abduction at the age of 16 in Virginia.[21] He was sentenced to two terms of life in prison without parole.[22] After the *Graham* decision, LeBlanc petitioned the state courts to vacate his sentence and afford him a sentence consistent with the *Graham* ruling that he have a meaningful opportunity for release.[23] While recognizing that Virginia had abolished parole for those convicted of felonies after 1995, the state insisted that LeBlanc's sentence was still compliant with *Graham* because the state had a geriatric release program.[24] Virginia's geriatric release program permits an inmate to apply for early release from a sentence if they are 60 years old (and have served at least 10 years of their sentence) or 65 years old (and have served at least 5 years of their sentence).[25] According to the state's position, LeBlanc already had a "meaningful opportunity" to obtain release because, under this provision, theoretically, he could seek conditional release when he turned 60, at which point he would have served more than 40 years of his life sentence.

The Fourth Circuit Court of Appeals rejected Virginia's defense of LeBlanc's sentence and held that the geriatric release program does not satisfy the "meaningful opportunity" standard from *Graham*. To begin, the appellate court noted that the Parole Board may deny geriatric release for *any reason whatsoever*, and that, by definition, such a protocol violates the *Graham* Court's requirement that the opportunity for release hinge on demonstrated "maturity and rehabilitation."[26] Second, the Court held that the geriatric release protocol failed to satisfy *Graham* because it took no account of juveniles' greater capacity for change. In fact, as the Court pointed out, more than 95 percent of the denials of geriatric release were based on the nature of the inmate's crime.[27] This approach—focusing on the nature of the crime, rather than the capacity for change—fundamentally violated *Graham's* premise that children are less culpable and more amenable to rehabilitation. Finally, the Court noted that youth was absent from the Parole Board's factors to consider in the geriatric release decision process.[28] For all of these reasons, the Court held that Virginia could not satisfy the requirement that inmates like Terrence Graham and Dennis LeBlanc have a "meaningful opportunity" for release with the theoretical possibility of geriatric release. The question of what remedy *is* satisfactory will continue to unfold in the years to come.

Similarly, when the Court held that *Miller* applies retroactively to all 2,500 inmates nationwide, it once again acknowledged the lurking question of what remedy would satisfy the Court's ruling. In fact, the Court suggested that states could satisfy its ruling by granting parole hearings to these individuals rather than resentencing hearings.

> Giving *Miller* retroactive effect, moreover, does not require States to relitigate sentences, let alone convictions, in every case where a juvenile offender received mandatory life without parole. A State may remedy a *Miller* violation by permitting juvenile homicide offenders to be considered for parole, rather than by resentencing them.... Allowing those offenders to be considered for parole ensures that juveniles whose crimes reflected only transient immaturity—and who have since matured—will not be forced to serve a disproportionate sentence in violation of the Eighth Amendment.[29]

However, there remains a question for defenders: is parole the better avenue? Or is a resentencing hearing optimal? On one hand, Parole

Boards may be more flexible and more narrowly targeted in their directives. On the other hand, Parole Boards fall under the executive branch, and there is some concern that the branch of government responsible for *enforcing* the criminal law ought not also to have a say in who enjoys a reprieve from those laws and when. As discussed in Chapter 6, Parole Boards can be fickle and subject to political winds. In any event, both Parole Board hearings and judicial resentencing for JLWOP individuals are underway. Time will tell whether judges or Parole Board members are better equipped to engage in analyzing which defendants have demonstrated maturity and rehabilitation.

It will be years, if not decades, before the Supreme Court can address these and other questions related to implementing the *Miller* trilogy. And there is no guarantee that the current Court or a future composition of the Court will have the appetite or inclination to do so. Until then, juvenile advocates will seek to ensure that the Court's message about kids is carried out to its fullest extent. Even as that litigation continues, there are separate but related legal and policy questions that should be pursued as part of the war for kids.

B. Put Juveniles Back in Juvenile Court

In the wake of the *Miller* trilogy, juvenile justice advocates can seek a return to the juvenile court model. While that model has had its shortcomings from the get-go, it was based on a fundamental notion that has been lost: children are different in their very constitution and, with rare exception, they should not be dealt with in the adult criminal justice system. Those who invented the concept of the juvenile court in the late 19th century understood that adult criminal court was no place for children—that sentiment required no proof or explanation. For decades, if the state sought to remove a child from the juvenile court's jurisdiction—to transfer that child to adult court—the state had to prove to a judge why that transfer was necessary on an individualized basis. Only because of fear-based and (now debunked) theories about juvenile super-predators did we move away from that model as a nation. Given what we know today about brain development and given what the Supreme Court has done in the juvenile sentencing arena, there is no reason for children to be transferred to adult court as a matter of course.

Instead, we should return to the default that a child who breaks the law ought to be dealt with in juvenile court unless a judge determines that extraordinary circumstances warrant a transfer to adult court. In some ways, this is a tall order. We have become accustomed to the legal fiction that a minor can be transformed into an adult through legislative fiat. As discussed in Chapter 3, transfer provisions that put kids in adult court are now the norm: all states have some mechanism, and many have several, that permit adult criminal prosecution of juvenile defendants.[30] Twenty-nine states have statutory exclusion transfer laws—laws that mandate adult criminal court for children charged with certain offenses.[31] Moreover, for years scholars have argued against transfer laws,[32] and lawyers have challenged various transfer laws in court—without success. [33]

But today, in the wake of the *Miller* trilogy, there is newfound traction to the claim that mandatory transfer laws are unconstitutional and nonsensical. As was addressed in Chapter 5, *Miller* and the cases that came before it changed the landscape for the treatment of children in the criminal justice system. After *Miller*, it is now possible to challenge automatic transfer laws as impermissible "one-size-fits-all" treatment of juveniles. In fact, the *Miller* Court not only took issue with conflating adult and juvenile sentencing generally, but it also criticized mandatory transfer provisions explicitly. The *Miller* Court explained that mandatory transfer laws, depending upon their operation, can vest prosecutors with too much unbridled discretion; can force judges into making extreme sentencing choices; and can jeopardize a child's well-being.[34]

The language, logic, and science of the *Miller* trilogy, then, have further eroded the legitimacy of transfer laws—laws that have been under attack for decades. Many scholars have mapped out this newfound basis for challenging juvenile transfer laws.[35] For example, Tulane Law Professor Janet Hoeffel has noted that transfer and death penalty proceedings have much in common in their stakes and in their finality. She argues that the transfer decision should be done on an individual basis, just as capital sentencing proceedings have to be, incorporating all relevant mitigation evidence.[36] Lawyers today can draw on this new law and scholarship to challenge juvenile transfer laws and to argue for a return to the default of keeping kids in juvenile court.

The goal of keeping more kids in the juvenile system is not unrealistic, and, in fact, efforts to accomplish this goal are already underway in several states. To begin, while most states and the District of Columbia deal with adolescents in juvenile court until they turn 17 (at least as a default), in the last seven years, five states have amended their laws to keep children in juvenile court until they turn 18: Illinois, Connecticut, New Hampshire, Massachusetts, and Mississippi.[37] Similar efforts are ongoing in Michigan and New York.[38] At the same time, legislators are trying to curb the power of prosecutors to "direct file" juvenile cases in adult court in California, Florida, and Vermont.[39] These efforts reflect a national recognition that both kids and society are better off when we keep juveniles in juvenile court.

C. Provide Age-Appropriate Sentencing for Kids

As long as kids continue to be charged in adult criminal court, juvenile advocates must insist upon age-appropriate sentencing for them. The *Miller* trilogy provides the foundation for this policy measure, as well. As a preliminary matter, age-appropriate sentencing for youth requires abolition of life without parole sentences for juveniles—across the board. The Supreme Court has said that LWOP for kids is akin to a death sentence, and given what we know about juvenile brain development, as a nation we should be no more comfortable with JLWOP than we are with juvenile execution. This objective—banning JLWOP—is priority number one, and it is achievable.

As discussed in Chapter 5, the Supreme Court only addressed the unconstitutionality of JLWOP in 2010, and in 2011 five states banned JLWOP.[40] Since then, the trend away from JLWOP has been remarkable. Today 17 states ban the practice of JLWOP; 5 additional jurisdictions ban JLWOP in nearly all cases; and 3 states that technically have JLWOP on the books have never imposed it.[41] In a very short period of time, the nation has reached a point where nearly half its jurisdictions have said no to JLWOP. Historically tough-on-crime states like Texas, Kansas, Florida, and California are part of this trend away from JLWOP.[42] Nationwide abolition of JLWOP is achievable and on the horizon.

At the same time, we must recognize that eliminating JLWOP is the first right step toward age-appropriate sentencing, but it is just the first step. A ban on JLWOP actually does not accomplish enough for kids in the adult criminal justice system. For example, a nationwide ban on JLWOP would not prevent a 16-year-old from getting a life sentence with the theoretical (but illusory) possibility of parole. Nor would a nationwide ban on JLWOP prevent a child from being exposed to decades in prison under a mandatory minimum sentencing scheme.

Instead, as long as children are charged in the adult system, we must work toward the goal that youth *always* counts as a mitigating variable on its own at the sentencing phase. This goal means a few things. At a minimum, it means that juvenile justice advocates should challenge presumptive and advisory sentencing guidelines if they do not account for youth as a mitigating factor. Recall from earlier chapters that sentencing guidelines range from mandatory to advisory. If a sentence is mandatory, it means that once the jury has convicted the defendant of a certain charge, the judge has no choice but to impose the sentence prescribed by the legislature for that crime.[43] A presumptive sentencing guideline, however, suggests a predetermined sentence for a crime, but permits the judge to impose a more lenient alternative sentence if the judge determines that there are mitigating circumstances. Typically, the legislature determines in advance what mitigating factors might justify a downward departure from the presumptive sentence.[44] Finally, advisory guidelines are voluntary in that they provide a benchmark for the sentencing judge, but the judge may depart from the suggested sentence with or without explanation.[45]

Post-*Miller*, juvenile justice advocates should insist that youth itself be a relevant mitigating factor when presumptive sentencing guidelines apply. As the *Miller* Court explained, there are many " 'mitigating qualities of youth.' "[46] Youth is a "time of immaturity, irresponsibility, 'impetuousness[,] and recklessness,' " and it is a period during which "a person may be most susceptible to influence and to psychological damage."[47] Thus, youth alone should at least be permissible grounds for a judge to impose a more lenient sentence than what the presumptive guideline suggests.

But not all presumptive sentencing guidelines include youth as a mitigating factor in its own right. For example, Alaska provides presumptive sentencing guidelines for felonies, and the statute separately lists aggravating factors and mitigating factors.[48] The Alaska statute lists 20 separate mitigating factors that may "allow imposition of a sentence below the presumptive range."[49] Only 1 of the 20 mitigating factors relates to youth, and it does not recognize youth in its own right as a mitigating variable. The statute permits a lesser sentence than the presumptive one if "the conduct of a youthful defendant was substantially influenced by another person more mature than the defendant."[50] Moreover, as with any of the mitigating variables, the burden is on the defendant to prove to the judge by clear and convincing evidence each mitigating factor.[51] Alaska is not alone in its disregard for youth as a mitigating factor in and of itself.[52]

Because the Supreme Court has elevated youth in its own right to a mitigating factor of constitutional significance, states must consider youth at sentencing even in a presumptive or advisory sentencing context. At the same time, the Supreme Court recently reiterated that a court's consideration of youth cannot be perfunctory in the JLWOP context. In *Tatum v. Arizona*, the Court sent back a handful of JLWOP cases to the Arizona courts for further consideration in light of *Montgomery v. Louisiana*.[53] While the lower courts had noted the juvenile defendant's age in each case before imposing LWOP, the Supreme Court found that judicial notice was insufficient. "It is clear after *Montgomery* that the Eighth Amendment requires more than mere consideration of a juvenile offender's age before the imposition of a sentence of life without parole. It requires that a sentencer decide whether the juvenile offender before it is a child 'whose crimes reflect transient immaturity' or is one of 'those rare children whose crimes reflect irreparable corruption' for whom a life without parole sentence may be appropriate. . . . There is thus a very meaningful task for the lower courts to carry out on remand."[54] In sum, youth must always be considered as a mitigating variable, regardless of the nature of the sentencing scheme, and consideration means more than recording the juvenile's age for the record. It requires analysis of the youth's environment and capacity for rehabilitation. This is a modest step toward age-appropriate sentencing.

The goal of age-appropriate sentencing for youth also requires something more radical—or at least radical in our current world where kids are treated like adults because of a legal fiction. It means that mandatory minimums should not apply to children. Ever.

As discussed in Chapter 3, mandatory minimums are especially harmful and unfair to children. After *Miller*, they are simply unjustifiable.[55] The *Miller* opinion is replete with discussion of process and the importance of discretion for juvenile sentencing. The Court explained, "[s]uch mandatory penalties, by their nature, preclude a sentencer from taking account of an offender's age and the wealth of characteristics and circumstances attendant to it."[56] And later, "Mandatory life without parole for a juvenile precludes consideration of his chronological age and its hallmark features—among them, immaturity, impetuosity, and failure to appreciate risks and consequences."[57] The *Miller* Court was examining and speaking of LWOP, but in an earlier part of the decision, the majority recognized that "none of what [*Graham*] said about children—about their distinctive (and transitory) mental traits and environmental vulnerabilities—is crime specific."[58] It is also true that none of what *Roper/Graham/Miller* said about children is *sentence*-specific. The sentencing process and discretion called for by the *Miller* Court are simply incompatible with a mandatory sentencing scheme—whether it is a mandatory sentence of life without parole or a mandatory sentence of 35 years.

To be sure, the claim that *Miller* precludes mandatory minimums for juveniles sounds radical, at least at first blush. Only one state supreme court to date has read *Miller* in this way.[59] In an expansive opinion, documenting the evolution of juvenile justice in this country and the United States Supreme Court's recent juvenile cases, the Iowa Supreme Court rejected the concept of mandatory minimums for children in *Iowa v. Lyle*.[60] "Mandatory minimum sentences for juveniles are simply too punitive for what we know about juveniles," the court held.[61] Moreover, the court anchored its decision in its reading of *Miller*: "*Miller* is properly read to support a new sentencing framework that reconsiders mandatory sentencing for all children. Mandatory minimum sentencing results in cruel and unusual punishment due to the differences between children and adults. This rationale applies to all crimes, and no principled basis exists to cabin the protection only for the most serious crimes."[62]

While several other state courts have rejected Iowa's position,[63] the Iowa Supreme Court's reading of *Miller* is entirely defensible. Again, the language of the *Miller* Court repeatedly emphasized the importance of process and discretion when sentencing juveniles. In addition to its language, the *logic* of the *Miller* decision also precludes mandatory sentencing for juveniles. The *Miller* Court drew on two separate strands of precedent: its cases dealing with categorical bans on certain sentencing practices and its line of cases prohibiting the mandatory imposition of capital punishment.[64] The first line of cases to which the *Miller* Court refers says "that children are constitutionally different from adults for purposes of sentencing."[65] It went on to reiterate what *Roper* and *Graham* had recognized: that brain and social science confirm children are less culpable and more amenable to reform and that these differences must be taken into account at sentencing.[66] Because the *Miller* Court cemented this "kids are different" approach, one cannot claim post-*Miller* that such differences are irrelevant outside the context of LWOP.

Second, the *Miller* Court drew on its line of cases requiring "that capital defendants have an opportunity to advance, and the judge or jury a chance to assess, any mitigating factors," especially those dealing with "the 'mitigating qualities of youth.'"[67] This line of cases requires the states to provide defendants with an opportunity to present mitigating factors that may impact the sentence—including youth, substance abuse, a history of violence within the family, developmental challenges, or traits that suggest amenability to rehabilitation. The *Miller* Court borrowed from this line of cases to say that kids are different, and that these differences should be illuminated in an individualized, discretionary sentencing scheme. Thus, the logic of *Miller*, in addition to its language, suggests that mandatory minimums—schemes that preclude individual consideration of mitigating factors, including youth— are incompatible with the *Miller* trilogy.

Now, beyond the question of whether mandatory minimums are permissible in the wake of *Miller*, critics will argue that eliminating mandatory minimums for juveniles will generate unworkable administrative burdens for state courts. The dissenting justices in the *Lyle* case emphasized this point. Justice Zager, for example, lamented that there were more than 100 Iowan inmates serving a mandatory sentence that was imposed upon them as juveniles, and that revisiting those sentences would "take hundreds, if not thousands, of hours."[68] Further, the dissenting justices posited that, without mandatory minimums for juveniles, trial courts would be required to hear expert witnesses regarding juveniles' diminished culpability.[69] "In sum, 'the trial court must consider all relevant evidence' of the distinctive youthful attributes of the juvenile offender. . . . The possibilities are nearly endless."[70] The logical conclusion of this type of administrative burden argument is that, if indeed juveniles cannot be subject to mandatory sentences, the entire process of sentencing juveniles in adult court is undermined, as determinate sentencing schemes are the national norm.[71]

To begin, that outcome does not necessarily follow. Prohibiting mandatory minimums for juveniles does not preclude their appearance in adult criminal court. It may make juvenile sentencing in adult court more time consuming and resource intensive, but the Supreme Court has consistently held that efficiency and fiscal constraints must yield to the observance of constitutional rights.[72] States may not, for example, refuse to provide lawyers to poor criminal defendants or doctors to inmates because those obligations are too expensive.[73] In the same way, states cannot defend a juvenile sentencing scheme simply on the grounds of administrative ease and cost containment.

Further, if it is simply too onerous for states to sentence juveniles in adult court without relying upon mandatory sentencing schemes, that reality may compel prosecutors and legislators to reconsider when, and how frequently, children should be transferred to adult court. Suppose, for example, that prosecutors in Iowa do not want to pursue an adult criminal sentence except in rare cases because of the burden of justifying such sentences under the *Miller* factors. It may turn out that precluding juvenile mandatory minimums forces state actors to internalize the full costs of prosecuting children as adults. And it may follow that, as a result of internalizing those costs, over time, state actors charge juveniles as adults only very sparingly. Given what science has revealed about juveniles and their capacity for change, and given the Supreme Court's incorporation of that science, such an outcome seems logical. Moreover, such an outcome—the reluctant charging of children in adult court—would merely be a return to the juvenile justice model that was founded in this country more than a century ago.

In sum, juvenile advocates must seek age-appropriate sentencing for all minors in adult court, regardless of the severity of the crime or the nature of the sentencing scheme. This entails several steps: nationwide abolition of JLWOP; youth as a mitigating variable in its own right even in presumptive and advisory sentencing schemes; and the end to adult mandatory minimums for kids.

D. Argue against Incarceration and for Rehabilitation

A war for kids also requires some immediate changes to juvenile incarceration nationwide. First, as discussed in Chapter 4, solitary confinement of youth is a common practice and it is incredibly damaging. Not only does solitary confinement cause psychological distress, but also youth in isolation are at the highest risk for suicide. In January 2016, President Obama issued an executive order recognizing the dangers of solitary confinement for youth and banning the practice in federal prisons.[74] Advocates should seek to abolish solitary for youth at the state level, too, by leveraging the brain science of the *Miller* trilogy and the example of the federal government.

In the longer term, though, a war for kids requires something more than eliminating the most threatening aspects of incarceration—it requires changing our concept of youth incarceration altogether. As discussed in Chapter 4, we currently rely upon youth detention where it is unnecessary, and it routinely does more harm than good. Only about 25 percent of children in detention facilities have been charged with or convicted of one of the four most serious felonies, and nearly a third are serving time based on a public order violation, a technical parole or probation violation, or a status offense.[75] At the same time, the majority of incarcerated youth enter the system with a mental health or special education need that often goes unmet and with a history of trauma that is only exacerbated by the hostility of detention. Once a child enters the correctional system he or she is more likely to have diminished educational and employment opportunities and to commit crime in the future. While we are spending almost 6 billion dollars a year on youth corrections, the prevailing method of juvenile detention is an utter failure: between 70 and 80 percent of juveniles released from detention centers are rearrested within two or three years for a new offense.[76] Youth incarceration is a tremendous waste of human potential and taxpayer dollars.

Going forward, incarceration for juveniles should be a rare measure of last resort, and it should be rehabilitative when it needs to happen. In recent years, states like Alabama, California, Louisiana, New York, and North Carolina have reduced their detained youth populations, and these jurisdictions can serve as a model for keeping youth out of the correctional system.[77] For example, Alabama lawmakers passed a juvenile justice reform act in 2008 that recognized the state was confining too many youths, often for minor offenses.[78] Since its passage, the state has cut its detained youth population roughly in half and has been able to redirect the money spent on incarceration to diversion programs set up in 52 counties. Through these diversion programs low-risk youth have access to substance abuse and mental health treatment, as well as counseling, and they avoid the harmful effects of incarceration.

Similarly, in the 1990s the Annie E. Casey Foundation began exploring alternatives to juvenile incarceration and launched the Juvenile Detention Alternatives Initiative (JDAI).[79] The goal of the JDAI was to demonstrate in pilot locations that youth detention populations could be substantially reduced without impacting public safety.[80] JDAI jurisdictions use objective indicators to screen out youth who do not pose a risk to public safety and to offer appropriate alternatives to detention, such as mental health treatment and Multisystemic Therapy, a family- and community-based approach to addressing the root cause of delinquency. As of 2013, more than 250 localities in 39 states and the District of Columbia were participating in the JDAI.[81] Overall these participating jurisdictions have achieved a cumulative 43 percent reduction in detention populations,[82] and 38 JDAI sites have reduced their average daily populations in detention by 50 percent or more.[83] At the same time, JDAI sites have experienced reductions in youth crime indicators, such as juvenile arrests and felony petitions.[84] These jurisdictions demonstrate that diverting youth away from incarceration can be a win-win proposition for taxpayers and youth.

In the small percentage of cases where youth represent a risk to society and must be incarcerated, we need to overhaul the mode of detention altogether. As discussed in Chapter 4, large prison-like detention centers are the most common mode of incarceration for kids in

America,[85] and they are the least effective, with recidivism rates hovering around 75 percent.[86] However, there is a well-documented, affordable, and more effective alternative that has been successfully employed in Missouri for nearly four decades with bipartisan support.[87] Instead of warehousing youth for long periods of time in large centers that offer few services, Missouri shifted to small centers that emphasize routine, therapy, and relationship building for detained youth. Politicians across the political spectrum, non-profit organizations, and mainstream media outlets have applauded this "Missouri Model" for its efficacy, humanity, and affordability.

The Missouri youth corrections model emphasizes treatment over punishment, and it has six defining features.[88] First, Missouri youth who require confinement are placed in small facilities near their homes when possible. Second, the correction model focuses heavily on group therapy and group accountability rather than leaving youth to find their own way among equally troubled youth in a large prison environment. Third, the model employs staff who are trained in therapy and supportive treatment, eschewing guards and coercive techniques that are the norm in juvenile prisons. Fourth, confined youth in Missouri are engaged in educational and vocational training that will enable them to transition back into society. At the same time they spend a great deal of time in group therapy seeking to discern the root cause of their delinquency so that they can avoid repeating that behavior in the future. Fifth, when possible, the staff in Missouri's system seeks to include family members in youth treatment and after-care plans. Finally, when youth are deemed rehabilitated and ready to return to society, Missouri provides intensive transition resources and after-care support as youth re-enter educational and job opportunities.

The radical differences between confinement in Missouri and in other states' juvenile correctional facilities cannot be overstated. Instead of being in an environment with 100 other delinquent youth, in Missouri, the largest youth confinement center has only 50 beds, and within facilities youth are assigned to 12-member teams of kids with whom they work.[89] Instead of sleeping on metal cots in cells, Missouri kids are in carpeted rooms with bunkmates and walls decorated with personal effects.[90] While many detained youth across the country are simply sitting in a cell waiting for their release date, kids in the Missouri system are scheduled all day, primarily working on academics, work details, and group therapy sessions. Moreover, Missouri youth are serving indeterminate sentences; release hinges not on the passage of time but on personal growth. Before they are released, Missouri youth must demonstrate self-awareness, personal growth, an ability to control their emotions, and the capacity to live and work in a community.

Perhaps the biggest difference between the juvenile incarceration status quo and the Missouri model is its underlying value system. The Missouri model is predicated on the "belief that delinquent youth can succeed and the expectation that most will."[91] With this value in mind, the entire program is geared toward enabling that success, giving youth the tools to understand their past behaviors, learn from them, and develop skills to make alternative choices in the future. Not only do youth develop self-awareness through group therapy and sharing with their peers, but they also develop leadership and responsibility for others. For example, while the group of 10–12 kids in each team "checks in" at least five times a day to discuss the group dynamics, share feelings and air tensions, at any point in time staff members and the youth themselves can "call a circle."[92] When a circle is called, all team members sit or stand facing each other so that a grievance can be aired or a conflict can be addressed. In this way, the youth learn self-care and regulation, but also interaction with others and positive conflict resolution.

It is easy to be cynical about delinquent youth and to dismiss the Missouri model as something only a Pollyanna would seriously consider. Yet the Missouri model has been in use now for nearly four decades, and it has a proven track record of success that far outstrips national average indicators of success. To begin, the Missouri model is far more effective at treating the underlying cause of delinquency than the traditional juvenile detention model. While recidivism measurements vary widely by state, Missouri's rates are typically half that of other states.[93] When looking at Missouri youth three years after release, more than 65 percent were law-abiding and had not been recommitted to the youth system or the adult system.[94] Despite the fact that the Missouri model rejects the use of coercive correctional measures like handcuffs and solitary confinement, its residential centers are safer than other facilities. In 2006, for example, Ohio's Youth Corrections performed a comparison of Ohio and Missouri detained youth safety. Even though Ohio had a little more than twice the number of youth in confinement, Ohio had four times as many youth on youth assaults, and nearly seven times as many youth on staff assaults, as Missouri.[95] Perhaps most revealing on the safety front, since closing its traditional detention centers, Missouri has not had a single youth in detention commit suicide.[96]

Because of the physical and emotional safety in Missouri's facilities, its detained youth are experiencing educational gains that detained youth elsewhere are not. One such indicator is the percentage of confined youth who are making at least one year of academic progress for every year in confinement. The national average is 25 percent, while in Missouri nearly 75 percent of detained youth are staying on track academically, if not accomplishing more than they could in a public school setting.[97] Finally, Missouri is achieving all of this success for its detained youth at a fraction of the cost of juvenile detention in other states. Criminologists estimate that "steering just one high-risk delinquent teen away from a life of crime saves society $3 million to $6 million in reduced victim costs and criminal justice expenses, plus increased wages and tax payments over the young person's lifetime."[98] In short, the Missouri model is not only more humane for the youth it treats, but it is also more productive and cost effective in the long run.

To date, a number of states and localities have attempted to pursue the Missouri model of juvenile justice. Louisiana, Washington, D.C., and counties within New Mexico, Virginia, and California are trying to implement parts of the Missouri model.[99] Yet, "emulation of the system has been slower than one might expect."[100] As I discuss in the Conclusion, some of the resistance may occur at the emotional level and thus not be responsive to statistics and studies. Going forward, though, the Missouri model is clearly superior, and it ought to be aggressively pursued nationwide.

E. Create Youth-Informed Panels for Periodic Sentencing Reviews

As long as children continue to be sentenced to lengthy prison terms, those who fight a war for kids must also seek periodic, youth-informed sentencing review on the back end. This requires several measures. First, there must be a lawful parole mechanism in place. In the late 20th century, amid fears of violent crime predictions, many jurisdictions scaled back the availability of parole.[101] By 2000, 16 states abolished discretionary parole altogether, while another 5 abolished discretionary parole for certain violent crimes.[102] In jurisdictions where discretionary parole has been abolished in whole or in part, lawmakers need to revise those statutes and create a parole mechanism again.

Once a basic parole mechanism is in place, it should be offered to youthful offenders on a periodic, regular basis. At the same time, those in charge of parole decisions need to be sufficiently knowledgeable about the mitigating aspects of youth and a juvenile's unique capacity for rehabilitation. In the wake of the *Miller* trilogy at least two states have attempted to implement some kind of youth-informed parole provision.

In 2012, California passed a law that permitted a resentencing hearing for those who were sentenced to life without parole as juveniles.[103] Soon thereafter, state legislators expanded the scope of back-end sentencing review for juvenile offenders. In 2014, the state established a youth-specific parole process for those who were under 18 at the time of a crime but who were tried and sentenced as adults.[104] In 2015, recognizing that neuroscience indicates brain development well into the mid-20s, the state extended the youth parole process to those who were under 23 at the time of their offense.[105] While an applicant for parole must demonstrate significant rehabilitation, the Parole Board is specifically instructed to "provide a meaningful opportunity for release."[106] Moreover, eligible prisoners may present testimony from friends and family members regarding their maturity over time.[107] Finally, "[i]n assessing growth and maturity, psychological evaluations and risk assessment instruments, if used by the board, shall be administered by licensed psychologists employed by the board and shall take into consideration the diminished culpability of juveniles as compared to that of adults, the hallmark features of youth, and any subsequent growth and increased maturity of the individual."[108] Over 12,000 prisoners are now eligible for parole consideration under these new laws, and to date more than 250 inmates have satisfied the Parole Board that they are rehabilitated and fit for parole.[109] California's youth parole provisions are consistent with scientific findings about the juvenile brain and with the Supreme Court's call to treat children differently in the criminal justice system.

Massachusetts has also been an early leader on implementing *Miller* with back-end sentencing review. As discussed in Chapter 6, even before the United States Supreme Court resolved the question whether *Miller* applied retroactively, the Massachusetts high court held that it did, banning JLWOP sentences in the state.[110] In 2014, the state enacted a tiered parole system for juveniles convicted of homicide, permitting parole for them after 20–30 years depending on the nature of the homicide conviction.[111] Last year, the state high court further held that youth offenders have a right to state-funded counsel at their initial parole hearing if they are indigent, that they have a right to reasonable expert assistance if necessary for the hearing, and that they have the right to judicial review of Parole Board decisions.[112] At least in its written policy, the Massachusetts Parole Board states that parole petitions from juveniles serving life sentences "will be evaluated with recognition of the distinctive attributes of youth, including immaturity, impetuosity, and a failure to appreciate risks and consequences."[113] As discussed in Chapter 6, Massachusetts has already paroled a number of individuals who were sentenced to JLWOP using this process.

States like California and Massachusetts that employ youth-informed parole measures accomplish at least two goals. First, these states recognize what the Supreme Court has reiterated in its recent juvenile sentencing decisions: children are different in the eyes of the law and sentencing practices should reflect that fact. Juveniles are different in two key ways: their incomplete brain development makes them both less culpable and more amenable to rehabilitation. Youth-informed parole mechanisms reflect this latter difference—that youth have a greater chance at rehabilitation and should have an ongoing opportunity to demonstrate that.

Perhaps even more important than compliance with federal law, these states are giving hope and motivation to young incarcerated individuals. Juveniles serving lengthy prison terms who see that they have a reason to work on themselves and a shot at a second chance will be more inclined to do both. Edel Gonzalez was one of the first individuals to be paroled under California's new youth parole provisions.[114]

At 16 years old, Gonzalez was involved in a carjacking in which his codefendant shot and killed the driver. Gonzalez was sentenced to life without parole and for two decades he thought he would die in prison. At his parole hearing, though, the board members recognized his significant maturity and change. Upon news of his release, Gonzalez said to other youthful offenders: "A light shines at the end . . . Keep hope and faith."[115]

At the same time, as Chapter 6 indicated, parole needs to be administered in a way that is consistent with the *Miller* principles. This means at least a few things. First, it means that whatever standard the Parole Board uses, it must also take account of the Supreme Court requirement that youth be given a "meaningful opportunity to obtain release based on demonstrated maturity and rehabilitation."[116] Parole should not be equal parts demonstration of maturity and luck. Nor should it be a process subject to the whims of political motives. Going forward, states need to ensure that Parole Board members have expertise in youth development and that the decisions are rendered in an even-handed manner, consistent with the vision of the Supreme Court.

In sum, a war for kids requires a number of bold policy and legislative moves—the implementation of the *Miller* trilogy; keeping kids in juvenile court; age-appropriate sentencing; a shift away from traditional youth incarceration; and periodic sentencing review for juveniles who are incarcerated.

Conclusion

UNRAVELING DECADES OF PUNITIVE, counterproductive juvenile justice laws and policies will take significant bipartisan effort. Today, there is the science and the case law to facilitate that effort, but the question remains: is there the political will?

On the one hand, state and federal efforts in recent years have suggested a political climate conducive to criminal justice reform. For example, in 2014, California voters passed Proposition 47, which reduced some felonies, such as nonviolent property crimes, to misdemeanors.[1] The new law enabled the early release of thousands of inmates and will prevent thousands more from entering California's prison system each year. In Alaska, the state's Criminal Justice Commission called for overhauling reliance upon incarceration, suggesting that only serious violent offenders should be imprisoned and that many misdemeanors could be reclassified as fine-only infractions.[2] Several states, including Florida, Massachusetts, Virginia, Maryland, and Oklahoma, have been reconsidering the use of mandatory minimums, recognizing that those sentencing schemes have been unfair to individuals as well as costly and unnecessary for the states.[3] Many states have enacted criminal justice reform measures grounded in social science that tells us long sentences do not deter crime; they are crushingly expensive for states; and they inhibit individuals from rejoining society.

Recent efforts at the federal level have been promising, too. In the summer of 2015, Obama became the first sitting president to visit a federal prison.[4] Acknowledging prison overcrowding and the $80 billion price tag of incarcerating more than 2 million people each year, the president said during his visit, "We have to consider whether this is the smartest way for us to both control crime and to rehabilitate individuals."[5] At the same time, by the end of his second term, President Obama had commuted the sentences of more than 1,000 individuals— more than the prior 11 presidents combined.[6]

By mid-2016, the House Judiciary Committee had passed eight bills dealing with issues such as sentencing laws, overcriminalization and prison reform, and Speaker Paul Ryan seemed committed to bringing them to the floor.[7] Around the same time, both Senator Cory Booker and Congressman Sean Patrick Maloney introduced versions of the Equal Justice Under Law Act to address public defense shortcomings nationwide.[8] Under Senator Chuck Grassley's leadership, federal lawmakers on both sides of the aisle seemed likely to pass sentencing reform with a focus on curtailing mandatory minimums for nonviolent offenders.[9]

Coupled with the Supreme Court's recent sentencing decisions, these executive and legislative actions appeared to confirm popular sentiment on several issues.

- Fear-based policies of the 1980s did not make us safer, but instead left our nation saddled with a bloated prison population and deprived millions of people of freedom and opportunity;
- We currently have a two-tiered justice system, one for the wealthy and one for the poor, and this inequity compromises freedom for us all;
- Public health problems like mental illness and addiction cannot be addressed with incarceration; and
- Decades of science have proven that children really are different— they are less culpable and more amenable to rehabilitation—and these differences must matter in the eyes of the law.

Yet even as the nation appeared to be moving away from the failed experiment of mass incarceration, other variables were at work. The latter half of 2016 revealed just how fragile the "smart on crime" movement was. On Thursday, July 9, 2016, demonstrators gathered in Dallas to protest the use of force on civilians, especially black men who had died at the hands of law enforcement. Demonstrations were peaceful until

25-year-old Micah Johnson opened fire on police, killing five officers and wounding seven more.[10] Less than two weeks later, another gunman shot and killed three law enforcement officers in Baton Rouge.[11] President Obama, recognizing the precarious state of affairs, called on the nation for calm, imploring Americans to "temper our words and open our hearts."[12]

By the time the Republican National Convention got underway in Ohio at the end of July, bipartisan criminal justice reform appeared a distant memory, and Nixon-era politics had taken center stage. Black Lives Matter seemed squarely in competition with Blue Lives Matter, as if liberty for citizens and safety for officers were mutually exclusive. To be sure, the issues had been percolating for months. Donald Trump had suggested the seemingly outrageous: a ban on Muslim immigrants;[13] a wall to prevent Mexicans from entering the United States;[14] and a whole array of isolationist foreign policy positions. During the Republican Convention Mr. Trump revived a law and order political agenda not seen in years, if not decades. He spoke of "violence in our streets" and "chaos in our communities."[15] He mentioned rising homicide rates and seemed to link gun violence with "illegal immigrants . . . roaming free to threaten peaceful citizens."[16] Citing lawlessness at home and abroad, Mr. Trump declared himself the law and order candidate: " I have a message for all of you: the crime and violence that afflicts our nation will soon come to an end. Beginning on January 20th, 2017, safety will be restored."[17] He used the expression "law and order" four times; it was the dominant theme of his speech.[18]

As Mr. Trump gained traction in crucial battleground states, he won voters not with detailed policy proposals, but with emotional appeals. For example, when Mr. Trump spoke of crime, he asserted that the murder rate in the United States was the highest that it had been in 45 years; this was flatly wrong, and the FBI statistics belied his claim.[19] While there had been an increase in the national murder rate between 2014 and 2015, the 2015 rate was still half of the nation's peak murder rate in the 1980s and 1990s.[20] But the facts did not matter.

Mr. Trump recognized that many Americans legitimately went to sleep scared about rogue acts of terrorism; that many Americans were distraught by their limited educational and economic opportunities; and that the nation seemed fragile both on its own streets and in the international arena. When he offered to make America great again, whether grounded in actionable steps or not, he met an emotional need for a large chunk of the voting public. And his ability to meet those emotional needs won him the Oval Office in perhaps the most improbable presidential election in modern history. As the pollsters—and the nation—were reeling from the shock of Mr. Trump's election, some recognized this blind spot in the Clinton camp for what it was. As FORBES magazine reported, "While polling data correctly predicted the popular-vote win for Clinton, it failed to make the more nuanced call that *anger* among working class white voters ran deep, and would drive them to the polls in larger numbers than the lukewarm Clinton supporters in the Democratic base."[21] In short, Mr. Trump won "by tapping into emotion, not by mapping data points."[22]

This emotional front is critical to recognize because before juvenile justice advocates can work for the reform measures I addressed in Chapter 7—abolition of JLWOP and the use of mandatory minimums for juveniles, for example—we must work to address the emotional front. The war for kids is not simply about legal and policy questions. It must be a war that counters the politics of fear and disenchantment and offers a vision of inclusion and redemption. How does one fight a war toward that end?

I think that the process begins with what lawyer and juvenile justice advocate Bryan Stevenson calls *proximity*. We tend to relate to the problems we have experienced or witnessed up close, and as Stevenson says, "We cannot make good decisions from a distance. . . . If you are not proximate, you cannot change the world."[23] So how does the average American get proximate to the issue of juvenile justice run amok? While contact with the criminal justice system has become very common—nearly a third of the American adult work force has a criminal record[24]—we still tend to think of a "criminal" as "other," different, and inferior. This emotional distancing is facilitated in large part by the discriminatory practices of the criminal justice system: poor minority communities have paid the greatest price for our increasingly punitive practices, and thus the majority of Americans can tell themselves that this is "their" problem.

A war for kids on an emotional front, then, must begin by humanizing the image of someone, particularly a child, who breaks the law.

Americans have to be proximate enough to the problem—or the child—to care. Names and faces are the first step toward proximity. It is much easier to write off Terrence Graham when his name is misspelled, or worse yet, when he is known only by D.O.C. # J25706. On the other hand, when one hears his story—his childhood fears and disappointments, his hopes for today, and his healing over time—one sees a man who has made the best of great adversity and some very bad adolescent choices.

In addition to prisoner names and faces, America needs to hear the stories of formerly incarcerated youth who are living proof that "no child is born bad"[25] and that youth have tremendous capacity for growth and rehabilitation. They need to hear stories like those of Sara Kruzan.[26] Sara grew up in Riverdale, California, with a drug-addicted single mother who had Borderline Personality Disorder. Because of its instability and the rotation of abusive men her mother brought home, Sarah recalls her childhood home as a "war zone."[27] Molested by a babysitter at 5 years old, Sara was later lured into prostitution by a man who offered her material goods and an otherwise missing father figure. At 13, this man, George Howard, had sex with Sara and told her "you don't need to give it up for free."[28] That same year, Howard put Sara on the streets as a prostitute, forcing her to work from 6 in the evening to 5 or 6 the next morning.[29] When she was 16 years old, after attempting to escape by suicide several times, Sara shot Howard in the back of the head as he prepared to have sex with her. She recalls kneeling down next to her victim immediately and apologizing.

Barred from presenting any mitigating evidence regarding her abuse at Howard's hands, Sara was convicted of first-degree murder in adult court and sentenced to life without parole. At sentencing, the judge told Sara that she "lacked moral scruples"; she recalls that she didn't even know what he meant.[30] After spending nearly two decades in prison, though, Sara learned what that term meant. She took college courses, as well as rehabilitative sessions on Victim Impact and Self Awareness among other topics.[31] She was accepted into her prison's "honor dorm," and in 2010 her peers recognized her as "Woman of the Year" for her participation in the facility's Young Women's Group.[32] Human Rights Watch profiled Sara in one of its documentaries on extreme

juvenile sentencing in America, and her story went viral.[33] She garnered the attention of pro bono attorneys from a private law firm, state
lawmakers, and ultimately, Governor Schwarzenegger. Because of her
youth and her victimization at the hands of sex traffickers, including her
mother, whom Sara considers her first trafficker, Sara received clemency
in late 2010.[34] Then Governor Schwarzenegger commuted her sentence
from LWOP to 25 years to life,[35] and, because of credit for her time
served, she became eligible for a Parole Board hearing. Sara was paroled
in 2013, and is now a mother and a contributing member of society.[36]

People also need to hear the story of Xavier McElrath-Bey.[37] Xavier
grew up in poverty with a mentally ill mother and an abusive alcoholic
stepfather on the south side of Chicago.[38] His family regularly lost their
power for nonpayment and moved from home to home as they were
evicted.[39] Eventually, Xavier was placed in the foster care system only
to experience further abuse. Xavier was deprived of normal childhood
opportunities and forced to perform hours of physical labor for his
foster mother.[40] By the time he was 11, he joined a gang, seeking safety,
love, a sense of belonging, and respect.[41] At 11, Xavier's best friend accidentally shot him in the face, and fearing the consequences for his
friend, Xavier told police that he didn't know who had shot him—that
it was some man in a black car.[42] Xavier was treated for his injuries and
then charged with obstruction of justice at 11. He spent some time in
detention, but ultimately received probation for failing to give up his
friend as his shooter.

Xavier admits that being shot in the face would be *the* wakeup call
to the reality of gang life for many, but for him it was not. The gang
was his family, so he persisted in gang activities. By the time he was 13,
Xavier had been arrested 19 times and he had been convicted of a crime
7 times.[43] Never once did he receive trauma services, counseling, or
diversion to treatment programs to deal with the abuse and dysfunction
of his family. When he was 13, he participated in a gang-related murder, and while he was not the actual "triggerman," he was transferred
to adult court, convicted of murder and sentenced to 25 years.[44] Xavier
did not know at the time of his trial that he could be sentenced to such
a long term, and he did not begin to wrap his head around his sentence
until he was 18 and in solitary confinement. Not only did he have time

to contemplate the choices he had made, but he also matured simply as a matter of neurological development. He left the gang world and pursued his education. He eventually was transferred to a medium-security facility and earned a bachelor's degree in social science with a 4.0 GPA.[45] Xavier was released in 2002 after serving 13 years in the Illinois Department of Corrections.[46]

Today his list of accomplishments is impressive. He completed his master's degree in counseling and human services.[47] He served as a field interviewer for a government-funded study on the mental health needs of formerly incarcerated youth,[48] and he later cofounded the advocacy group "ICAN"—Incarcerated Children's Advocacy Network.[49] He strives to set a positive example for his daughter and for other youth who come into contact with the criminal justice system. Xavier says that "[his] life course is a testament of the human potential for positive change, and [that he is] in no way an exception."[50]

He is right. Sara and Xavier present compelling, heart-wrenching stories, but their experiences are not outliers and neither are their paths of growth and redemption. To begin, recall from Chapter 4 that juvenile detention has a deleterious effect on children, and it is not reserved for serious crimes, as demonstrated by Xavier's detention at 11 for being a noncooperative *victim*. In fact, nearly a third of detained youth are serving time based on a public order violation, a technical parole or probation violation, or a status offense.[51] This practice is misguided in its own right, but to make matters worse, more than 90 percent of children in juvenile detention have experienced trauma, defined as physical abuse, sexual abuse, domestic violence, community violence, and/or disaster.[52] Sending kids in need of trauma therapy into a correctional system only exacerbates their underlying psychological and emotional issues. It is poor policy, and it is morally inexcusable—especially today in light of the scientific evidence of the capacity for youth rehabilitation.

There are children born into terrible circumstances, but, as Xavier says, there is no such thing as a child "born bad."[53] In order to get proximate to this issue, America needs to listen more keenly to people like Xavier who are living that truth. And listening to stories of formerly incarcerated youth does not mean we give juveniles who commit crime a "pass." Instead, it means we learn the keys to explaining and, ultimately, preventing youth crime. It means we intervene sooner than when a child is accused of crime, and it means our intervention methods must defy the status quo.

In addition to hearing from youth who have been incarcerated, we also need to get proximate to the pain experienced by victims and their families. Some victims' organizations argue against any sweeping reform and favor finality of sentences over periodic sentencing review. Most want to be considered crucial stakeholders in any reform process. These concerns are legitimate and need to be honored as states seek to correct misguided juvenile justice practices without re-traumatizing victims and their family members.

At the same time, though, the victims' rights community is not monolithic. We also need to hear from those victims and victims' family members who support juvenile justice reform—despite suffering tremendous loss at the hands of a juvenile. For example, Jeanne Bishop's pregnant younger sister and her brother-in-law were killed when a 16-year-old broke into their home.[54] Jeanne attended every day of the teenager's two-week trial, and when he was sentenced to mandatory LWOP, Jeanne was happy. After the *Miller* decision, though, Jeanne realized that her sister's killer may be resentenced, and she wrote to him and then offered to visit him in prison. Having served 20 years in prison, her sister's killer was remorseful and able to confess and apologize to Jeanne in person. They have now had more than a dozen visits, and Jeanne has come to believe that "[o]ur loved ones are not honored by mercilessly throwing a young person's life away."[55] Jeanne is not alone in thinking that sentencing a child to die in prison only exacerbates the suffering caused by juvenile crime.[56]

We also need to get proximate to the experience of family members of youth offenders; they, too, are often traumatized by their child's actions and the correctional experience. A relatively new family movement called *Mothers at the Gate* seeks to give voice to the family members, statistically most often the mothers, of youth in the criminal justice system.[57] These family members are sharing their emotional experiences of watching their children be treated as adults and confined in correctional facilities. More important, though, they are challenging the status quo of American juvenile corrections. As the report on their recent efforts describes, "Our use of prisons to deal with everything from serious acts of violence to minor affronts to authority relies on a particularly American premise: that a child who breaks the law becomes in that moment a radical individual, connected to no one, 'accountable' only to an abstract notion of the state—and that our response to a child's law-breaking affects only that child."[58] And they are advocating for much needed reform: breaking the school-to-prison pipeline; raising the age at which a child can be transferred to adult court, and seeking transfer abolition where possible; ending JLWOP; and enacting holistic juvenile sentencing reform.[59] We can get proximate to the experience of juvenile justice by also hearing from these family members.

Finally, Americans can get proximate to the broken nature of our juvenile justice system by engaging in a thought experiment. Bart Lubow, who joined the Annie E. Casey Foundation 25 years ago to launch its Juvenile Detention Alternatives Initiative (JDAI), coined a concise shorthand for assessing juvenile justice practices; he called it the "my child test."[60] The concept is this: when we examine a juvenile justice practice—whether it is unfettered prosecutorial transfer of kids to adult court, the use of shackles and solitary confinement, the housing of juveniles in adult facilities, or the sentencing of children to die in prison—the only metric we ought to use is the question whether that practice would be acceptable for *my child*. If not, then we should abandon the practice on moral grounds. Lubow's proposed test, which he has tried to operationalize for decades now, is the ultimate gut check, especially for people who already have children. If you have ever discovered a teenager who had a schoolyard fight, or drank beer at an unsupervised party, or snuck out of the house at night and drove the family car without a license, or smoked marijuana because all his friends were trying it, then the "my child" test speaks to you. It reminds you that, as Bryan Stevenson says, we are all broken humans.[61] It also reminds you that every child deserves the opportunity to thrive mentally and physically, whether or not they are born into a family that can give them that chance.

In sum, the war for kids must be fought on an emotional and a policy front. We must remind people, as Xavier says, that no child is born bad; that our laws and policies should foster growth and development, rather than punish age-appropriate acting out; that children in poverty and trauma scenarios need our care, not our spite; that youth is a biologically significant factor that must count in the eyes of the law; and that children are our future and we have a collective responsibility to safeguard them. Only with these principles in mind can we win the war for kids.

NOTES

⟞⟝⧫⟞⟝

Introduction

1. *See generally infra* Chapter 1 (providing an overview of American juvenile justice).
2. U.S. Dept. of Justice, *Juvenile Arrests* (2014) (noting a 50 percent decline in arrests since 2005), available at: https://www.ojjdp.gov/ojstatbb/crime/qa05101.asp?qa.
3. Campaign for Youth Justice, *Key Facts: Youth in the Justice System* (2012), available at: http://www.campaignforyouthjustice.org/documents/KeyYouthCrimeFacts.pdf.
4. *See generally infra* Chapter 1 (discussing transfer provisions).
5. *Id.*
6. *See generally infra* Chapter 4 (discussing conditions of confinement).
7. *Infra* Chapter 1.
8. The Sentencing Project, *Trends in U.S. Corrections* 1 (2014) (noting state and federal inmate population between 200,000 and 400,000 in the 1970s), available at: http://sentencingproject.org/wp-content/uploads/2016/01/Trends-in-US-Corrections.pdf.
9. Charles C.W. Cooke, *Careful with the Panic: Violent Crime and Gun Crime Are Both Dropping*, NAT'L. REV. (Nov. 30, 2015), available at: http://www.nationalreview.com/corner/427758/careful-panic-violent-crime-and-gun-crime-are-both-dropping-charles-c-w-cooke.
10. Peter Wagner and Bernadette Rabuy, *Mass Incarceration: The Whole Pie 2016*, Prison Policy Initiative, (Mar. 14, 2016) available at: http://www.prisonpolicy.org/reports/pie2016.html.

11. The Pew Center on the States, *One in 31: The Long Reach of American Corrections*, at 5 (Mar. 2, 2009), available at: http://www.pewtrusts.org/en/research-and-analysis/reports/2009/03/02/one-in-31-the-long-reach-of-american-corrections (calculating that one in thirty-one Americans are under some form of correctional control).

12. Adam Liptak, *U.S. Prison Population Dwarfs That of Other Nations*, N.Y. TIMES (Apr. 23, 2008), available at: http://www.nytimes.com/2008/04/23/world/americas/23iht-23prison.12253738.html.

13. Brown v. Plata, 563 U.S. 493, 501 (2011).

14. *Id.* at 503.

15. *Id.* at 505.

16. *See generally* Michelle Alexander, THE NEW JIM CROW: MASS INCARCERATION IN THE AGE OF COLORBLINDNESS (The New Press, 2d ed. 2012).

17. U.S. Census Bureau., *Population QuickFacts* (last visited Feb. 4, 2017), available at: https://www.census.gov/quickfacts/table/PST045215/00 (citing African Americans and Latinos as less than 30 percent of 2010 population).

18. E. Ann Carson, *Prisoners in 2013* at 8. U.S. Dept. of Justice (Sept. 30, 2014), *available at:* https://www.bjs.gov/content/pub/pdf/p13.pdf ("On December 31, 2013, about 37% of imprisoned males were black, 32% were white, and 22% were Hispanic.")

19. Marc Mauer & Ryan S. King, *Uneven Justice: State Rates of Incarceration by Race and Ethnicity* at 1, THE SENTENCING PROJECT (2007), available at: http://www.sentencingproject.org/wp-content/uploads/2016/01/Uneven-Justice-State-Rates-of-Incarceration-by-Race-and-Ethnicity.pdf.

20. *Id.*

21. Marc Mauer, *Bill Clinton, "Black Lives," and the Myths of the 1994 Crime Bill*, THE MARSHALL PROJECT, (Apr. 11, 2016), available at: https://www.themarshallproject.org/2016/04/11/bill-clinton-black-lives-and-the-myths-of-the-1994-crime-bill#.BZtfVit6w.

22. Nell Bernstein, BURNING DOWN THE HOUSE: THE END OF JUVENILE PRISON, 71–80 (The New Press 2014).

23. *Id.*

24. Mauer, *Bill Clinton, supra* note 21.

25. *See generally* Brown v. Plata, 563 U.S. 493.

26. Tracey Kaplan, *Proposition 36: Voters Overwhelmingly Ease Three Strikes Law*, MERCURY NEWS (Nov. 6, 2012), available at: http://www.mercurynews.com/2012/11/06/proposition-36-voters-overwhelmingly-ease-three-strikes-law/.

27. Howard Mintz & Matt O'Brien, *Proposition 34: Death Penalty Repeal Fails*, MERCURY NEWS (Nov. 6, 2012), available at: http://www.mercurynews.com/2012/11/06/proposition-34-death-penalty-repeal-fails/.

28. Shane Bauer, *How Conservatives Learned to Love Prison Reform*, MOTHER JONES, (Mar./Apr. 2014), available at: http://www.motherjones.com/politics/

2014/02/conservatives-prison-reform-right-on-crime; *see generally, Right on Crime* (last visited Feb. 4, 2017), available at: http://rightoncrime.com/.

29. Carl Hulse, *Unlikely Cause Unites the Left and the Right: Justice Reform*, N.Y. TIMES (Feb. 18, 2015), available at: http://www.nytimes.com/2015/02/19/us/politics/unlikely-cause-unites-the-left-and-the-right-justice-reform.html.

30. Elizabeth S. Scott, Miller v. Alabama *and the (Past and) Future of Juvenile Crime Regulation*, 31 LAW & INEQ. 535, 541 (2013).

31. Graham v. Florida, 560 U.S. 48, 53. (2010).

32. *Id.*

33. *Id.* at 57.

34. *Id.* at 82.

35. *Id.* at 75.

36. Miller v. Alabama, 132 S. Ct. 2455 (2012).

37. *Id.* at 2466.

38. *Id.* at 2468; *see generally infra* Chapter 5.

39. *Id.* at 2466.

40. The Campaign for the Fair Sentencing of Youth, *Righting Wrongs: The Five Year Groundswell of State Bans on Life Without Parole for Children*, at 4 (2016), available at: http://fairsentencingofyouth.org/wp-content/uploads/2016/09/Righting-Wrongs-.pdf?utm_source=Five+Year+Report+KI+Rollout &utm_campaign=Righting+Wrongs&utm_medium=email.

41. *See generally infra* Chapter 5.

42. *See generally infra* Chapters 5 and 6.

43. *See, e.g.,* Donna St. George, *"Free Range" Parents Cleared in Second Neglect Case, After Kids Walked Alone*, WASH. POST (Jun. 22, 2015), available at: https://www.washingtonpost.com/local/education/free-range-parents-cleared-in-second-neglect-case-after-children-walked-alone/2015/06/22/82283c24-188c-11e5-bd7f-4611a60dd8e5_story.html.

44. Elizabeth Kolbert, *Spoiled Rotten: Why Do Kids Rule the Roost?*, THE NEW YORKER, (July 2, 2012), available at: http://www.newyorker.com/magazine/2012/07/02/spoiled-rotten.

45. *See generally infra* Chapter 4.

Chapter 1

1. *Miller*, 132 S. Ct. at 2461.

2. *Id.*

3. *Id.*

4. *Id.*

5. *Id.*

6. *Id.*

7. *Miller*, 132 S. Ct. at 2461.

8. Graham v. Florida, 560 U.S. at 53–54 .

9. *Id.* at 53.

10. *Id.* at 54.

11. *Id.*
12. *Id.*
13. Graham v. Florida, 560 U.S. at 55.
14. *Id.*
15. *Id.* at 56.
16. *Id.*
17. *Id.*
18. *Id.* at 57.
19. *Graham*, 560 U.S. at 56.
20. *See generally infra* Chapter 2.
21. Campaign for Youth Justice, *Key Facts: Youth in the Justice System* 1 (April 2012), available at: http://www.campaignforyouthjustice.org/documents/ KeyYouthCrimeFacts.pdf.
22. *See generally infra* Chapter 1, Part B.
23. *See generally infra* Chapter 3.
24. *Id.*
25. *See generally infra* Chapter 4.
26. *Id.*
27. *Id.*
28. Franklin E. Zimring & David S. Tanenhaus, Introduction to Choosing the Future for American Juvenile Justice 1 (Franklin E. Zimring & David S. Tanenhaus eds., 2014) [hereinafter Choosing the Future].
29. Aaron Kupchik, Judging Juveniles: prosecuting adolescents in adult and juvenile courts 10–11 (2006) [hereinafter Judging Juveniles].
30. Kupchik, Judging Juveniles 11.
31. Franklin E. Zimring, American Juvenile Justice 6–7 (2005) [hereinafter American Juvenile Justice]; *see also* Kupchik, Judging Juveniles 51.
32. Zimring & Tanenhaus, Choosing the Future 1; *see also* Zimring, American Juvenile Justice 33 ("No legal institution in Anglo-American legal history has achieved such universal acceptance among the diverse legal systems of the industrial democracies.").
33. Terry A. Maroney, *The Once and Future Juvenile Brain*, Choosing the Future 189. Juvenile justice scholars agree that we have entered a new era of policy in the last decade. *See, e.g., id.* ("We surely now have moved into a new era of juvenile justice."); Elizabeth S. Scott, Miller v. Alabama *and the (Past and) Future of Juvenile Crime Regulation*, 31 Law & Ineq. 535 (2013) (discussing the moral panic that drove policies of the 1990s and the shifts that have emerged in the last decade).
34. Maroney, *supra* note 33, at 189.
35. *In re* Gault, 387 U.S. 1, 15–16 (1967) (citations omitted).
36. Kent v. U.S., 383 U.S. 541 (1966).
37. *Id.* at 543.
38. *Id.*
39. *Id.* at 550.

40. *Id.* at 553.
41. *Id.*
42. *Kent*, 383 U.S. at 550, 551.
43. *Id.* at 550, 559–62.
44. 387 U.S. 1 (1967).
45. *Id.* at 4.
46. *Id.*
47. *Id.* at 5.
48. *Id.* at 6–7.
49. *Id.* at 8.
50. *Id.* at 8–9.
51. *Id.* at 1–2.
52. Maroney, *supra* note 33. at 189. It is worth noting that some academics have suggested that juvenile defendants have fared worse in the post-*Gault* era. *See, e.g.,* Franklin E. Zimring & David S. Tanenhaus, *On Strategy and Tactics for Contemporary Reforms*, in CHOOSING THE FUTURE 231–32 (describing the contrast between an early juvenile court where the judge had tremendous power and discretion and the post-*Gault* expansion of prosecutorial power at the expense of judicial and probation authority).
53. Clyde Haberman, *When Youth Violence Spurred Superpredator Fear*, N.Y. TIMES (Apr. 6, 2014), available at: http://www.nytimes.com/2014/04/07/us/ politics/killing-on-bus-recalls-superpredator-threat-of-90s.html?_r=0.
54. *Id.*
55. Terry A. Maroney, *The Once and Future Juvenile Brain,* in CHOOSING THE FUTURE 189. *See generally* Franklin E. Zimring, *American Youth Violence: A Cautionary Tale*, in CHOOSING THE FUTURE 7; *see also* Elizabeth S. Scott, Miller v. Alabama *and the (Past and) Future of Juvenile Crime Regulation*, 31 LAW & INEQ. 535, 537–41.
56. Roper v. Simmons, 543 U.S. 551, 575 (2005) ("Our determination that the death penalty is disproportionate punishment for offenders under 18 finds confirmation in the stark reality that the United States is the only country in the world that continues to give official sanction to the juvenile death penalty.").
57. Brief for Amnesty International et al. as Amici Curiae Supporting Petitioners, *Miller v. Alabama*, 132 S. Ct. 2455 (2012) (Nos. 10-9646, 10-9647), 2012 WL 174238.
58. Kupchik, JUDGING JUVENILES 1.
59. *Id. at* 11 ("The founders of the juvenile court imagined a judge and probation officer, assisted by medical and psychological treatment professionals, diagnosing and remedying youth's problems without the need to constrict due process rules.").
60. Franklin E. Zimring, *The Power Politics of Juvenile Court Transfer in the 1990's,* in CHOOSING THE FUTURE 42 ("The long-standing method of transfer

was a hearing held before a juvenile court judge who had the power to waive the juvenile court's jurisdiction.").

61. *Cf.* Franklin E. Zimring, AMERICAN JUVENILE JUSTICE 141–44 (2005) (discussing mission of juvenile court as being its primary limitation in that some juvenile cases warrant a punishment response the juvenile court cannot impose).

62. Kupchik, JUDGING JUVENILES 154–59 (discussing the three primary methods for transfer of jurisdiction from juvenile to adult court).

63. *Id.*

64. U.S. Dep't. of Justice, *Trying Juveniles as Adults: An Analysis of State Transfer Laws and Reporting* 2 (Sept. 2011), available at: https://www.ncjrs.gov/pdffiles1/ojjdp/232434.pdf, (hereinafter *Trying Juveniles as Adults*).

65. *Id.* at 3.

66. *Id.*

67. *Id.*

68. *Id.* at 6.

69. *Id.* at 5.

70. *Trying Juveniles as Adults*, at 5.

71. *Id.*

72. *Id.* at 3.

73. Kupchik, JUDGING JUVENILES 156 (defining the process and explaining its problems).

74. Franklin E. Zimring, *The Power Politics of Juvenile Court Transfer in the 1990's*, in CHOOSING THE FUTURE 44 ("So the proliferation of direct file provisions is really an enhancement of prosecutorial power as much as it is a legislative judgment about which juveniles should be transferred to criminal court, because it is contingent on prosecutorial charging discretions."). *Id.* at 45.

75. Zimring, *The Power Politics of Juvenile Court Transfer in the 1990's*, in CHOOSING THE FUTURE 44.

76. *Miller*, 132 S. Ct. at 2474 (citation omitted).

77. The *Miller* Court noted that state legislators were not necessarily considering the interaction of these separate legislative efforts, and yet the consequences were dire for juveniles. *Miller*, 132 S. Ct. at 2472.

78. As discussed above, Evan Miller was sentenced under a mandatory sentencing scheme.

79. Kim S. Hunt & Michael Connelly, *Advisory Guidelines in the Post-Blakely Era*, 17 FED. SENT'G REP. 233, 233–35 (2005) (providing overview of presumptive sentencing guidelines and the rationales for them); *see also* CONN. GEN. ASSEMBLY, LEGISLATIVE PROGRAM REVIEW AND INVESTIGATIONS COMM., CONNECTICUT MANDATORY MINIMUM SENTENCES BRIEFING (2005), available at: http://www.cga.ct.gov/2005/pridata/Studies/Mandatory_Minimum_Senteces_Briefing.htm (providing examples of crimes that carry a presumptive minimum versus those that carry a mandatory minimum).

80. *See, e.g., Sentencing Guidelines Overview*, MD. ST. COMMISSION ON CRIM. SENT'G POL'Y, available at http://www.msccsp.org/Guidelines/Overview. aspx (last visited Mar. 7, 2017). ("The sentencing guidelines are advisory and judges may, at their discretion, impose a sentence outside of the guidelines. If judges choose to depart from the sentencing guidelines, the Code of Maryland Regulations (COMAR) 14.22.01.05(A) mandates 'The judge shall document on the guidelines worksheet the reason or reasons for imposing a sentence outside of the recommended guidelines range.' In practice, however, the judiciary has generally neglected to provide an explanation for departure. For example, in 61% of the fiscal year 2005 cases that resulted in a departure from the guidelines, the reason(s) for departure was not provided."). *See generally* Hunt & Connelly, *Advisory Guidelines in the Post-Blakely Era*.

81. Marc Mauer, *The Race to Incarcerate: The Causes and Consequences of Mass Incarceration*, 21 ROGER WILLIAMS U. L. REV. 447, 449–50 (2016).

82. *Id.* at 450.

83. Robert J. Anello & Jodi Misher Peikin, *Evolving Roles in Federal Sentencing: The Post-*Booker/Fanfan *World*, 2005 FED. CTS. L. REV. 9 (2005); Margaret P. Spencer, *Sentencing Drug Offenders: The Incarceration Addiction*, 40 VILL. L. REV. 335, 347–48 (1995).

84. Spencer, *supra* note 83, at 347–51.

85. *Id.* at 350–51.

86. U.S. Sentencing Comm'n, Special Report to the Congress: Mandatory Minimum Penalties in the Federal Criminal Justice System 9 (1991), available at: http://www.ussc.gov/sites/default/files/pdf/news/congressional-testimony-and-reports/mandatory-minimum-penalties/1991_Mand_Min_Report.pdf.

87. *Cf.* Gary Fields & John R. Emshwiller, *Many Failed Efforts to Count Nation's Federal Criminal Laws*, WALL ST. J. (July 23, 2001), *available* at: http://online.wsj.com/news/articles/SB10001424052702304319804576389601079 728920 (estimating that there are at least 3,000 federal criminal laws and recognizing that the true number is probably beyond estimation).

88. Paul J. Larkin, Jr., *Parole: Corpse or Phoenix?*, 50 AM. CRIM. L. REV. 303, 315–20 (2013) (describing the "death of parole" at the state and federal level).

89. Mauer, *supra* note 81, at 451.

90. *Id.* at 452.

91. *Id.* at 456–57 (explaining research indicating that deterrence comes from certainty rather than severity of punishment).

92. *Miller*, 132 S. Ct. at 2461.

93. *Id.*

94. *Id.*

95. *Id.* at 2463.

96. *Id.* at 2462.

97. *Id.* at 2462–63.

98. *Miller*, 132 S. Ct. at 2471.
99. *Id.* at 2474.
100. *See generally infra* Chapter 3.

Chapter 2

1. 560 U.S. at 56.
2. *Id.*
3. Report of Sarah Flynn, M.S.W., Dec. 7, 2011, *In re* State v. Terrence Graham, on file with author.
4. Interview with Terrence Graham, August 1, 2012. Notes on file with author.
5. Mary Sue Backus & Paul Marcus, *The Right to Counsel in Criminal Cases: A National Crisis*, 57 HASTINGS L.J. 1031, 1034 (2006).
6. Nat'l Center for Children in Poverty, *Child Poverty*, available at http://www.nccp.org/topics/childpoverty.html (last visited Mar. 7, 2017).
7. DEPT. OF HEALTH & HUMAN SERVS., *Annual Update of the HHS Poverty Guidelines* (2015), available at: https://www.federalregister.gov/articles/2015/01/22/2015-01120/annual-update-of-the-hhs-poverty-guidelines#t-1.
8. Max Fisher, Map: *How 35 Countries Compare on Child Poverty* (the United States is ranked 34th), WASH. POST (Apr. 15, 2013), available at: https://www.washingtonpost.com/news/worldviews/wp/2013/04/15/map-how-35-countries-compare-on-child-poverty-the-u-s-is-ranked-34th/.
9. American Psychological Ass'n, *Effects of Poverty, Hunger and Homelessness on Children and Youth*, available at http://www.apa.org/pi/families/poverty.aspx (last visited Mar. 7, 2017).
10. *Id.*
11. Abby C. Winer & Ross Thompson, *How Poverty and Depression Impact a Child's Social and Emotional Competence*, POLICY BRIEF: CENTER FOR POVERTY RESEARCH, available at: http://poverty.ucdavis.edu/sites/main/files/file-attachments/policy_brief_thompson_risk_print.pdf.
12. *Id.*
13. *Id.*
14. American Psychological Ass'n, *Effects of Poverty, Hunger and Homelessness on Children and Youth*, available at: http://www.apa.org/pi/families/poverty.aspx (last visited Mar. 7, 2017).
15. *Id.*
16. *Id.*
17. *Id.*
18. Eric Jensen, TEACHING WITH POVERTY IN MIND, *Ch. Two: How Poverty Affects Behavior and Academic Performance* (2009), available at: http://www.ascd.org/publications/books/109074/chapters/How-Poverty-Affects-Behavior-and-Academic-Performance.aspx.
19. *Id.*
20. *Id.*

21. *Id.* (citations omitted).

22. Valerie Strauss, *Why "No Excuses" Makes No Sense: Revisiting the Coleman Report*, Wash. Post (July 23, 2011), available at https://www.washingtonpost.com/blogs/answer-sheet/post/why-no-excuses-makes-no-sense-revisiting-the-coleman-report/2011/07/23/gIQAo7W7UI_blog.html; *see also* Mark G. Yudof, *Equal Opportunity and the Courts*, 51 Tex. L. Rev. 411, 422–23 (1973) (discussing the report and subsequent related findings).

23. Sean F. Reardon, *The Widening Income Achievement Gap*, Educ. Leadership (May 2013), available at: https://assets.documentcloud.org/documents/2190993/the-widening-income-achievement-gap.pdf; *see also* Jeanne L. Reid, *The Racial and Ethnic Composition of Pre-Kindergarten Classrooms and Children's Language Development*, 119 Penn St. L. Rev. 645, 649 (2015) (attributing at least half of the white-black and white-Hispanic gaps in average assessment scores among children at Kindergarten entry to socioeconomic status).

24. Tamar Birckhead, *Delinquent by Reason of Poverty*, 38 Wash. U. J.L. & Pol'y 53, 59 (2012).

25. *Id.* at 81.

26. *Id.* at 82.

27. *Id.* at 83–84.

28. *Id.* at 61.

29. Barbara Fedders, *Losing Hold of the Guiding Hand: Ineffective Assistance of Counsel in Juvenile Delinquency Representation*, 14 Lewis & Clark L. Rev. 771, 797–98 (2010).

30. *Id.*

31. *Id.*

32. Maryland v. King, 133 S. Ct. 1958 (2013) (upholding police practice of obtaining DNA with mouth swab upon arrest).

33. *See generally* Justice Policy Institute, *The Dangers of Detention: The Impact of Incarcerating Youth in Detention and Other Secure Facilities*, available at: http://www.justicepolicy.org/images/upload/06-11_rep_dangersofdetention_jj.pdf.

34. *Id.* at 3.

35. *Id.* at 8.

36. *Id.* at 8–9.

37. *Id.* at 4–6.

38. Michelle Alexander, The New Jim Crow: Mass Incarceration in an Age of Colorblindness (2d Ed. 2012).

39. NAACP, *Criminal Justice Fact Sheet*, available at http://www.naacp.org/pages/criminal-justice-fact-sheet (last visited Mar. 7, 2017).

40. *Id.*

41. *Id.*

42. *See generally* Edward J. Smith & Shaun R. Harper, *Disproportionate Impact of K–12 School Suspension and Expulsion on Black Students in Southern States*

(2015), available at: http://www.gse.upenn.edu/equity/sites/gse.upenn.edu.equity/files/publications/Smith_Harper_Report.pdf [*hereinafter* The Smith Harper Report].

43. The Smith Harper Report at 1.

44. *Id.* at 5.

45. *Id.* at 1.

46. *Id.*

47. *Id.*

48. *Id.* at 87.

49. Motoko Rich, *Analysis Finds Higher Expulsion Rates for Black Students*, N.Y. Times (Aug. 25, 2015), available at http://www.nytimes.com/2015/08/25/us/higher-expulsion-rates-for-black-students-are-found.html?_r=0.

50. Sharon LaFranier & Andrew W. Lehren, *The Disproportionate Risks of Driving While Black*, N.Y. Times (Oct. 24, 2015), available at: http://www.nytimes.com/2015/10/25/us/racial-disparity-traffic-stops-driving-black.html.

51. *Id.*

52. *Id.*

53. *Id.*

54. Bureau of Justice Statistics, *Traffic Stops* (2011), available at: http://www.bjs.gov/index.cfm?ty=tp&tid=702 (last visited Mar. 7, 2017).

55. George L. Kelling & James Q. Wilson, *Broken Windows: The Police and Neighborhood Safety*, The Atlantic (Mar. 1982), available at: http://www.theatlantic.com/magazine/archive/1982/03/broken-windows/304465/.

56. *Id.*

57. 88 S. Ct. 1868 (1968).

58. *Id.* at 1880–1881.

59. *Id.* at 1883.

60. N.Y. Civ. Lib. Union, *Stop and Frisk During the Bloomberg Administration 2002–2013* at 1–2 (2014), available at: http://www.nyclu.org/files/publications/stopandfrisk_briefer_2002-2013_final.pdf [hereinafter *Stop and Frisk During the Bloomberg Administration*].

61. *Id.* at 2.

62. Petition, *New York Civ. Lib. Union v. New York Police Dept.* (N.Y. Sup. Ct.,Nov. 13, 2007), available at: https://www.clearinghouse.net/chDocs/public/PN-NY-0026-0001.pdf

63. *Stop and Frisk During the Bloomberg Administration*, at 2.

64. *Id.* at 4.

65. *Id.* at 14.

66. *See generally* Floyd v. City of New York, 959 F. Supp. 2d 540 (S.D.N.Y. 2013).

67. *Id.* at 658–67.

68. Mike Bostock & Ford Fessenden, *Stop and Frisk Is All but Gone from New York*, N.Y. Times (Sept. 9, 2014), available at: http://www.nytimes.com/

interactive/2014/09/19/nyregion/stop-and-frisk-is-all-but-gone-from-new-york.html.

69. Aamer Madhani, *Chicago Police and ACLU Agree to Stop and Frisk Safeguards*, USA TODAY (Aug. 7, 2015), available at: http://www.usatoday.com/story/news/2015/08/07/chicago-police-agree-reform-stop-and-frisk/31277041/.

70. American Civ. Lib. Union of Illinois, *Stop and Frisk in Chicago* 11 (2015), available at: http://www.aclu-il.org/wp-content/uploads/2015/03/ACLU_StopandFrisk_6.pdf.

71. *Id.* at 9.

72. Aamer Madhani, *Chicago Police*, supra note 69.

73. Brad Heath, *Racial Gap in U.S. Arrest Rates: Staggering Disparity*, USA TODAY (Nov. 19, 2014), available at: http://www.usatoday.com/story/news/nation/2014/11/18/ferguson-black-arrest-rates/19043207/.

74. *See generally* Black Lives Matter, *Guiding Principles*, available at: http://blacklivesmatter.com/guiding-principles/(last visited Mar. 7, 2017).

75. U.S. Dept. of Justice, *Prisoners in 2013* at 8 (2014) ("On December 31, 2013, about 37 percent of imprisoned males were black, 32 percent were white, and 22 percent were Hispanic."). *Id. See also* NAACP, Criminal Justice Fact Sheet, available at: http://www.naacp.org/pages/criminal-justice-fact-sheet (last visited Mar. 7, 2017).

76. Death Penalty Information Center, *National Statistics on Death Penalty and Race* (Nov. 9, 2016), available at http://www.deathpenaltyinfo.org/race-death-row-inmates-executed-1976#deathrowpop.

77. 481 U.S. 279 (1987).

78. *Id.* at 286.

79. *Id.* at 287.

80. *Id.* at 297.

81. Death Penalty Information Center, *National Statistics on Death Penalty and Race*, (Nov. 9, 2016), available at: http://www.deathpenaltyinfo.org/race-death-row-inmates-executed-1976#deathrowpop.

82. The Pew Charitable Trust, *Collateral Costs: Incarceration's Effect on Economic Mobility* at 4 (2010), available at: http://www.pewtrusts.org/~/media/legacy/uploadedfiles/pcs_assets/2010/collateralcosts1pdf. [hereinafter *Collateral Costs*].

83. DEPT. HEALTH & HUMAN SERVS., *Effects of Parental Incarceration on Young Children* (2001), available at: http://aspe.hhs.gov/basic-report/effects-parental-incarceration-young-children [hereinafter *Effects of Parental Incarceration*].

84. *Collateral Costs* at 4.

85. *Id.*

86. The Osborne Ass'n, *Children of Incarcerated Parents Fact Sheet*, available at: http://www.osborneny.org/images/uploads/printMedia/Initiative%20CIP%20Stats_Fact%20Sheet.pdf (last visited Mar. 7, 2017).

87. *Id.*
88. *Effects of Parental Incarceration, supra* note 83.
89. *Id.*
90. Bureau of Justice Stat., *Parents in Prison and their Minor Children* at 5 (2010), available at: http://www.bjs.gov/content/pub/pdf/pptmc.pdf.
91. *Id.* at 18 (App. Table 10).
92. Bernadette Rabuy & Daniel Kopff, *Separation by Bars and Miles: Visitation in State Prisons* , Prison Policy Initiative, (2015), available at: http://www.prisonpolicy.org/reports/prisonvisits.html.
93. *See generally Effects of Parental Incarceration, supra* note 83.
94. Sarah D. Sparks, *Parents' Incarceration takes Toll on Children, Studies Say*, Educ. Week (Feb. 24, 2015), available at: http://www.edweek.org/ew/articles/2015/02/25/parents-incarceration-takes-toll-on-children-studies.html.
95. *See generally Effects of Parental Incarceration, supra* note 83.
96. Sarah D. Sparks, *supra* note 94.
97. *Id.*
98. Nat'l Conf. State Legislators, *Children of Incarcerated Parents* at 2 (2009), available at: http://www.ncsl.org/documents/cyf/childrenofincarceratedparents.pdf.
99. American Academy of Child and Adolescent Psychiatry, Children and TV Violence (2014), available at: https://www.aacap.org/AACAP/Families_and_Youth/Facts_for_Families/FFF-Guide/Children-And-TV-Violence-013.aspx.
100. Children's Defense Fund, *Protect Children from Abuse and Neglect,* available at: http://www.childrensdefense.org/policy/policy-priorities-overviews/ProtectChildrenFromAbuse.html(last visited Mar. 11, 2017).
101. *See, e.g.*, Cathy Spatz Wisdom, *Understanding Child Maltreatment and Juvenile Delinquency: The Research,* available at: http://66.227.70.18/programs/juvenilejustice/ucmjd03.pdf.
102. Campaign for the Fair Sentencing of Youth, *Facts and Infographics about Life without Parole for Children*, available at: http://fairsentencingofyouth.org/what-is-jlwop/ (last visited Mar. 11, 2017).
103. Domestic Violence Roundtable, *The Effects of Domestic Violence on Children, available at* http://www.domesticviolenceroundtable.org/effect-on-children.html (last visited Mar. 11, 2017).
104. *Id.*
105. *Id.*
106. *Id.*
107. Campaign for the Fair Sentencing of Youth, *Facts and Infographics about Life without Parole for Children,* available at: http://fairsentencingofyouth.org/what-is-jlwop/ (last visited Mar. 11, 2017).
108. *See generally* Michele Cooley-Strickland et al., *Community Violence and Youth: Affect, Behavior, Substance Use and Academics*, Clin. Child &

Family Psych. Rev. (2009), *available at* https://www.ncbi.nlm.nih.gov/pmc/articles/PMC2700237/.

109. Glenn D. Braunstein, *Violent Events Have Long-Term Effects on Children*, Huffington Post (Sept. 24, 2012), available at: http://www.huffingtonpost.com/glenn-d-braunstein-md/children-ptsd_b_1901651.html.

110. *Id.*

111. *Id.*

112. Campaign for the Fair Sentencing of Youth, *Facts and Infographics about Life without Parole for Children,* available at: http://fairsentencingofyouth.org/what-is-jlwop/ (last visited Mar. 11, 2017).

113. 132 S. Ct. 2455, 2462.

114. *Id.*

115. *Id.*

Chapter 3

1. State v. Lyle, 854 N.W.2d 378, 381 (Iowa 2014).

2. *Id.*

3. *Id.*

4. *Id.* at 404.

5. *See generally* Chapter 1 *supra* (discussing proliferation of mandatory minimum sentencing schemes nationally).

6. *Lyle,* 854 N.W.2d at 401.

7. Richard Fausset, Richard Perez-Pena, & Alan Blinder, *Race and Discipline in Spotlight After South Carolina Officer Drags Student*, N.Y. Times (Oct. 27, 2015), at: http://www.nytimes.com/2015/10/28/us/spring-valley-high-school-sc-officer-arrest.html.

8. *Id.*

9. *Id.*

10. Bill Chappell, *S.C. Sheriff's Deputy Is Fired After Review of High School Student's Arrest*, Nat'l Public Radio, (Oct. 28, 2015), available at: http://www.npr.org/sections/thetwo-way/2015/10/28/452501995/s-c-sheriff-will-decide-deputy-s-future-with-department.

11. Meg Kinnard, *F.B.I. Getting Involved in S.C. Girl's Arrest*, U.S. News & World Rep., (Oct. 27, 2015), available at: http://www.usnews.com/news/us/articles/2015/10/27/sheriff-seeks-information-on-officer-student-confrontation.

12. Bill Chappell, *supra* note 10 .

13. Meg Kinnard, *supra* note 11.

14. Aaron Kupchik, *The School to Prison Pipeline: Rhetoric and Reality*, in Choosing the Future 98.

15. Melinda D. Anderson, *When Schooling Meets Policing*, The Atlantic (Sept. 21, 2015), available at: http://www.theatlantic.com/education/archive/2015/09/when-schooling-meets-policing/406348/.

16. Josh Sanburn, *Do Cops in Schools Do More Harm Than Good?* Time, (Oct. 29, 2015), available at: http://time.com/4093517/south-carolina-school-police-ben-fields/.

17. Aaron Kupchik, *The School to Prison Pipeline: Rhetoric and Reality*, in Choosing the Future 96 (noting that school security was initially driven by rising crime rates but that expansion continued even as crime rates dropped and expansion was into schools across all sectors of society).

18. *Id.* at 95.

19. *Id. at* 103.

20. *Id.*

21. Melinda D. Anderson, *supra* note 15.

22. *Id.*

23. Michael Pinard, *From the Classroom to the Courtroom: Reassessing Fourth Amendment Standards in Public School Searches Involving Law Enforcement Authorities*, 45 Ariz. L. Rev. 1067, 1077 (2003).

24. Melinda D. Anderson, *supra* note 15.

25. *See* Nat'l Ass'n School Res. Officers, *Frequently Asked Questions*, available at: https://nasro.org/frequently-asked-questions/ (last visited Mar. 11, 2017). ("The National Association of School Resource Officers (NASRO), estimates that between 14,000 and 20,000 SROs are in service nationwide, based on DOJ data and the number of SROs that NASRO has trained."). *Id.*

26. *See, e.g.*, Total Security Solutions, *School Resource Officers Are Fastest Growing Area of Law Enforcement*, (Jan. 20, 2016), available at: http://www.tssbulletproof.com/school-resource-officers-fastest-growing-area-law-enforcement/.

27. American Psychological Ass'n Zero Tolerance Task Force, *Are Zero Tolerance Policies Effective in the Schools? An Evidentiary Review and Recommendations*, Am. Psychologist 852 (2008).

28. *Id.*

29. Gary Fields & John R. Emshwiller, *For More Teens, Arrests by Police Replace School Discipline*, Wall St. J. (Oct. 20, 2014), available at: http://www.wsj.com/articles/for-more-teens-arrests-by-police-replace-school-discipline-1413858602.

30. Aaron Kupchik, *The School to Prison Pipeline: Rhetoric and Reality*, in Choosing the Future 96.

31. *Id.*

32. Tierney Sneed, *School Resource Officers: Safety Priority or Part of the Problem?* U.S. News & World Rep. (Jan. 30, 2015), available at: http://www.usnews.com/news/articles/2015/01/30/are-school-resource-officers-part-of-the-school-to-prison-pipeline-problem.

33. Josh Verges, *Here's How St. Paul Police Describe a Teen's Arrest at Central High*, Pioneer Press (May 26, 2016), available at: http://www.twincities.com/2016/05/26/heres-how-st-paul-police-describe-a-students-arrest-at-central-high/.

34. Kayla Ruble, *School System That Had Student Arrested for Throwing Skittles Accused of Racial Discrimination*, VICE NEWS (May 13, 2015), available at: https://news.vice.com/article/school-system-that-had-student-arrested-for-throwing-skittles-accused-of-racial-discrimination.

35. Lydia Wright, *Story from the Field: Mississippi High School Sending Children to Jail for "Disorderly Conduct,"* S. POVERTY L. CENTER (Apr. 19, 2016), available at: https://www.splcenter.org/news/2016/04/19/story-field-mississippi-high-school-sending-children-jail-%E2%80%98disorderly-conduct%E2%80%99.

36. Melinda D. Anderson, *supra* note 15.

37. Allie Bidwell, *Florida Suspends More Students Than Any Other State*, U.S. NEWS & WORLD REP. (Feb. 24, 2015), available at: http://www.usnews.com/news/blogs/data-mine/2015/02/24/florida-suspends-more-students-than-any-other-state.

38. *Id.*

39. Joe Davidson, *Preschool Suspensions Are Made Worse by Racial Disparities*, WASH. POST (June 13, 2016), available at: https://www.washingtonpost.com/news/powerpost/wp/2016/06/13/preschool-suspensions-are-made-worse-by-racial-disparities/.

40. U.S. Dept. of Educ. Office for Civil Rights, *Data Snapshot: Early Childhood Education* 15 (2014), available at: http://www2.ed.gov/about/offices/list/ocr/docs/crdc-early-learning-snapshot.pdf.

41. Christina A. Samuels, *Pre-K Suspension Data Prompt Focus on Intervention*, EDUC. WEEK (April 2, 2014), available at: http://www.edweek.org/ew/articles/2014/04/02/27ocrprek.h33.html.

42. Meredith Bouchein, *School to Prison Pipeline: A Comparison in Discipline Policy Between Maryland and Texas Public Schools* 3 (2015), available at: http://www.education.umd.edu/TLPL/centers/MEP/Research/k12Education/Bouchein_School_to_Prison_Final_8.26.15.pdf.

43. *School Crime Is Down, Suspension Rate Still High*, CRIME REP., (Aug. 19, 2016), available at: http://thecrimereport.org/2016/08/19/school-crime-is-down-suspension-rate-still-high/.

44. 557 U.S. 364 (2009).

45. *Id.* at 368–69.

46. *Id.* at 374–77.

47. The Civil Rights Project, *Opportunities Suspended: The Devastating Consequences of Zero Tolerance and School Discipline* 17 (2000), available at: https://civilrightsproject.ucla.edu/research/k-12-education/school-discipline/opportunities-suspended-the-devastating-consequences-of-zero-tolerance-and-school-discipline-policies/crp-opportunities-suspended-zero-tolerance-2000.pdf [hereinafter *Opportunities Suspended*].

48. *Opportunities Suspended* at 17.

49. *See generally* Jason Nance, *Students, Police and the School to Prison Pipeline*, 93 Wash. U. L. Rev. 919 (2016) ("Not only is there no evidence that zero tolerance policies have made schools safer, these policies have also pushed more students out of schools and into the juvenile justice system.") (citations omitted). *Id.* at 934.

50. *Opportunities Suspended*, at 13.

51. *Opportunities Suspended*, at 10–11.

52. *Opportunities Suspended*, at 13.

53. *See, e.g.*, Sam Dillon, *Study Finds High Rate of Imprisonment Among Dropouts*, N.Y. Times (Oct. 8, 2009), available at: http://www.nytimes.com/2009/10/09/education/09dropout.html.

54. *Id.*

55. *Id.*

56. Joe Robertson, *Metal Detectors in School: Source of Safety or Anxiety?* Kan. City Star (Oct. 11, 2014), available at: http://www.kansascity.com/news/local/article2680258.html.

57. *Id.*

58. Greg Toppo, *Civil Rights Groups: Cops in School Don't Make Students Safer*, USA Today (Oct. 28, 2015), available at: http://www.usatoday.com/story/news/2015/10/28/school-resource-officer-civil-rights/74751574/.

59. Tamar Lewin, *Black Students Face More Discipline, Data Suggests*, N.Y. Times (Mar. 6, 2012), available at: http://www.nytimes.com/2012/03/06/education/black-students-face-more-harsh-discipline-data-shows.html.

60. *See, e.g.*, Jack Holmes, *White Kids Get Medicated When They Misbehave, Black Kids Get Suspended—Or Arrested*, N.Y. Mag., (Aug. 6, 2015), available at: http://nymag.com/scienceofus/2015/08/white-kids-get-meds-black-kids-get-suspended.html.

61. Kupchik, *The School to Prison Pipelinem* at 97.

62. *See generally* Chapter 1 *supra*.

63. *See generally* U.S. Dept. of Justice, *Trying Juveniles as Adults: An Analysis of State Transfer Laws and Reporting* 1 (2011), available at: https://www.ncjrs.gov/pdffiles1/ojjdp/232434.pdf, [hereinafter *Trying Juveniles as Adults*].

64. *Trying Juveniles as Adults*, at 8–9.

65. *Id.*

66. Campaign for Youth Justice, *Key Facts: Youth in the Justice System* 3 (2012), available at: http://www.campaignforyouthjustice.org/documents/KeyYouthCrimeFacts.pdf.

67. *See generally* Chapter 1 *supra*.

68. *See e.g.*, Cal. Welf. & Inst. Code § 202 (b) ("Minors under the jurisdiction of the juvenile court who are in need of protective services will receive care, treatment, and guidance consistent with their best interest and the best interest of the public.").

69. David O. Brink, *Immaturity, Normative Competence, and Juvenile Transfer: How (Not) to Punish Minors for Major Crimes*, 82 Tex. L. Rev. 1555, 1559 (2004).

70. *Cf.* Brink, *supra* note 69, at 1558.

71. *Cf.* U.S. Dept. of Justice, *Extended Age of Juvenile Court Jurisdiction* (2012) available at: https://www.ojjdp.gov/ojstatbb/structure_process/qa04106. asp?qaDate=2012(noting that 33 states extend the juvenile court's jurisdictional age limit to 20 and another 7 extend it even further in some cases).

72. *See generally* James B. Jacobs, *Juvenile Criminal Record Confidentiality* 149–68, in Choosing the Future (describing the protective rationale behind confidentiality and its erosion in recent years).

73. *See generally* Elizabeth S. Scott & Thomas Grisso, *Developmental Incompetence, Due Process and Juvenile Justice Policy*, 83 N.C. L. Rev. 793, 811–16 (2005).

74. Scott & Grisso, *supra* note 73, at 820.

75. *Id.* at 822.

76. *Id.* at 823–25.

77. *Id.* at 824.

78. *Id.* at 824–25.

79. Jessica Lahey, *The Steep Costs of Keeping Juveniles in Adult Prisons*, The Atlantic (Jan. 8, 2016), available at: http://www.theatlantic.com/education/archive/2016/01/the-cost-of-keeping-juveniles-in-adult-prisons/423201/ ("These children lose more than their freedom when they enter adult prisons; they lose out on the educational and psychological benefits offered by juvenile-detention facilities.").

80. *See, e.g.*, Justice Policy Institute, *The Dangers of Detention: The Impact of Incarcerating Youth in Detention and Other Secure Facilities* 4. available at: http://www.justicepolicy.org/images/upload/06-11_rep_dangersofdetention_ jj.pdf(citing prior commitment as greatest predictor of recidivism).

81. Prison Rape Elimination Act, 42 U.S.C.A. § 15601(4) (2003).

82. *See generally infra* Chapter 4.

83. Lahey, *supra* note 79.

84. Campaign for Youth Justice, *Key Facts: Youth in the Justice System* 4 (2012).

85. U.S. Dept. of Just., *Juveniles Tried as Adults* (2011), available at: http://www.ojjdp.gov/ojstatbb/structure_process/qa04105.asp?qaDate=2011.

86. *Id.*

87. Dana Canedy, *Boy Convicted of Murder in Wrestling Death*, N.Y. Times (Jan. 26, 2001), available at: http://www.nytimes.com/2001/01/26/us/boy-convicted-of-murder-in-wrestling-death.html.

88. *Id.*

89. Tate v. State, 864 So. 2d 44, 50 (2003 Ct. App. Fl. 4th Dist.) ("Even if a child of Tate's age is deemed to have the capacity to understand less serious charges, or common place juvenile court proceedings, it cannot be determined, absent a hearing, whether Tate could meet competency standards incident to facing a first-degree murder charge involving profound decisions regarding strategy, whether to make disclosures, intelligently analyze plea offers, and consider waiving important rights."). *Id.*

90. Felicia Fonseca, *No Clear Way to Handle Arizona 8 Year Old's Case*, ASSOCIATED PRESS (Dec. 14, 2008) available at: http://www.sfgate.com/crime/article/No-clear-way-to-handle-Arizona-8-year-old-s-case-3180432.php.

91. *Id; see also* Felicia Fonseca, *Arizona 9 Year Old Pleads Guilty in Shooting Death*, ASSOCIATED PRESS (Feb. 19, 2009) available at: http://www.sandiegouniontribune.com/sdut-child-charged-021909-2009feb19-story.html.

92. Philip Holloway, *Should 11-Year Olds Be Charged with Adult Crimes?* CNN (Oct. 14, 2015), available at: http://www.cnn.com/2015/10/14/opinions/holloway-charging-juveniles-as-adults/.

93. Jacquellena Carrero, *Judge Rules Girls in "Slender Man" Case to Be Tried as Adults*, NBC (Aug. 10, 2015), available at: http://www.nbcnews.com/storyline/slender-man-stabbing/judge-rules-girls-slender-man-case-be-tried-adults-n407351.

94. *Id.*

95. Bryan Stevenson, *We Need to Talk About an Injustice*, TED TALK (Mar. 2012), *available at* https://www.ted.com/talks/bryan_stevenson_we_need_to_talk_about_an_injustice/transcript?language=en.

96. Mary Sue Backus & Paul Marcus, *The Right to Counsel in Criminal Cases: A National Crisis*, 57 HASTINGS L.J. 1031, 1034 (2006).

97. 372 U.S. 335 (1963).

98. *Id.* at 344.

99. See, e.g., Douglas v. California, 372 U.S. 353 (1963) (providing poor defendants with right to counsel for direct appeal); Strickland v. Washington, 466 U.S. 668 (1984) (establishing test for evaluating whether counsel satisfies constitutional standard for effective representation); Ake v. Oklahoma, 470 U.S. 68 (1985) (holding poor defendant entitled to psychiatric expert at state's expense if necessary).

100. *Cf.* David A. Love, *Why It's One Law for the Rich in America and McJustice for the Rest*, THE GUARDIAN (March 14, 2013), available at: https://www.theguardian.com/commentisfree/2013/mar/14/law-rich-america-mcjustice.

101. Anthony Lewis, *Abroad at Home: A Muted Trumpet*, N.Y. TIMES (Mar. 17, 1988), available at: http://www.nytimes.com/1988/03/17/opinion/abroad-at-home-a-muted-trumpet.html.

102. Paul Butler, *Gideon's Muted Trumpet*, N.Y. TIMES (Mar. 17, 2013), available at: http://www.nytimes.com/2013/03/18/opinion/gideons-muted-trumpet.html?_r=o.

103. Stephen B. Bright, *Turning Celebrated Principles into Reality*, 27-FEB CHAMPION 6 (2003).

104. American Bar Ass'n, Juvenile Justice Center, *A Call for Justice: An Assessment of Access to Counsel and Quality of Representation in Delinquency Proceedings* 21 (1995), available at: http://njdc.info/wp-content/uploads/2013/11/A-Call-for-Justice_

An-Assessment-of-Access-to-Counsel-and-Quality-of-Representation-in-Delinquency-Proceedings.pdf [*hereinafter A Call for Justice*].

105. *A Call for Justice*, at 22.

106. Sarah Barr, *Campaign Says Juveniles Need Better Access to Quality Legal Counsel*, Juv. Just. Info. Exchange (May 17, 2016), available at: http://jjie.org/campaign-says-juveniles-need-better-access-to-quality-legal-counsel/246782/.

107. *Id.*

108. *Id.*

109. *A Call for Justice*, at 6.

110. *Id.*

111. The Constitution Project, *Excessive Caseloads* 2, at: http://www.constitutionproject.org/pdf/excessive_caseloads.pdf [hereinafter *Excessive Caseloads*].

112. American Bar Ass'n, Gideon's *Broken Promise: America's Continuing Quest for Equal Justice* 17 (2004), available at: http://www.americanbar.org/content/dam/aba/administrative/legal_aid_indigent_defendants/ls_sclaid_def_bp_right_to_counsel_in_criminal_proceedings.authcheckdam.pdf.

113. The Constitution Project, *Justice Denied: America's Continuing Neglect of Our Constitutional Right to Counsel* 65 (2009), available at: http://www.constitutionproject.org/wp-content/uploads/2012/10/139.pdf [hereinafter *Justice Denied*]; *see also* Nat'l Ass'n Crim. Def. Attys., *Minor Crimes, Massive Waste: The Terrible Toll of America's Broken Misdemeanor Courts* 22–26 (2009), available at: https://www.nacdl.org/reports/misdemeanor/.

114. *A Call for Justice*, at 7.

115. *Excessive Caseloads, supra* note III, at 1.

116. *Id.*

117. *See generally* American Bar Ass'n, *Ten Principles of a Public Defense Delivery System* (2002), available at: http://www.americanbar.org/content/dam/aba/administrative/legal_aid_indigent_defendants/ls_sclaid_def_tenprinciplesbooklet.authcheckdam.pdf.

118. Nat'l Juv. Def. Ctr. & Nat'l. Legal Aid and Def. Ass'n, *Ten Core Principles for Providing Quality Delinquency Representation through Public Defense Delivery Systems* Principle 2 (2008), available at: http://njdc.info/wp-content/uploads/2013/11/10-Core-Principles.pdf.

119. *Id.* at Principle 7.

120. *A Call for Justice*, at 11.

121. *Justice Denied*, at 82, 93.

122. *Cf. A Call for Justice*, at 24–25.

123. *A Call for Justice*, at 27.

124. *See generally* Molly M. Gill, *Let's Abolish Mandatory Minimums, The Punishment Must Fit the Crime*, 36-SPG Hum. Rts. 4 (2009).

125. *Id.* at 4–5.

126. *Id.*

127. *Id.*
128. Sari Horwitz, *Former Federal Judge to President Obama: Free the Man I Sentenced to 55 Years in Prison*, Wash. Post (Feb. 9, 2016), available at: https://www.washingtonpost.com/news/post-nation/wp/2016/02/09/former-federal-judge-to-president-obama-free-the-man-i-sentenced-to-55-years-in-prison/?utm_term=.4fa9d73f968e.
129. *Id.*
130. *Id.*
131. *Id.*
132. Greg Jaffe & Sari Horwitz, *Utah Man Whose Long Drug Sentence Stirred Controversy Is Released*, Wash. Post (June 3, 2016), available at: https://www.washingtonpost.com/politics/president-obama-just-commuted-the-sentences-of-42-people-here-are-their-names/2016/06/03/08f23b7c-29c3-11e6-a3c4-0724e8e24f3f_story.html.
133. Gill, *supra* note 124 at 4, 5.
134. *See generally* Chapter 1, Part C *supra.*
135. *Graham*, 560 U.S. at 70.
136. *See generally infra* Chapter 5.
137. *State v. Lyle*, 854 N.W.2d 378, 381.
138. *Id.*
139. *Id.*
140. *Id.*
141. *Id.*
142. *Id.*
143. *Lyle*, 854 N.W. 2d 378, 381.
144. *Id.* at 401.
145. *Id.* at 399.
146. *Id.* at 403.
147. *Id.* at 419 (Zager, J., dissenting).

Chapter 4

1. Letter from De'Andre (Jan. 26, 2016) (on file with author).
2. *See* U.N. Int'l Covenant on Civil and Pol. Rights, Human Rights Committee Report, (Apr. 23, 2014), available at: http://www.ushrnetwork.org/sites/ushrnetwork.org/files/iccpr_concluding_obs_2014.pdf.
3. U.S. Dept. of Justice, *Juveniles in Residential Placement, 2013* 3 (2016), available at: http://www.ojjdp.gov/pubs/249507.pdf?ed2f26df2d9c416fbddd dd2330a778c6=ixggxbbxfa-icgedfbc [hereinafter *Residential Placement*].
4. For example: Mountain View Youth Development Center (Maine); Green Oaks Detention Center (Louisiana); Adobe Mountain School (Arizona); Walnut Grove Correctional Facility (Mississippi).
5. *Residential Placement*, at 6.
6. *Id.*
7. *Id.*

8. *Id.*

9. Eleanor Hinton Hoytt et al., *Reducing Racial Disparities in Juvenile Detention* 4–5 (2001), available at: http://www.aecf.org/m/resourcedoc/aecf-Pathways8reducingracialdisparities-2001.pdf.

10. *Residential Placement*, at 5.

11. Annie E. Casey Foundation, *No Place for Kids*, 3, Fig. 1 (2011), available at: http://www.aecf.org/m/resourcedoc/aecf-NoPlaceForKidsFullReport-2011.pdf.

12. *Reducing Racial Disparities in Juvenile Detention, supra* note 9, at 5.

13. *Residential Placement*, at 12.

14. Nell Bernstein, Burning Down the House: The End of Juvenile Prison 38 (2014).

15. *Id.*

16. *Id.* at 39.

17. *Id.* at 41.

18. *Id.* at 45.

19. U.S. Dept. of Justice, *Juveniles in Corrections, Facility Characteristics, Juveniles in Residential Placement by Facility Size and Facility Type* (2014), available at: http://www.ojjdp.gov/ojstatbb/corrections/qa08501.asp?qaDate=2014.

20. U.S. Dept. of Justice, *Juveniles in Corrections, Facility Characteristics, Juvenile Offender Population by Facility Operation* (2014), available at: http://www.ojjdp.gov/ojstatbb/corrections/qa08502.asp?qaDate=2014.

21. U.S. Dept. of Justice, *Juveniles in Corrections, Facility Characteristics, Offense Mix by Facility Type* (2013), available at: http://www.ojjdp.gov/ojstatbb/corrections/qa08509.asp?qaDate=2013.

22. Campaign for Youth Justice, *Key Facts: Youth in the Justice System*, at 2 (2012), available at: http://www.campaignforyouthjustice.org/documents/KeyYouthCrimeFacts.pdf [hereinafter *Key Facts*].

23. U.S. Dept. of Justice, *Juveniles in Corrections, Facility Characteristics, Percent of Facilities Providing Treatment Services, by Facility Operation* (2014), available at: http://www.ojjdp.gov/ojstatbb/corrections/qa08520.asp?qaDate=2014.

24. Youth First, *54,000 Children: The Geography of America's Dysfunctional & Racially Disparate Youth Incarceration Complex,* available at: http://www.youthfirstinitiative.org/the54000/# (last visited Apr. 18, 2017).

25. Patrick Marley & Jason Stein, *Agents Raid School for Juvenile Offenders Amid Secret Probe*, J. Sentinel (Dec. 7, 2015), available at: http://archive.jsonline.com/news/wisconsin/agents-descend-on-wisconsin-juvenile-facility-amid-secret-probe-b99629753z1-360823921.html.

26. Don Behm, *Crowding, Chronic Understaffing Plague Juvenile Detention Center,* J. Sentinel (Apr. 19, 2016), *available at* http://archive.jsonline.com/news/milwaukee/crowding-chronic-understaffing-plague-juvenile-detention-center-b99709172z1-376155261.html.

27. Dan Lawton, *San Mateo: Lawsuit Details Rape of 14 Year Old at Juvenile Detention Facility*, MERCURY NEWS (Dec. 4, 2015), available at: http://www.mercurynews.com/news/ci_29199379/san-mateo-lawsuit-details-rape-14-year-old.

28. Kate Brumback, *Lawsuit: Mistreatment of 14 Year Old in Juvenile Detention Caused Him to Hang Himself*, Talking Points Memo (Dec. 18, 2015), available at: http://talkingpointsmemo.com/news/georgia-teen-suicide-juvenile-detention-center.

29. *Key Facts: Youth in the Justice System, supra* note 22, at 2.

30. *Reducing Racial Disparities in Juvenile Detention, supra* note 9, at 6.

31. *See generally No Place for Kids, supra* note 11, at 22–25; Kaukab Jhumra Smith, *Advocates Say Schools in Juvenile Detention Facilities Are Failing Kids*, JUV. JUSTICE INF. EXCH., (July 24, 2012), available at: http://jjie.org/advocates-say-schools-juvenile-detention-facilities-failure/90195/.

32. Nat'l Ctr. on Educ., Disability and Juv. Justice, *Juvenile Correction Education Programs, available at* http://www.edjj.org/focus/education/ (last visited Apr. 18, 2017).

33. Melinda D. Anderson, *Learning Behind Bars*, THE ATLANTIC (June 6, 2016), available at: http://www.theatlantic.com/education/archive/2016/06/learning-behind-bars/485663/.

34. Nat'l Ctr. on Educ., Disability and Juv. Justice, *Juvenile Correction Education Programs.*

35. Anderson, *supra* note 33.

36. *No Place for Kids, supra* note 11, at 22.

37. *Id.*

38. *Id.* at 24.

39. U.S. Dept. of Justice, *Juvenile Residential Facility Census*, at 16 (2010), available at: http://www.ojjdp.gov/pubs/241134.pdf.

40. Am. Civ. Lib. Union, *Alone & Afraid: Children Held in Solitary Confinement and Isolation in Juvenile Detention and Correctional Facilities* 7 (2014), available at: https://www.aclu.org/files/assets/Alone%20and%20Afraid%20COMPLETE%20FINAL.pdf [hereinafter *Alone & Afraid*].

41. *Alone & Afraid, supra* note 40, at 7.

42. *Id.* at 4.

43. *Id.* at 5.

44. *Id.*

45. *No Place for Kids, supra* note 11, at 2.

46. *See generally No Place for Kids, supra* note 11; *see also* Bernstein, BURNING DOWN THE HOUSE, at 50–51.

47. Jeff Fleischer & Shaena Fazal, *A Much- Needed Alternative to Youth Prisons*, HUFFINGTON POST (July 15, 2016), available at: http://www.huffingtonpost.com/shaena-fazal/youth-prisons_b_7772722.html.

48. Nell Bernstein et al, *Mothers at the Gate* 16 (2016), available at: http://www.ips-dc.org/wp-content/uploads/2016/05/k-dolan-mothers-at-the-gate-5.3.pdf; *see also* Bridget DiCosmo, *Jonathan McClard Speaks about the Jackson Shooting That Sent Him to Prison*, SOUTHEAST MISSOURIAN (Dec. 28, 2007), available at: http://www.semissourian.com/story/1300327.html.

49. Bridget DiCosmo, *supra* note 48.

50. *Id.*

51. *Id.*

52. *Id.*

53. *Id.*

54. Bridget DiCosmo, *supra* note 48.

55. *Id.*

56. *Id.*

57. *Id.*

58. Jessica Lahey, *The Steep Costs of Keeping Juveniles in Adult Prisons*, THE ATLANTIC (Jan. 8, 2016), available at: http://www.theatlantic.com/education/archive/2016/01/the-cost-of-keeping-juveniles-in-adult-prisons/423201/.

59. Youth in the Adult System: Fact Sheet (2014), available at: http://www.act4jj.org/sites/default/files/ckfinder/files/ACT4JJ%20Youth%20In%20Adult%20System%20Fact%20Sheet%20Aug%202014%20FINAL.pdf.

60. *Key Facts, supra* note 22, at 4.

61. *Id.*

62. *See generally* Lahey, *supra* note 58.

63. U.S. Dept. of Justice, *Trying Juveniles as Adults: An Analysis of State Laws and Reporting* 22 (2011), *available at* https://www.ncjrs.gov/pdffiles1/ojjdp/232434.pdf.

64. *Id.*

65. *Id.*

66. Interview with Mary Graham, Terrence Graham's mother (Jacksonville, Florida, Aug. 7, 2016) (notes on file with author).

67. Judi Villa, *Young Offenders Groomed for Life of Crime*, ARIZ. REPUBLIC (Nov. 14, 2004).

68. Nancy Wolff & Jing Shi, *Contextualization of Physical and Sexual Assault in Male Prisons: Incidents and Their Aftermath*, J. CORRECT. HEALTH CARE (2009), available at: http://www.ncbi.nlm.nih.gov/pmc/articles/PMC2811042/.

69. James E. Robertson, *"Fight or F…"and Constitutional Liberty: An Inmate's Right to Self Defense When Targeted by Aggressors*, 29 IND. L. REV. 339, 343–44 (1995).

70. Hum. Rts. Watch & The Am. Civ. Lib. Union, *Growing up Locked Down: Youth in Solitary Confinement in Jails and Prisons Across the United States* 19 (2012), available at: https://www.hrw.org/report/2012/10/10/growing-locked-down/youth-solitary-confinement-jails-and-prisons-across-united [hereinafter *Growing up Locked Down*].

71. R.W. v. Bruce A. Kiser, Jr. (Middle Dist. Fl. Jan. 27, 2016) (Comp. at 3-10); *see also* Elyssa Cherney, *Sex Assault on Teen at Florida Prison Spurs Federal Lawsuit*, Orlando Sentinel (Jan. 28, 2016), available at: http://www. orlandosentinel.com/news/breaking-news/os-sumter-correctional-institute-juvenile-abuse-lawsuit-20160128-story.html.

72. Letter from Terrence Graham (Oct. 29, 2013) (on file with author).

73. Florida Dept. of Corrections, *Inmate Mortality*, available at: http://www. dc.state.fl.us/pub/mortality/(last visited Apr. 18, 2017).

74. *Id.*

75. *Id.*

76. Interview with Terrence Graham (Taylor Correctional Institute, Perry, Florida, Aug. 1, 2012) (notes on file with author).

77. Letter from Terrence Graham (Aug. 3, 2016) (on file with author).

78. *Id.*

79. Letter from Terrence Graham (Oct. 29, 2013) (on file with author).

80. Letter from Terrence Graham (Aug. 3, 2016) (on file with author).

81. U.S. Dept. of Justice, *PREA Data Collection Activities*(2015), available at: http://www.bjs.gov/content/pub/pdf/pdca15.pdf.

82. Bureau of Justice Stat., *Sexual Victimization Reported by Adult Correctional Authorities*, 2009–2011, available at: http://www.bjs.gov/index. cfm?ty=pbdetail&iid=4882.

83. *Id.*

84. Justice Policy Inst., *The Risks Juveniles Face When They Are Incarcerated with Adults* 3 (1997), available at: http://www.justicepolicy.org/images/upload/97-02_rep_riskjuvenilesface_jj.pdf.

85. T.J. Parsell, *Unsafe Behind Bars*, N.Y. Times (Sept. 18, 2005), available at: http://query.nytimes.com/gst/fullpage.html?res=9C06E2D81131F93BA25 75AC0A9639C8B63.

86. *Id.*

87. Prison Rape Elimination Act, 42 U.S.C.A. § 15601(4) (2003).

88. Prison Rape Elimination Commission, 42 U.S.C.A. § 15606.

89. U.S. Dept. of Justice, Press Release: *Justice Department Releases Final Rule to Prevent, Detect and Respond to Prison Rape* (May 17, 2012), available at: https://www.justice.gov/opa/pr/justice-department-releases-final-rule-prevent-detect-and-respond-prison-rape.

90. Nat'l Public Radio, *Enforcing Prison Rape Elimination Standards Proves Tricky* (Apr. 2, 2014), available at: http://www.npr.org/2014/04/02/ 298332579/enforcing-prison-rape-elimination-standards-proves-tricky.

91. Bureau of Justice Stat., *FY 2015 List of Certification and Assurance Submissions*, available at: https://www.bja.gov/Programs/15PREA-AssurancesCertifications.pdf .

92. Rebecca Boone, *Utah Now One of Just Three States Not Complying with Federal Prison Rape Law*, Salt Lake Trib. (Dec. 12, 2015) available at: http:// www.sltrib.com/home/3300263-155/idaho-finally-agrees-to-comply-with (citing Utah, Arkansas, and Alaska).

93. Interview with Terrence Graham (Taylor Correctional Institute, Perry, Florida Aug. 1, 2012) (notes on file with author).

94. Letter from Jackson (Oct. 28, 2013) (on file with author).

95. Letter from Jackson (Aug. 22, 2013) (on file with author).

96. Letter from Jackson (Oct. 28, 2013) (on file with author).

97. *Growing up Locked Down, supra* note 70, at 51–52; *see also* Dep't of Justice, *Prison Rule Violators* 1 (1989), available at: https://www.ncjrs.gov/pdffiles1/Digitization/120344NCJRS.pdf.

98. *Growing up Locked Down*, at 51.

99. *Growing up Locked Down*, at 52.

100. Judi Villa, *Young Offenders Groomed for Life of Crime*, Ariz. Republic (Nov. 14, 2004).

101. Dep't of Justice, *Prison Rule Violators* at 2 (1989).

102. *See, e.g.,* Bureau of Prisons, *Inmate Discipline Program* (2011), available at: https://www.bop.gov/policy/progstat/5270_009.pdf.

103. *Id.*

104. *Id.*

105. Dep't of Just., *Prison Rule Violators*, at 4 (1989) (Table 6).

106. Letter from Jamie (June 4, 2015) (on file with author).

107. Letter from Jackson (Dec. 12, 2015) (on file with author).

108. Letter from Terrence Graham (Aug. 3, 2016) (on file with author).

109. Dep't of Justice, *Prison Rule Violators*, at 6 (1989) (Table 12).

110. *Id.*

111. Terms and definitions vary by jurisdiction. *See generally Solitary Watch*, available at: http://solitarywatch.com/facts/faq/ (defining solitary confinement as "the practice of isolating people in closed cells for 22–24 hours a day, virtually free of human contact, for periods of time ranging from days to decades.").

112. *Growing up Locked Down, supra* note 70, at 48–63 (discussing common types of solitary confinement across jurisdictions).

113. *Id.*

114. Elizabeth Landau, *Solitary Confinement and the Angola 3* (Feb. 23, 2014), CNN, *available at* http://www.cnn.com/2014/02/23/health/solitary-confinement-psychology/.

115. *Growing up Locked Down, supra* note 70, at 29–33.

116. Letter from Terrence Graham (July 11, 2016) (on file with author).

117. Justice Policy Inst., *The Risks Juveniles Face When They Are Incarcerated with Adults* 1, 2 (1997), available at: http://www.justicepolicy.org/images/upload/97-02_rep_riskjuvenilesface_jj.pdf.

118. *Growing up Locked Down, supra* note 70, at 30.

119. Letter from Terrence Graham (Aug. 22, 2012) (on file with author).

120. Interviews with Mary Graham (Aug. 1, 2016 and Aug. 7, 2016) (notes on file with author).

121. Interview with Terrence Graham (Taylor Correctional Institute, Perry, Florida Aug. 1, 2012) (notes on file with author).

122. For an example of a schedule of an inmate's day, see N.C. Dept. Public Safety, *24 Hours in Prison*, available at: http://www.doc.state.nc.us/DOP/HOURS24.htm. The federal Bureau of Prisons also makes available handbooks given to inmates upon arrival at each facility, and these handbooks indicate a similar structure. *See, e.g.,* U.S. Penitentiary Satellite Prison Camp, Big Sandy, Inez, KY, available at: https://www.bop.gov/locations/institutions/bsy/BSY_aohandbook.pdf.

123. N.C. Dept. Public Safety, *24 Hours in Prison*, available at: http://www.doc.state.nc.us/DOP/HOURS24.htm.

124. The Editorial Board, *A College Education for Prisoners*, N.Y. TIMES (Feb. 16, 2016), available at: http://www.nytimes.com/2016/02/16/opinion/a-college-education-for-prisoners.html?_r=0; *see also,* Edward L. Rubin, *The Inevitability of Rehabilitation*, 19 LAW & INEQ. 343, 343-344 (2001).

125. Letter from De'Andre (Jan. 26, 2016) (on file with author).

126. Letter from Alex (Feb. 19, 2014) (on file with author).

127. Letter from Jaime (June 4, 2015) (on file with author).

128. Letter from Terrence Graham (Aug. 22, 2012) (on file with author).

129. Letter from Terrence Graham (Aug. 22, 2012) (on file with author).

130. Letter from Jackson (Aug. 22, 2012) (on file with author).

131. *Id.*

132. Letter from Jaime (June 4, 2015) (on file with author).

133. *Miller*, 132 S. Ct. 2455, 2475. (Breyer J., concurring).

134. Letter from Alex (Feb. 19, 2014) (on file with author).

135. *Key Facts, supra* note 22, at 4.

Chapter 5

1. Roper v. Simmons, 543 U.S. 551 (2005).

2. *Roper,* 543 U.S. at 578.

3. *Id.* at 564.

4. *Id.* at 564.

5. *Id.* at 567–68.

6. *Id.* at 551, 568.

7. *Id.* at 569–70.

8. *Id.* at 571–72.

9. *Id.* at 569–70 (discussing the lack of maturity and recklessness, susceptibility to negative outside influences, and transient character of youth and citing the science behind each point).

10. *Id.* at 575.

11. Graham v. Florida, 560 U.S. 48 (2010).

12. *Graham,* 560 U.S. at 79.

13. *Id.* at 59.

14. *Id.* at 59–61.

15. *Id.* at 61–62.

16. *Id.* at 64.

17. *Id.* at 67.
18. *Id.*
19. *Id..*
20. *Id.* at 69.
21. *Id.* at 75.
22. *Id.* at 64 ("Thus, adding the individuals counted by the study to those we have been able to locate independently, there are 123 juvenile nonhomicide offenders serving life without parole sentences. A significant majority of those, 77 in total, are serving sentences imposed in Florida . . . The other 46 are imprisoned in just 10 States—California, Delaware, Iowa, Louisiana, Mississippi, Nebraska, Nevada, Oklahoma, South Carolina, and Virginia.") (citations omitted).
23. Miller v. Alabama, 132 S. Ct. 2455 (2012).
24. *Miller,* 132 S. Ct. at 2463.
25. *Id.* at 2463–64.
26. *Id.* at 2466.
27. *Id.* at 2466. ("[T]he mandatory penalty schemes at issue here prevent the sentencer from taking account of these central considerations. By removing youth from the balance—by subjecting a juvenile to the same life-without-parole sentence applicable to an adult—these laws prohibit a sentencing authority from assessing whether the law's harshest term of imprisonment proportionately punishes a juvenile offender. That contravenes Graham's (and also Roper's) foundational principle: that imposition of a state's most severe penalties on juvenile offenders cannot proceed as though they were not children.").
28. *Id.* at 2482 (Roberts, C.J., dissenting) (emphasis added).
29. *Id.* at 2481 (Roberts, C.J., dissenting).
30. *Id.* at 2486 (Thomas, J., dissenting).
31. Solem v. Helm, 463 U.S. 277 (1983) (finding unconstitutional life without parole sentence under South Dakota recidivist statute for defendant who passed a bad check).
32. Harmelin v. Michigan, 111 S. Ct. 2680 (1990) (rejecting petitioner's proportionality challenge to sentence of mandatory term of life in prison without possibility of parole for possessing more than 650 grams of cocaine); Ewing v. California, 123 S. Ct. 1179 (2003) (rejecting petitioner's proportionality challenge to sentence of 25 years to life under state's three-strikes law).
33. *Miller,* 132 S. Ct. at 2468.
34. *Id.* at 2468–69 ("The features that distinguish juveniles from adults also put them at a significant disadvantage in criminal proceedings.") (*citing* J.D.B. v. North Carolina, 131 S. Ct. 2394, 2400–01 (2011)).
35. *Id.* at 2466.
36. *Id.* at 2467 (*quoting* Eddings v. Oklahoma, 455 U.S. 104, 116 (1982)).
37. *Id.* at 2464.

38. *Id.*

39. *Id..*

40. *Id.* at 2464–65.

41. *Id.* at 2474–75.

42. *Id.* at 2474.

43. *Id.*

44. *Id.* at 2469 ("[G]iven all we have said in *Roper, Graham* and this decision about children's diminished culpability and heightened capacity for change, we think appropriate occasions for sentencing juveniles to this harshest possible penalty will be uncommon.").

45. *See generally* Cara H. Drinan, *Graham on the Ground*, 87 Wash. L. Rev. 51, 64–69 (2012) (explaining retroactivity doctrine in general and as applied to the *Graham* case).

46. *See, e.g.,* Diatchenko v. District Att'y for Suffolk Dist., 1 N.E. 3d 270 (2013) (finding *Miller* retroactively applicable); People v. Davis, 6 N.E. 3d 709 (Ill. 2014).

47. *See, e.g.,* Chambers v. State, 831 N.W.2d 311 (Minn. 2013) (holding *Miller* does not apply retroactively); People v. Carp, 852 N.W.2d 801 (Mich. 2014) (also holding *Miller* does not apply retroactively).

48. Montgomery v. Louisiana, 131 S. Ct. 718 (2016).

49. Garrett Epps, *What Happens to Old Sentences When the Law Changes*, The Atlantic, Oct. 14, 2015, http://www.theatlantic.com/politics/archive/2015/10/what-happens-to-old-sentences-when-the-law-changes/410455/.

50. *Id.*

51. *Id.*

52. The Court spent much of the argument time on the question whether it had jurisdiction to resolve the retroactivity question. *See, e.g., Montgomery*, 131 S. Ct. 718, 737 (Scalia, J., dissenting) (arguing that Court did not have that jurisdiction).

53. 131 S.Ct. at 736 ("The Court now holds that *Miller* announced a substantive rule of constitutional law. The conclusion that *Miller* states a substantive rule comports with the principles that informed *Teague*. *Teague* sought to balance the important goals of finality and comity with the liberty interests of those imprisoned pursuant to rules later deemed unconstitutional. *Miller*'s conclusion that the sentence of life without parole is disproportionate for the vast majority of juvenile offenders raises a grave risk that many are being held in violation of the Constitution.").

54. *Id.* ("A State may remedy a *Miller* violation by permitting juvenile homicide offenders to be considered for parole, rather than by resentencing them.").

55. The Campaign for the Fair Sentencing of Youth, *Righting Wrongs: The Five Year Groundswell of State Bans on Life Without Parole for Children*, at 4 (2016), available at: http://fairsentencingofyouth.org/wp-content/uploads/2016/09/Righting-Wrongs-.pdf?utm_source=Five+Year+Report+KI+Rollo

ut&utm_campaign=Righting+Wrongs&utm_medium=email [hereinafter *Righting Wrongs*].

56. *Righting Wrongs, supra* note 55, at 4.
57. *Id.*
58. *Id.*
59. *See* H.B. 4210, 82d Leg., 1st Sess. (W. Va. 2014); S.B. 9, 147th Gen. Assemb., Reg. Sess. (Del. 2013).
60. W. Va. H.B. 4210 (codified at W. Va. Code §§ 61-11-23 (c)(1-15) (listing the following 15 factors: (1) Age at the time of the offense; (2) Impetuosity; (3) Family and community environment; (4) Ability to appreciate the risks and consequences of the conduct; (5) Intellectual capacity; (6) The outcomes of a comprehensive mental health evaluation conducted by a mental health professional licensed to treat adolescents in the state of West Virginia; (7) Peer or familial pressure; (8) Level of participation in the offense; (9) Ability to participate meaningfully in his or her defense; (10) Capacity for rehabilitation; (11) School records and special education evaluations; (12) Trauma history; (13) Faith and community involvement; (14) Involvement in the child welfare system; and (15) Any other mitigating factor or circumstances). The new legislation similarly sets forth factors that the Parole Board should take into account when periodically assessing the parole eligibility of juveniles. *See id.* (codified at W. Va. Code §62-12-13b(b)) (requiring the Parole Board to consider "the diminished culpability of juveniles as compared to that of adults, the hallmark features of youth, and any subsequent growth and increased maturity of the prisoner during incarceration" and requiring the board to consider "educational and court documents . . . Participation in available rehabilitative and educational programs while in prison. Age at the time of the offense . . . Immaturity at the time of the offense . . . Home and community environment at the time of the offense; Efforts made toward rehabilitation . . . evidence of remorse; and Any other factors or circumstances the board considers relevant").
61. *See* Del S.B. 9; *see also Delaware Enacts Sentencing Review Process for Youth*, Campaign for Fair Sent'g Youth (June 10, 2013), at: http://fairsentencingofyouth.org/2013/06/10/delaware-entacts-sentence-review-process-for-youth/.
62. *Delaware Eliminates Death in Prison Sentences for Children*, Equal Justice Initiative, (June 13, 2013), http://www.eji.org/node/779.
63. Diatchenko v. District Att'y for Suffolk Dist., 466 Mass. 655 (Mass. 2013) (holding that *Miller* applies retroactively and that the Massachusetts state constitution forbids LWOP sentence for juveniles).
64. Diatchenko v. District Att'y for Suffolk Dist., 27 N.E.3d 349 (Mass. 2015).
65. State v. Lyle, 854 N.W.2d 378, 400 (Iowa 2014) (interpreting Iowa state constitution to prohibit "all mandatory minimum sentences of imprisonment for youthful offenders"); *see also* Chapter 7 *infra* discussing the *Lyle* decision and its broader implications.

66. *See, e.g.,* Gridine v. State, 175 So. 3d 672 (Fla. 2015) (holding that 70-year prison sentence for juvenile non-homicide defendant was de facto life sentence precluded by *Graham*).

67. *See generally* The Sentencing Project, *Slow to Act: State Responses to 2012 Supreme Court Mandate on Life Without Parole,* June 2014 available at: http://sentencingproject.org/doc/publications/jj_State_Responses_to_ Miller.pdf (documenting states' responses to Miller decision) [hereinafter "Slow to Act"].

68. *See generally* Act of Oct. 25, 2012, Pa. Laws 1655 (2012), available at: www. legis.state.pa.us/WU01/LI/LI/US/HTM/2012/0/0204..HTM; *See also,* Juv. L. Ctr., *Juvenile Life Without Parole (JLWOP) in Pennsylvania,* Juv. L. Ctr., available at: http://www.jlc.orgcurrent-initiatives/promoting-fairness-courts/ juvenile-life-without-parole/jlwop-pennsylvania (last updated Mar. 26, 2013).

69. H.B. 152, 2013 Leg., Reg. Sess. (La. 2013). The same terms also apply under Florida's post-*Miller* legislation. *See* The Sentencing Project, *Slow to Act, supra* note 67, at 2.

70. The Sentencing Project, *Slow to Act, supra* note 67, at 2.

Chapter 6

1. *See generally* John Simerman, *George Toca, La. Inmate at Center of Debate on Juvenile Life Sentences, to Go Free,* THE ADVOCATE, Jan. 30, 2015, *available at* http://www.theadvocate.com/new_orleans/news/article_5586e606-745b-5ea8-ab51-7c9830f3303b.html; *see also* George Toca v. Burl Cain, Petitioner's Memorandum in Support of Application for Supervisory Writ, filed Oct. 14, 2010 (4th Cir. Ct. App. La.) (on file with author) [hereinafter Supervisory Writ Memo].

2. Telephone interview with George Toca (Aug. 23, 2016) (notes on file with author) [hereinafter Aug. 23, 2016 Intvw.].

3. Supervisory Writ Memo. at 1.

4. *See, e.g.,* Human Rights Watch, *California: New Hope for Young Offenders,* Oct. 5, 2015, available at: https://www.hrw.org/news/2015/10/05/california-new-hope-young-offenders (estimating that more than 12,000 youthful offenders are eligible for parole hearings under the state's post-*Miller* sentencing laws and more than 250 have already been paroled).

5. Louis R. Costa's Memorandum in Support of Parole, In the Matter of Louis R. Costa, W44737, Mass. Parole Board (filed Feb. 18, 2016) (on file with author) [hereinafter Costa Parole Memo.].

6. Telephone Interview with George Toca (Aug. 23, 2016) (notes on file with author); Interview with George Toca, (New Orleans, LA) (Oct. 1, 2016) (notes on file with author).

7. Aug. 23, 2016 Intvw.

8. *Id.*

9. *Id.*

10. *Id..*

11. Supervisory Writ Memo., at 4.

12. *Id.*

13. *Id.*

14. Supervisory Writ Memo., at 3.

15. *Id.*

16. Supervisory Writ Memo., at 4; *see also* Gwen Filosa, *Judge Refuses to Reopen 25 Year Old Murder Case*, TIMES-PICAYUNE (June 16, 2010), available at: http://www.nola.com/crime/index.ssf/2010/06/orleans_judge_refuses_to_re-op.html.

17. Supervisory Writ Memo., at 4.

18. Aug. 23, 2016 Intvw.

19. Supervisory Writ Memo., at 4.

20. *Id.* at 14.

21. *Id.*

22. John Simerman, *Free After Three Decades in Prison, George Toca Sprints Toward a New Life*, NEW ORLEANS ADVOCATE, Mar. 19, 2015, available at: http://www.theadvocate.com/new_orleans/news/article_c9298184-7758-5979-a0ae-934161a7645d.html.

23. Supervisory Writ Memo. at 13.

24. *Id.* at 14.

25. *Id.* at 4.

26. Because they are unique in their degree of guaranteed procedural safeguards, death penalty cases provide the best information about wrongful convictions. A 2014 study on the issue showed that 4.1 percent of defendants sentenced to death in the United States are later proven innocent. Samuel R. Gross et al., *Rate of False Conviction of Criminal Defendants Who Are Sentenced to Death*, PROC. NAT'L. ACAD. SCI. (2014), available at: http://www.pnas.org/content/111/20/7230. It is hard to know whether this rate of error applies across the system, but there are millions of people in prison, so even if it were lower, thousands of lives would be lost to wrongful convictions.

27. Laren-Brooke Eisen & Oliver Roeder, *America's Faulty Perception of Crime Rates*, Mar. 16, 2015, available at: https://www.brennancenter.org/blog/americas-faulty-perception-crime-rates (showing that violent crime rate in the United States rose fairly consistently until 1980, before a small dip, and then a peak in the late 1990s).

28. The Drug Policy Alliance provides a brief history of the War on Drugs and notes that, while President Nixon declared a war on drugs in the 1970s, the social focus on drugs reached its peak in the 1980s. The Drug Policy Alliance, *A Brief History of the Drug War,* available at: http://www.drugpolicy.org/facts/new-solutions-drug-policy/brief-history-drug-war-0.

29. *See generally* The Innocence Project website: http://www.innocenceproject.org/about/.

30. *See generally* The National Registry of Exonerations, Newkirk Center for Science & Society at University of California Irvine, the University of Michigan Law School and Michigan State University College of Law, http://www.law.umich.edu/special/exoneration/Pages/about.aspx.

31. The National Registry of Exonerations website updates its figures regularly. The National Registry of Exonerations, Newkirk Center for Science & Society at University of California Irvine, the University of Michigan Law School and Michigan State University College of Law, http://www.law.umich.edu/special/exoneration/Pages/about.aspx. (visited on Oct. 6, 2016, and listing 1,895 exonerations on that date).

32. The Registry tracks factors, like these mentioned and others, that contributed to the wrongful convictions . The National Registry of Exonerations, available at: http://www.law.umich.edu/special/exoneration/Pages/detaillist.aspx.

33. *See Exonerations by Year: DNA and non-DNA (1989–2015),* The National Registry of Exonerations, *available at* http://www.law.umich.edu/special/exoneration/Pages/Exoneration-by-Year.aspx.

34. *See Exonerations in the United States,* The National Registry of Exonerations (a map, which permits researchers to search the documented cases by contributing factors), available at: http://www.law.umich.edu/special/exoneration/Pages/Exonerations-in-the-United-States-Map.aspx.

35. *Id.*

36. *See* generally Perry v. New Hampshire, 132 S. Ct. 716, 730–40 (2012) (Sotomayor, J., dissenting) (discussing the Court's long-standing concern with the problem of eyewitness identification).

37. Amy D. Trenary, State v. Henderson: *A Model for Admitting Eyewitness Identification Testimony,* 84 U. Colo. L. Rev. 1257, 1275 (2013).

38. *See generally* Gary L. Wells & Elizabeth A. Olson, *The Other-Race Effect in Eyewitness Identification: What Do We Do About It?,* 7 Psychol. Pub. Pol'y & L. 230 (2001).

39. *See generally* Steven Penrod & Brian Cutler, *Witness Confidence and Witness Accuracy: Assessing Their Forensic Relation,* 1 Psychol. Pub. Pol'y & L. 817 (1995).

40. Brief for the American Psychological Ass'n as Amicus Curiae Supporting Petitioner at 3, Perry v. New Hampshire, 565 U.S. 228 (2012).

41. *See* Jules Epstein, *Irreparable Misidentifications and Reliability: Reassessing the Threshold for Admissibility of Eyewitness Identification,* 58 Vill. L. Rev. 69, 89–91 (2013) (surveying studies showing that jurors consistently are unaware of the many ways in which a witness's ability to accurately recall what she has seen may be compromised).

42. *See generally* Lauren Tallent, *Through the Lens of Federal Evidence Rule 403: An Examination of Eyewitness Identification Expert Testimony Admissibility in the Federal Circuit Courts,* 68 Wash. & Lee L. Rev. 765 (2011) (discussing the debate around use of such experts and related circuit split).

43. *Id.*
44. Jeffrey Goldberg, *The End of the Line: Rehabilitation and Reform in Angola Penitentiary*, THE ATLANTIC (Sept. 9, 2015) available at: http://www.theatlantic.com/politics/archive/2015/09/a-look-inside-angola-prison/404377/Atlantic.
45. *Id.*
46. *Life, Death and Raging Bulls*, THE ECONOMIST (May 10, 2014), *available at* http://www.economist.com/news/united-states/21601853-god-and-daredevilry-give-prisoners-hope-and-dignity-says-burl-cain-life-death-and-raging.
47. Whitney Benns, *American Slavery, Reinvented*, THE ATLANTIC (Sep. 21, 2015), available at: http://www.theatlantic.com/business/archive/2015/09/prison-labor-in-america/406177/.
48. *See* Andrea C. Armstrong, *Slavery Revisited in Penal Plantation Labor*, 35 SEATTLE U. L. REV. 869, 903–05 (2012) (discussing the state's takeover of what had been a private convict leasing system).
49. *See History of Angola Prison*, Angola Museum, Louisiana State Penitentiary Museum Foundation, available at: http://www.angolamuseum.org/history/history/.
50. Williams v. Edwards, 547 F.2d 1206, 1208 (5th Cir. 1977).
51. *Williams*, 547 F.2d at 1211.
52. *Id.* at 1208.
53. Massarah Mikati, *Faith-Based Prison Seminaries Help "Moral Rehabilitation" of Inmates*, DESERET NEWS (July 10, 2015), available at: http://www.washingtontimes.com/news/2015/jul/10/faith-based-prison-seminaries-help-moral-rehabilit/.
54. Maya Lau, *Burl Cain Claims Angola Transformation, But Prison's Violent Era Preceded Him by Decades*, THE ADVOCATE (Jan. 3 2016), available at: http://www.theadvocate.com/baton_rouge/news/crime_police/article_c2c84230-f700-5c00-936c-85933b4b73be.html.
55. Erik Eckholm, *Bible College Helps Some at Louisiana Prison Find Peace*, N.Y. TIMES (Oct. 5, 2013), available at: http://www.nytimes.com/2013/10/06/us/bible-college-helps-some-at-louisiana-prison-find-peace.html?pagewanted=all&_r=0.
56. *See* Chad Calder, *Special Angola Program Aims to Ease Ex-Cons' Reentry into Society and Workforce*, THE ADVOCATE, July 3, 2015, available at: http://www.theadvocate.com/new_orleans/news/article_1811b53a-0424-5f66-a0f0-6dffa02aa617.html.
57. Erik Eckholm, *Bible College Helps Some at Louisiana Prison Find Peace*, N.Y. TIMES (Oct. 5, 2013).
58. Ball v. LeBlanc, 792 F.3d 584 (5th Cir. 2015).
59. Aug. 23, 2016 Intvw.
60. Motion to Correct Illegal Sentence in Light of *Miller v. Alabama*, at 5, Toca v. Cain, Case No. 301-875 "G" (Crim. Dist. Ct. Orleans Parish, filed May 1,

2013) (on file with author) [*hereinafter* Motion to Correct Illegal Sentence];
Aug. 23, 2016 Intvw.

61. Aug. 23, 2016 Intvw.

62. Oct. 1, 2016 Intvw.

63. *Id.*

64. Supervisory Writ Memo. at 5; *see also id.* at 22.

65. *Id.*

66. Supervisory Writ Memo. at 12–13; *see also id.* at 21.

67. *Id.*

68. Toca v. Louisiana, Petit. for Writ Cert. 2014 WL 7366267 (Sept. 8, 2014).

69. Motion to Correct Illegal Sentence, *supra* note 60, at 4.

70. *Id.* at 5.

71. Toca v. Louisiana, 135 S. Ct. 781 (Dec. 12, 2014).

72. John Simerman, *George Toca, La. Inmate at Center of Debate on Juvenile Life Sentences, to Go Free,* THE ADVOCATE, Jan. 30, 2015, available at: http://theadvocate.com/news/neworleans/11462053-148/george-toca-louisiana-inmate-at.

73. *Id.*

74. Lex Talamo, *Watchdog: State Reviewing Life Sentences,* SHREVEPORT TIMES (Feb. 4, 2016) (estimating 247 JLWOP cases), available at: http://www.shreveporttimes.com/story/news/2016/02/01/supreme-court-rules-re-open-cases-juvenile-offenders-sentenced-life-without-parole/78846364/.

75. John Simerman, *George Toca, La. Inmate at Center of Debate on Juvenile Life Sentences, to Go Free,* THE ADVOCATE, Jan. 30, 2015, available at: http://theadvocate.com/news/neworleans/11462053-148/george-toca-louisiana-inmate-at.

76. *Id.*

77. *Id.*

78. Aug. 23, 2016 Intvw.

79. Aug. 23, 2016 Intvw.

80. Aug. 23, 2016 Intvw.

81. Toca v. Louisiana, 135 S. Ct. 1197 (Feb. 3, 2015).

82. John Simerman, *George Toca, La. Inmate at Center of Debate on Juvenile Life Sentences, to Go Free,* THE ADVOCATE, Jan. 30, 2015, available at: http://theadvocate.com/news/neworleans/11462053-148/george-toca-louisiana-inmate-at.

83. Montgomery v. Louisiana, 135 S. Ct. 1546 (March 23, 2015).

84. Aug. 23, 2016 Intvw.

85. Oct. 1, 2016 Intvw.

86. Bloomberg Business Week, *Prisoners Dilemma: Life on the Outside,* available at: http://www.bloomberg.com/news/articles/2015-02-19/prisoners-sentenced-to-life-as-kids-just-lost-their-best-chance-for-freedom.

87. Oct. 1, 2016 Intvw.; Matt Sledge, *Obama Grants Clemency to Two New Orleans Drug Offenders, One with Life Sentence,* THE ADVOCATE (Aug. 30,

2016), available at: http://www.theadvocate.com/new_orleans/news/crime_police/article_c8093488-6f06-11e6-8f36-3379167c67a1.html.

88. Oct. 1, 2016 Intvw.

89. *See* United States Courts, *Supreme Court Procedures,* available at: http://www.uscourts.gov/about-federal-courts/educational-resources/about-educational-outreach/activity-resources/supreme-1. The Supreme Court accepts between 100 and 150 cases per year out of the approximately 7,000 cases in which the Court is petitioned. *Id.*

90. Decision in the Matter of Gregory Diatchenko, W38579, Comm. of Mass. Parole Board at 1 (Oct. 31, 2014) [hereinafter Diatchenko Parole Dec.].

91. Diatchenko Parole Dec., at 1.

92. *Id.* at 5; *see also* Interview with Gregory Diatchenko (Cambridge, MA) (Oct. 19 and 20, 2016) (notes on file with author) [hereinafter Diatchenko Intvw.].

93. Diatchenko Parole Dec., at 5.

94. *Id.*

95. Beth Schwartzapfel, *Would You Let This Man Go Free?* Boston Mag. (July 2014), available at: http://www.bostonmagazine.com/news/article/2014/07/22/let-free-greg-diatchenko/; *see also* Diatchenko Parole Dec. at 5.

96. Diatchenko Parole Dec., at 5.

97. *Id.*

98. Diatchenko Parole Dec., at 3.

99. Beth Schwartzapfel, *Would You Let This Man Go Free?* Boston Mag., (July 2014); *see also* Diatchenko Parole Dec. at 5.

100. Diatchenko Parole Dec., at 5.

101. *Id.*

102. Diatchenko Parole Dec., at 5, 6; Diatchenko Intvw.

103. Diatchenko Parole Dec., at 5.

104. *Id.*

105. *Id.* at 6.

106. *Id.*

107. *Id.*

108. Beth Schwartzapfel, *Would You Let This Man Go Free?, supra* note 95.

109. Comm. v. Diatchenko, 443 N.E.2d 397, 399 (Mass. 1982); Diatchenko Parole Dec., at 2.

110. *Id.*

111. *Id.*

112. *Id.*

113. *Id.*

114. *Id.*

115. Diatchenko Parole Dec., at 2.

116. Diatchenko Parole Dec., at 6.

117. *Id.*

118. *Id.*

119. Diatchenko Intvw.

120. *See, e.g.,* Carlo v. Gunter, 520 F.2d 1293 (1st Cir. 1975) (describing "near riot conditions," murders, and assaults at the facility).

121. Arruda v. Fair, 547 F. Supp. 1324, 1326 (U.S. Dist. Ct. Mass. 1982).

122. Diatchenko Intvw.

123. *Id.*

124. *Id.* The name of this individual has been changed for purposes of anonymity and safety.

125. David Abel, *An Inside Look at Mass. Prison Life,* THE BOSTON GLOBE (Nov. 14, 2011), available at: https://www.bostonglobe.com/metro/2011/11/14/ inside-look-massachusetts-prison-life/pCM2p6X4Hfcs51gAPR8vUO/story. html.

126. Diatchenko Parole Dec., at 4.

127. Diatchenko Intvw.

128. Diatchenko Parole Dec., at 4.

129. Diatchenko Parole Dec., at 4; Diatchenko Intvw.

130. Diatchenko Parole Dec., at 4.

131. Diatchenko Intvw.

132. *See generally* Beth Schwartzapfel & Bill Keller, *Willie Horton Revisited,* THE MARSHALL PROJECT (May13, 2015), *available at:* https://www. themarshallproject.org/2015/05/13/willie-horton-revisited#.TDPn5JVh5.

133. Diatchenko Parole Dec., at 4; Diatchenko Intvw.

134. Diatchenko Intvw.

135. Greg Diatchenko, as told to Beth Schwartzapfel, *Why It's Hard to Be a Lifer Who's Getting Out of Prison,* THE MARSHALL PROJECT (Dec. 4, 2015).

136. *Id.*

137. Diatchenko v. District Att'y for Suffolk Dist., 1 N.E.3d 270 (Mass. 2013).

138. *Diatchenko,* 1 N.E.3d at 279.

139. *Id.* at 281.

140. *Id.* at 284.

141. Diatchenko Parole Dec., at 7.

142. *Id.*

143. *Id.* at 4.

144. *Id.* at 7.

145. *Id.*

146. Diatchenko Intvw.

147. Decision in the Matter of Louis Costa, W44737, Comm. of Mass. Parole Board at 4 (July 28, 2016) [hereinafter Costa Parole Dec.].

148. Biographical facts are based on interviews with Louis Costa (both by phone and in person); Deborah Salvucci, Louis's maternal aunt; and Louis's counsel, David Apfel, between the months of July 2016 and November 2016 (notes on file with author).

149. Louis R. Costa's Memorandum in Support of Parole, In the Matter of Louis R. Costa, Case No. W 44737 (filed Feb. 18, 2016, Mass. Parole Board) [hereinafter Costa Parole Memo.].
150. Letter from Louis Costa (Oct. 23, 2016) (on file with author).
151. Costa Parole Dec., at 3.
152. Costa Parole Dec., at 3.
153. Interview with Deborah Salvucci, Louis's maternal aunt (Nov. 19, 2016) (notes on file with author).
154. Costa Parole Dec., at 3.
155. *Id.*
156. Costa Parole Dec., at 3.
157. *Id.*
158. *Id.*
159. *Id.*
160. Costa Parole Dec., at 2.
161. *Id.*
162. *See* Costa Parole Dec., at 1. There was a third shooter that night. Mr. Costa has maintained that Richard Storella, who was a fully immunized witness at his and Mr. DiBenedetto's trial, was that third shooter. Mr. Storella himself at one point claimed that he had been one of the murderers. The state argued that Mr. Tanso had been the third shooter, and Mr. Tanso was ultimately acquitted. *Id.*
163. Costa Parole Dec., at 2.
164. *Id.*
165. Costa Parole Memo., at 25.
166. Costa Parole Dec., at 1–2.
167. Costa Parole Dec., at 2.
168. Costa Parole Dec., at 2; interview with David Apfel, Esq., counsel for Mr. Costa (Boston, MA) (July 18, 2016) (notes on file with author).
169. Interview with David Apfel, Esq., counsel for Mr. Costa, (July 18, 2016) (notes on file with author).
170. Costa Parole Dec., at 2.
171. Commw. v. DeBenedetto, 693 N.E.2d 1007 (Mass. 1998) (denying direct appeal of conviction after second trial); Costa v. Hall, 673 F.3d 16 (1st Cir. 2012) (denying petition for writ of habeas corpus based on claim of ineffective assistance of counsel); Commw. v. DeBenedetto, 30 Mass. L. Rptr. 280 (Sup. Ct., Suffolk County 2012) (denying codefendant's motion for new trial based on new evidence).
172. Costa Parole Dec., at 3.
173. *See generally* Diatchenko v. District Att'y for Suffolk Dist., 1 N.E.3d 270 (Mass. 2013).
174. *Diatchenko*, 1 N.E.3d at 284–86.
175. Commw. v. Costa, 33 N.E.3d 412, 417 (Mass. 2015) ("This court's decisions in *Diatchenko* and *Brown* transformed a choice that could be regarded as

'somewhat symbolic' into one of some consequence, since a consecutive sentence doubles the amount of time the defendant must serve before he becomes eligible for parole."). *Id.*

176. *Id.* at 415.
177. *See generally Costa.*
178. *Id.* at 416.
179. *Id. at* 419.
180. *Id. at* 420–21.
181. Costa Parole Dec., at 2.
182. Costa Parole Memo., at 5.
183. Costa Parole Memo., at 5.
184. Costa Parole Dec., at 5.
185. Costa Parole Memo., at 8.
186. *Id.*
187. *Id.* at 9.
188. *Id.*
189. *Id.* at 10.
190. *Id.*
191. *Id.*
192. *Id.* at 10–11.
193. *Id.* at 17–20.
194. *Id.* at 19–20.
195. *Id.* at 18.
196. *Id.* at 19.
197. *Id.*
198. *Id.* at 20.
199. *Id.* at 3.
200. Costa Parole Dec., at 1.
201. Costa Parole Dec., at 4.
202. *Id.*
203. 120 C.M.R. 300.04.
204. Costa Parole Dec., at 4.
205. Costa Parole Memo., at 33–39 (cataloguing each of the cases the Board had considered as of 2016 and noting that Louis's case compared favorably to all cases in which parole had been granted).
206. Decision in the Matter of Ernest Fernandes, W56833, Commw. of Mass. Parole Board (Aug. 26, 2015); *see also* Costa Parole Memo. at 34.
207. Decision in the Matter of Keyma Mack W55540 at 7, Comm. of Mass. Parole Board (Nov. 20, 2014); *see also* Costa Parole Memo., at 34–35.
208. Costa Parole Memo., at 36–38, 39.
209. *See generally* Chapter 5 *supra; see also* Cara H. Drinan, *Graham on the Ground*, 87 Wash. L. Rev. 51, 78–82 (2012) (arguing that implementation of *Graham* decision requires affirmative improvement to youth conditions of confinement).

210. Graham v. Florida, 560 U.S. 48, 79 (2010) ("Maturity can lead to that considered reflection which is the foundation for remorse, renewal, and rehabilitation."). *Id.*

211. *Miller,* 132 S. Ct. at 2468.

212. Matt Smith, *Long After Landmark Decision, Evan Miller Still Waits for Resentencing*, Mar. 18, 2016, at: http://jjie.org/long-after-landmark-decision-evan-miller-still-waits-for-resentencing/209630/.

213. *Id.*

214. Bryn Stole, *Life Sentence for Henry Montgomery in Murder of East Baton Rouge Deputy to be Reconsidered*, THE ADVOCATE (June 28, 2016), available at: http://www.theadvocate.com/baton_rouge/news/courts/article_436e58c2-3da9-11e6-baec-fbc24a3fe470.html.

215. *Id.*

Chapter 7

1. The Campaign for the Fair Sentencing of Youth, *Righting Wrongs: The Five Year Groundswell of State Bans on Life Without Parole for Children*, at 8–9 (2016) available at: http://fairsentencingofyouth.org/wp-content/uploads/2016/09/Righting-Wrongs-.pdf?utm_source=Five+Year+Report+KI+Rollout&utm_campaign=Righting+Wrongs&utm_medium=email.

2. The Editorial Board, *Michigan Prosecutors Defy the Supreme Court*, N.Y. TIMES (Sept. 10, 2016), available at: http://www.nytimes.com/2016/09/11/opinion/sunday/michigan-prosecutors-defy-the-supreme-court.html?mabReward=A1&action=click&pgtype=Homepage&region=CColumn&module=Recommendation&src=rechp&WT.nav=RecEngine&_r=0.

3. Miller v. Alabama, 132 S. Ct 2455, 2469.

4. The Editorial Board, *Michigan Prosecutors Defy the Supreme Court, supra* note 2.

5. Jones v. Commw., 763 S.E.2d 823 (Va. 2014), *vacated by* Jones v. Virginia, 136 S. Ct. 1358 (2016).

6. Foster v. State, 754 S.E.2d 33, 37 (Ga. 2014) (confining application of *Miller*'s principles to mandatory sentences and treating statute permitting death, life, or LWOP as discretionary); State v. Redman, No. 13-0225, 2014 WL 1272553 at *3 (W. Va. Mar. 28, 2014) (finding that *"Miller* has no applicability" where sentences are not mandatory).

7. There are additional states that have found *Miller* inapplicable because the state sentencing scheme permits some sentencing discretion, say a range from 50 years to death. While this is more of a choice than the binary one described above in Georgia and West Virginia, I would argue that these schemes are still not "discretionary" in the way that the *Miller* Court envisioned. *Cf.* Conley v. State, 972 N.E.2d 864 (Ind. 2012); Rohweder v. State, No. 63596, 2014 WL 495465 (Nev. Jan. 15, 2014), *cert. denied*, Rohweder v. Nevada, 134 S. Ct. 1896 (2014).

8. *Miller,* 132 S. Ct. 2455, 2458.

9. *Id.* at 2468. (explaining the factors, "Mandatory life without parole for a juvenile precludes consideration of his chronological age and its hallmark features—among them, immaturity, impetuosity, and failure to appreciate risks and consequences. It prevents taking into account the family and home environment that surrounds him—and from which he cannot usually extricate himself—no matter how brutal or dysfunctional. It neglects the circumstances of the homicide offense, including the extent of his participation in the conduct and the way familial and peer pressures may have affected him. Indeed, it ignores that he might have been charged and convicted of a lesser offense if not for incompetencies associated with youth—for example, his inability to deal with police officers or prosecutors (including on a plea agreement) or his incapacity to assist his own attorneys. . . . And finally, this mandatory punishment disregards the possibility of rehabilitation even when the circumstances most suggest it.") (citations omitted).

10. Rohweder v. State, No. 63596, 2014 WL 495465, *cert. denied*, Rohweder v. Nevada, 134 S. Ct. 1896 (2014).

11. Graham v. Florida, 130 S. Ct. 2011, 2030 (2010).

12. Bear Cloud v. State, 334 P.3d 132 (Wyo. 2014).

13. Casiano v. Comm'r of Corr., 115 A.3d 1031, 1043–44 (Conn. 2015).

14. State v. Null, 836 N.W.2d 41 (Iowa 2013).

15. People v. Caballero, 282 P.3d 291 (Cal. 2012).

16. *Null*, 836 N.W.2d at 71.

17. Bunch v. Smith, 685 F.3d 546, 550–51 (6th Cir. 2012).

18. State v. James, 2012 WL 3870349 (N.J. App. Sept. 7, 2012).

19. *Graham*, 560 U.S. 48, 75. Because the *Graham* decision dealt with a relatively small pool of individuals most of whom were in Florida, the question of what remedy there would be for "*Graham* inmates" was initially left to Florida judges. State court judges resentenced people on an ad hoc basis until the Florida legislature was able to pass modified juvenile sentencing laws. *See generally* Gary Blankenship, *Supreme Court Clarifies Guidelines for Resentencing Juveniles Tried as Adults*, FLA. BAR NEWS, Apr. 15, 2015, available at: http://www.floridabar.org/divcom/jn/jnnews01.nsf/ 8c9f13012b96736985256aa900624829/6fa66bc1472cb32b85257e1f00484c15! OpenDocument.

20. LeBlanc v. Mathena, 2016 WL 6652438 (4th Cir. Nov. 10, 2016).

21. *Mathena*, 2016 WL 6652438 at *1.

22. *Id.*

23. *Id.*

24. *Id.*

25. *Id.* at *2.

26. *Id.* at *8–9.

27. *Id.* at *10.

28. *Id.* at *11.

29. Montgomery v. Louisiana, 136 S. Ct. 718, 736 (2016).

30. U.S. Dept. of Justice, *Trying Juveniles as Adults: An Analysis of State Transfer Laws and Reporting*, at 2 (2011), available at: https://www.ncjrs.gov/pdffiles1/ojjdp/232434.pdf.

31. *Id.* at 3.

32. *See, e.g.*, David O. Brink, *Immaturity, Normative Competence, and Juvenile Transfer: How (Not) to Punish Minors for Major Crimes*, 82 Tex. L. Rev. 1555 (2004).

33. *See e.g., In re* Interest of D.M.L., 254 N.W.2d 457, 459 (S.D. 1977) (rejecting claim that juvenile transfer statute was unconstitutionally vague); Commonwealth v. Cotto, 753 A.2d 217, 224 (Pa. 2000) (rejecting claim that juvenile transfer statute violated Due Process Clause).

34. *Miller*, 132. S. Ct. at 2474.

35. Wendy N. Hess, *Kids Can Change, Reforming South Dakota's Juvenile Transfer Law to Rehabilitate Children and Protect Safety*, 59 S.D. L. Rev. 312, 331–32 (2014) (arguing for a return to discretionary, individual juvenile transfer post-*Miller*); Brice Hamack, *Go Directly to Jail, Do Not Pass Juvenile Court, Do Not Collect Due Process: Why Waiving Juveniles into Adult Court Without a Fitness Hearing is a Denial of their Basic Due Process Rights*, 14 Wyo. L. Rev. 775, 805–27 (2014) (relying upon the "juveniles are different" line of cases to argue that transfer without a hearing violates due process rights); Christopher Slobogin, *Treating Juveniles Like Juveniles: Getting Rid of Transfer and Expanded Adult Court Jurisdiction*, 46 Tex. Tech L. Rev. 103, 121–29 (2013) (arguing for a juvenile justice system without waiver post-*Miller*); Rachel Jacobs, Note, *Waiving Goodbye to Due Process: The Juvenile Waiver System*, 19 Cardozo J.L. & Gender 989, 992 (2013) (arguing that existing waiver procedures violate Due Process).

36. Janet C. Hoeffel, *The Jurisprudence of Death and Youth: Now the Twain Should Meet*, 46 Tex. Tech L. Rev. 29, 51–55 (2013).

37. Sarah Childress, *More States Consider Raising the Age for Juvenile Crime*, Frontline, June 2, 2016, available at: http://www.pbs.org/wgbh/frontline/article/more-states-consider-raising-the-age-for-juvenile-crime/.

38. Jeree Thomas, *Support of Michigan's Bill Package to Raise the Age*, Campaign for Youth Justice, Oct. 17, 2016, available at: http://cfyj.org/news/blog/tag/Campaign%20for%20Youth%20Justice.

39. Brian Evans, *"Raise the Age," "Direct File," and More: States Pursuing Youth Justice Reforms in 2016*, Campaign for Youth Justice, May 11, 2016, available at: http://cfyj.org/news/blog/tag/Campaign%20for%20Youth%20Justice.

40. The Campaign for the Fair Sentencing of Youth, *Righting Wrongs: The Five Year Groundswell of State Bans on Life Without Parole for Children*, at 4 (2016).

41. *Id.*

42. *Id.*

43. As discussed in Chapter 5, Evan Miller was sentenced to life without parole in Alabama under a mandatory sentencing scheme.

44. Kim S. Hunt & Michael Connelly, *Advisory Guidelines in the Post-*Blakely *Era*, 17 Fed. Sent'g Rep. 233, 233–35 (2005) (providing overview of presumptive sentencing guidelines and the rationales for them); *see also* Conn. Gen. Assembly, Legislative Program Review and Investigations Comm., Connecticut Mandatory Minimum Sentences Briefing (2005), http://www.cga.ct.gov/2005/pridata/Studies/Mandatory_Minimum_Senteces_Briefing.htm (providing examples of crimes that carry a presumptive minimum versus those that carry a mandatory minimum).

45. *See, e.g., Sentencing Guidelines Overview*, Md. St. Commission on Crim. Sent'g Pol'y, http://www.msccsp.org/Guidelines/Overview.aspx. ("The sentencing guidelines are advisory and judges may, at their discretion, impose a sentence outside of the guidelines. If judges choose to depart from the sentencing guidelines, the Code of Maryland Regulations (COMAR) 14.22.01.05(A) mandates 'The judge shall document on the guidelines worksheet the reason or reasons for imposing a sentence outside of the recommended guidelines range.' In practice, however, the judiciary has generally neglected to provide an explanation for departure. For example, in 61% of the fiscal year 2005 cases that resulted in a departure from the guidelines, the reason(s) for departure was not provided."). *See generally* Hunt & Connelly, *Advisory Guidelines in the Post-*Blakely *Era, supra* note 44.

46. Miller v. Alabama, 132 S. Ct. 2455, 2467 (2012) (citation omitted).

47. *Miller*, 132 S. Ct. at 2467 (citations omitted).

48. Alaska Stat. § 12.55.155(c) (2014) (listing aggravating factors); *Id.* § 12.55.155(d) (listing mitigating factors).

49. *Id.* § 12.55.155(d).

50. *Id.* § 12.55.155(d)(4).

51. *Id.* § 12.55.155(f)(1).

52. *See, e.g.,* Considerations in Imposing Sentence, Ind. Code § 35-38-1-7.1 (2015) (listing 11 mitigating circumstances the court may consider, none of which relate to youth); *Imposition of Presumptive Sentence; Jury Requirements; Departure Sentencing; Substantial and Compelling Reasons for Departure; Mitigating and Aggravating Powers*, Kan. Stat. Ann. 21-6815(c)(1) (2014) (listing non-exhaustive mitigating factors, none of which include youth); *Factors to Consider in Felony Sentencing*, Oh. Stat. Ann. § 2929.12 (2014) (same).

53. Tatum v. Arizona, 2016 WL 1381849 (Oct. 31, 2016).

54. *Id.* at *2 (citations omitted).

55. I first made this argument in two related law review articles. *See* Cara H. Drinan, *Misconstruing* Graham *&* Miller, 91 Wash. U. L. Rev. 785, 789, n. 26 (2014); Cara H. Drinan, *The* Miller *Revolution*, 101 Iowa. L. Rev. 1787, 1816–24 (2016). *See also* Martin Guggenheim, Graham v. Florida *and a*

Juvenile's Right to Age-Appropriate Sentencing, 47 Harv. C.R.-C.L. L. Rev. 457 (2012).

56. Miller v. Alabama, 132 S. Ct. 2455, 2467 (2012).

57. *Miller*, 132 S.Ct. at 2468.

58. *Id.* at 2465.

59. It is worth noting that other state *legislatures* have implicitly recognized the harshness of mandatory minimum sentences as they apply to children in adult court. For example, Oregon and Washington statutory law prohibits mandatory minimums for juveniles tried as adults, except for very serious crimes, such as aggravated murder. *See* Or. Rev. Stat. § 161.620 (2003) (providing juvenile tried as an adult shall not receive a mandatory minimum sentence except for aggravated murder or felonies committed with a firearm); *see also* Wash. Rev. Code. Ann. § 9.94A.540(3)(a) (2010) (prohibiting mandatory minimum sentences for juvenile offenders except for aggravated first-degree murder).

60. State v. Lyle, 854 N.W. 2d 378 (Iowa 2014).

61. *Lyle*, 854 N.W. 2d. at 400.

62. *Id.* at 402.

63. *See, e.g.,* People v. Banks, 36 N.E. 3d 432, 506 (Ill. 2015) (mandatory minimum sentence for first-degree murder did not violate juvenile's Eighth Amendment rights); State v. Vang, 847 N.W. 2d 248, 262–63 (Minn. 2014) (mandatory minimum of life with possibility of parole after 30 years for first-degree felony murder for juvenile did not violate Eighth Amendment); Commonwealth v. Lawrence, 99 A.3d 116, 121–22 (Pa. Super. Ct. 2014) (statute giving mandatory minimum of 35 years to juvenile defendant convicted of first-degree murder did not violate Eighth Amendment).

64. Miller v. Alabama, 132 S. Ct. 2455, 2463–64.

65. *Id.* at 2464.

66. *Id.* at 2464-65.

67. *Id.* at 2467.

68. 854 N.W.2d 378, 419 (Zager, J., dissenting).

69. *Id.* ("And, of course, there will be expert witnesses: social workers, psychologists, psychiatrists, substance-abuse counselors, and any number of related social scientists. And, other witnesses: mothers, fathers, sisters, and brothers."); *see also id.* ("After the parade of witnesses ends, the district court must then produce for each juvenile offender a detailed, reasoned sentencing decision. District courts must consider the 'juvenile's lack of maturity, underdeveloped sense of responsibility, vulnerability to peer pressure, and the less fixed nature of the juvenile's character,' keeping in mind that these are 'mitigating, not aggravating factors' in the decision to impose a sentence. It does not end there. District courts must recognize juveniles' capacity for change and 'that most juveniles who engage in criminal activity are not destined to become lifelong criminals.' If tempted to impose a harsh sentence on even a particularly deserving offender, 'the district court should

recognize that a lengthy prison sentence . . . is appropriate, if at all, only in rare or uncommon cases.'") (citations omitted).

70. *Id.* at 420.

71. *See* Chapter 1 *supra.*

72. *See, e.g.,* Gideon v. Wainwright, 372 U.S. 335 (1963) (holding Sixth Amendment right to counsel applies to states and thus imposing burden on states to pay for that representation); Brown v. Plata, 131 S. Ct. 1910 (2011) (affirming finding of Eighth Amendment violation due to prison overcrowding and requiring state to either improve conditions at state's expense or release inmates).

73. *Id.*

74. Juliet Eilperin, *Obama Bans Solitary Confinement for Juveniles in Federal Prisons,* WASH. POST (Jan. 26, 2016), available at: https://www.washingtonpost.com/politics/obama-bans-solitary-confinement-for-juveniles-in-federal-prisons/2016/01/25/056e14b2-c3a2-11e5-9693-933a4d31bcc8_story.html.

75. U.S. Dept. of Justice, *Juveniles in Residential Placement, 2013,* at 6 (2016), available at: http://www.ojjdp.gov/pubs/249507.pdf?ed2f26df2d9c416fbdddd d2330a778c6=ixggxbbxfa-icgedfbc [hereinafter *Residential Placement*].

76. Annie E. Casey Foundation, *The Missouri Model: Reinventing the Practice of Rehabilitating Youthful Offenders,* at 2, 2010, available at: http://static1.1.sqspcdn.com/static/f/658313/9749173/1291845016987/aecf_mo_fullreport_webfinal.pdf?token=qFAbECf2WN5xmvuKsMQloWE58do%3D [hereinafter *The Missouri Model*].

77. *The Missouri Model, supra* note 76, at 5.

78. Mike Cason, *New DYS Girls Facility Reflects Alabama's Reformed Approach to Juvenile Crime,* Oct. 9. 2015, available at: http://www.al.com/news/index.ssf/2015/10/new_dys_girls_facility_reflect.html.

79. *See generally* the Annie E. Casey Foundation, *Juvenile Detention Alternatives Initiative: Progress Report 2014,* available at: http://cms.aecf.org/m/resourcedoc/aecf-2014JDAIProgressReport-2014.pdf#page=5 [hereinafter *Progress Report 2014*].

80. *Progress Report 2014, supra* note 79, at 8.

81. *Id.* at 10.

82. *Id.* at 13.

83. *Id.* at 15.

84. *Id.* at 17–18.

85. *See* Chapter 4 *supra; see also* Nat'l Center for Juvenile Justice, *Juvenile Offenders and Victims: 2006 National Report* at 222 (2006) (noting that nearly half of juvenile offenders were held in large facilities), available at: https://www.ojjdp.gov/ojstatbb/nr2006/downloads/chapter7.pdf.

86. *The Missouri Model, supra* note 76, at 2 ("In state after state, 70 to 80 percent of juveniles released from youth corrections facilities are rearrested within two or three years for a new offense.").

87. *See generally id.; see also* Marian Wright Edelman, *Juvenile Justice Reform: Making the "Missouri Model" the American Model*, Huffington Post (May 25, 2011), available at: http://www.huffingtonpost.com/marian-wright-edelman/juvenile-justice-reform-m_b_498976.html.

88. *The Missouri Model, supra* note 76, at 13–14.

89. *Id.* at 15, 20.

90. *Id.* at 19.

91. *Id.* at 47.

92. *Id.* at 29.

93. *Id.* at 6–7.

94. *Id.* at 7, Fig. 4.

95. *Id.* at 9.

96. *Id.* at 10.

97. *Id.*.

98. *Id.* at 12.

99. Kim Taylor-Thompson, *Minority Rule: Redefining the Age of Criminality*, 38 N.Y.U. Rev. L. & Soc. Change 143, 198, n. 389 (2014); *see also The Missouri Model, supra* note 76, at 51–52.

100. Thompson, *Minority Rule,* 38 N.Y.U. Rev. L. & Soc. Change, at 197.

101. *See* Jeff Bleich, *The Politics of Prison Crowding*, 77 Cal. L Rev. 1125, 1147–48 (1989) (describing states abolishing parole during this period); *The Future of Parole as a Key Partner in Assuring Public Safety*, U.S. Dept. of Justice Nat'l Inst. Corrections 1–2 (2011), at: http:// static.nicic.gov/Library/024201.pdf.

102. Timothy A. Huges et al., *Trends in State Parole*, 1990–2000, Bureau of Justice Stat. 1 (Oct. 2001), http://www.bjs.gov/content/pub/pdf/tsp00.pdf.

103. Sen. Bill No. 9, Sentencing, available at: http://leginfo.legislature.ca.gov/faces/billNavClient.xhtml?bill_id=201120120SB9. (2012).

104. Human Rights Watch, *California: New Hope for Young Offenders*, Oct. 5, 2015, https://www.hrw.org/news/2015/10/05/california-new-hope-young-offenders.

105. See Ann. Cal. Code § 3051 (2016).

106. Ann. Cal. Code § 3051(e).

107. Ann. Cal. Code § 3051(f)(2).

108. Ann. Cal. Code § 3051(f)(1).

109. Human Rights Watch, *California: New Hope for Young Offenders*, Oct. 5, 2015, https://www.hrw.org/news/2015/10/05/california-new-hope-young-offenders.

110. *See* Chapter 6 *supra* (discussing the legal developments in Massachusetts post-*Miller*).

111. State House News Service, *Mass. Gov. Deval Patrick Signs Bill Allowing Parole for Juvenile Murderers*, July 25, 2014, http://www.masslive.com/politics/index.ssf/2014/07/massachusetts_gov_deval_patric_36.html.

112. Diatchenko v. District Att'y for Suff. Dist., 27 N.E.3d 349 (Mass. 2015).

113. Mass. Parole Board, *Guidelines for Life Sentence Decisions* (2014), available at: http://www.mass.gov/eopss/agencies/parole-board/guidelines-for-life-sentence-decisions.html.

114. Marisa Gerber, *California Inmate's Parole Reflects Rethinking of Life Terms for Youths*, L.A. Times (Mar. 24, 2015), available at: http://www.latimes.com/local/crime/la-me-juvenile-lwop-20150325-story.html.

115. *Id.*

116. Graham v. Florida, 560 U.S. 48, 75 (2010); *cf.* Montgomery v. Louisiana, 136 S. Ct. 718, 736 (2016) ("Allowing those offenders to be considered for parole ensures that juveniles whose crimes reflected only transient immaturity—and who have since matured—will not be forced to serve a disproportionate sentence in violation of the Eighth Amendment.").

Conclusion

1. Rebecca Beitsch, *States at a Crossroads on Criminal Justice Reform,* Stateline (Jan. 28, 2016), available at: http://www.pewtrusts.org/en/research-and-analysis/blogs/stateline/2016/01/28/states-at-a-crossroads-on-criminal-justice-reform.

2. *Id.*

3. *Id.*

4. Scott Horsley, *Obama Visits Federal Prison, A First for Sitting President*, National Pub. Radio, (July 16, 2015), available at: http://www.npr.org/sections/itsallpolitics/2015/07/16/423612441/obama-visits-federal-prison-a-first-for-a-sitting-president.

5. *Id.*

6. *A Nation of Second Chances: Obama's Record on Clemency* (Nov. 22, 2016), available at: https://www.whitehouse.gov/issues/clemency.

7. Seung Min Kim & Burgess Everett, *Time Running Out for Major Criminal Justice Bill*, Politico (Apr. 20, 2016), available at: http://www.politico.com/story/2016/04/senate-justice-crime-bill-222225.

8. *Booker, Maloney Announce Bicameral Effort to Fix Our Strained Public Defender System*, Cory Booker, United States Senator for New Jersey, available at: https://www.booker.senate.gov/?p=press_release&id=451.

9. *Senators Introduce Landmark Bipartisan Sentencing and Corrections Reform Act of 2015*, Chuck Grassley, United States Senator for Iowa, available at: http://www.grassley.senate.gov/news/news-releases/senators-introduce-landmark-bimsdbfkjashdfkjahsdfkjhsapartisan-sentencing-reform-and-corrections-act-2015.

10. Sewell Chan, *Shootings in Dallas, Minnesota, and Baton Rouge: What We Know*, N.Y. Times (July 8, 2016), http://www.nytimes.com/2016/07/09/us/dallas-attacks-what-we-know-baton-rouge-minnesota.html.

11. Steve Visser, *Baton Rouge Shooting: 3 Officers Dead*, CNN (July 18, 2016), http://www.cnn.com/2016/07/17/us/baton-route-police-shooting/.

12. Eric Bradner, *Obama: Temper Our Words and Open Our Hearts*, WDSU News (July 18, 2016), http://www.wdsu.com/news/local-news/new-orleans/obama-temper-our-words-and-open-our-hearts/40760254.

13. Philip Rucker, *Trump Pushes Expanded Ban on Muslims Entering the U.S.*, WASH. POST (June 13, 2016), https://www.washingtonpost.com/politics/trump-pushes-expanded-ban-on-muslims-and-other-foreigners/2016/06/13/c9988e96-317d-11e6-8ff7-7b6c1998b7a0_story.html.

14. Bob Woodward & Robert Costa, *Trump Reveals How He Would Force Mexico to Pay for Border Wall*, WASH. POST (Apr. 5, 2016), https://www.washingtonpost.com/politics/trump-would-seek-to-block-money-transfers-to-force-mexico-to-fund-border-wall/2016/04/05/c0196314-fa7c-11e5-80e4-c381214de1a3_story.html.

15. See transcripts of Mr. Trump's acceptance speech, available at: http://www.vox.com/2016/7/21/12253426/donald-trump-acceptance-speech-transcript-republican-nomination-transcript.

16. *Id.*

17. *Id.*

18. Patrick Healy & Jonathan Martin, *His Tone Dark, Donald Trump Takes G.O.P Mantle*, N.Y. TIMES (July 21, 2016), http://www.nytimes.com/2016/07/22/us/politics/donald-trump-rnc-speech.html.

19. D'Angelo Gore, *Trump Wrong on Murder Rate*, Oct. 28, 2016, available at: http://www.factcheck.org/2016/10/trump-wrong-on-murder-rate/.

20. *Id.*

21. John Carpenter, *Trump Win Shows Limits of Big Data, Power of Emotional Intelligence*, FORBES, Nov. 10, 2016, available at: http://www.forbes.com/sites/johncarpenter1/2016/11/10/trump-win-shows-limits-of-big-data-power-of-emotional-intelligence/#57bae6a25539 (emphasis added).

22. *Id.*

23. *Bryan Stevenson Urges USCA Audience to Get Proximate*, BLACK AIDS INST., available at: https://www.blackaids.org/news-2015/2527-bryan-stevenson-urges-usca-audience-to-qget-proximateq.

24. Matthew Friedman, *Just Facts: As Many Americans Have Criminal Records as College Diplomas*, BRENNAN CTR., Nov. 17, 2015, available at: https://www.brennancenter.org/blog/just-facts-many-americans-have-criminal-records-college-diplomas.

25. Xavier McElrath-Bay, *No Child is Born Bad*, TEDX Talk, Apr. 22, 2014, at: http://tedxtalks.ted.com/video/No-Child-Is-Born-Bad-Xavier-McEl.

26. Ms. Kruzan has shared her story widely in academic settings and mainstream media outlets. For details of her abusive childhood, her victimization by sex traffickers as an adolescent, incarceration, and ultimate release, *see, e.g.,* Human Rights Watch, *When I Die, They'll Send Me Home: Youth Behind Bars* (Apr. 21, 2009), available at: https://www.youtube.com/watch?v=bGL_p7BcJqk. *See, also* Crime Watch Daily, *Woman Freed*

After Killing Pimp as Teen Turns Life Around, Jan. 11, 2016, available at: http://crimewatchdaily.com/2016/01/11/teen-sentenced-to-life-for-murdering-her-pimp/.

27. *Woman Freed After Killing Pimp as Teen Turns Life Around, supra* note 26.

28. Human Rights Watch, *When I Die, They'll Send Me Home: Youth Behind Bars.*

29. *Id.*

30. *Id.*

31. Gov. Arnold Schwarzenegger, *Acts of Executive Clemency for the State of California,* Granted for the Period Jan. 1, 2010, through Dec. 31, 2010, at: https://assets.documentcloud.org/documents/1373290/executive-clemency-for-california-2010.pdf.

32. *Id.*

33. Human Rights Watch, *When I Die, They'll Send Me Home: Youth Behind Bars*; Scott Hechinger, *Juvenile Life Without Parole: An Antidote to Congress's One-Way Criminal Law Ratchet?* 35 N.Y.U. Rev. L. & Soc. Change 408, 457–58 (2011).

34. Gov. Arnold Schwarzenegger, *Acts of Executive Clemency for the State of California,* Granted for the Period Jan. 1, 2010, through Dec. 31, 2010.

35. *Id.*

36. Paige St. John, *Jerry Brown OK's Freedom for Woman Imprisoned at 16 for Killing Pimp,* L.A. Times, Oct. 26, 2013, at: http://articles.latimes.com/2013/oct/26/local/la-me-ff-kruzan-20131027. *See also* Camp. for Fair Sent'g Youth, Sara Kruzan, ICAN Member, available at: http://fairsentencingofyouth. org/sara-kruzan/. ICAN, the Incarcerated Children's Advocacy Network, is a group of youth who were incarcerated for committing serious crimes as youth and who now advocate for age-appropriate sentencing. *See generally,* The Campaign for Fair Sentencing Youth, *Incarcerated Children's Advocacy Network,* available at: http://fairsentencingofyouth.org/incarcerated-childrens-advocacy-network/.

37. *See generally* Xavier McElrath-Bey, *No Child is Born Bad,* TEDX Talk, Apr. 22, 2014, available at: http://tedxtalks.ted.com/video/No-Child-Is-Born-Bad-Xavier-McEl.

38. *Id.*

39. *Id.*

40. *Id.*

41. Xavier McElrath-Bey, *No Child is Born Bad,* TEDX Talk, Apr. 22, 2014.

42. *Id.*

43. *Id.*

44. Xavier McElrath-Bey, *The Light at the End of the Tunnel,* Huffington Post (June 21, 2013), at: http://www.huffingtonpost.com/xavier-mcelrathbey/the-light-at-the-end_b_3480715.html.

45. Xavier McElrath-Bey, *The Light at the End of the Tunnel.*

46. *Id.*

47. *Id.*
48. *Id.*
49. *See generally,* The Campaign for Fair Sentencing Youth, *Incarcerated Children's Advocacy Network,* available at: http://fairsentencingofyouth.org/incarcerated-childrens-advocacy-network/.
50. Xavier McElrath-Bey, *The Light at the End of the Tunnel, supra* note 44.
51. *See generally* Chapter 4 *supra.*
52. Julian D. Ford et al., *Trauma Among Youth in the Juvenile Justice System: Critical Issues and New Directions,* at 1–2 (2007), at: http://www.ncmhjj.com/wp-content/uploads/2013/10/2007_Trauma-Among-Youth-in-the-Juvenile-Justice-System.pdf.
53. *See generally* Xavier McElrath-Bey, *No Child is Born Bad,* TEDX Talk, Apr. 22, 2014.
54. Campaign for the Fair Sentencing of Youth, *Victim Family Member Profiles: Jeanne Bishop,* available at: http://fairsentencingofyouth.org/voices/voices-of-families-of-victims/victim-family-member-profiles/jeanne-bishop/.
55. *Id.*
56. The Campaign for the Fair Sentencing of Youth makes an effort to include victims and victims' advocates in their reform agenda. The Campaign highlights at conferences and on their website the positions of the many victims who, despite suffering, believe that youth deserve to be sentenced in an age-appropriate way. Profiles of additional victim family members can be found at: Campaign for the Fair Sentencing of Youth, Victim Family Member Profiles, http://fairsentencingofyouth.org/voices/voices-of-families-of-victims/victim-family-member-profiles/.
57. *See generally* Nell Bernstein et al., *Mothers at the Gate: How a Powerful Family Movement Is Transforming the Juvenile Justice System* (2016), at: http://www.ips-dc.org/wp-content/uploads/2016/05/k-dolan-mothers-at-the-gate-5.3.pdf [hereinafter *Mothers at the Gate*].
58. *Mothers at the Gate,* at 9.
59. *Id.* at 11.
60. *See generally* Bart Lubow, *Juvenile Justice in 25 Years: A System That Passes the "My Child" Test,* in Marc Mauer & Kate Epstein, eds., *To Build a Better Criminal Justice System: 25 Experts Envision the Next 25 Years of Reform* (2012), at: http://sentencingproject.org/wp-content/uploads/2016/01/To-Build-a-Better-Criminal-Justice-System.pdf.
61. See generally, Bryan Stevenson, *Just Mercy: A Story of Justice and Redemption* (Random House, 2014).

INDEX